# Praise for
## *The Bank On Yourself Revolution…*

"Even if you aren't ready to actually fire your banker, you need all the helpful information you can find in these uncertain economic times. Pamela Yellen once again is 'right on the money' when it comes to financial security."

—HARVEY MACKAY,
Author of the *New York Times* #1 bestseller *Swim With The Sharks Without Being Eaten Alive*, www.harveymackay.com

"Pamela Yellen should definitely win a Nobel Prize. With her guidance, you can grow a nest egg into a small fortune without the risks of conventional investments and political uncertainty. I urge you … no, I beg you … to get *The Bank On Yourself Revolution*. It's an investment in yourself and a book that will make a major difference in your life."

—JOSEPH SUGARMAN,
Entrepreneur, Author, and BluBlocker Corporation Founder,
www.BluBlocker.com

"*The Bank On Yourself Revolution* provides a pathway to building your wealth and puts the traditional bank, stock and real estate markets firmly in the back seat. If you are searching for an alternative path to a secure retirement, this is a must read to grow your money safely and predictably ever year—even when the markets are crashing."

—KRISTI FRANK,
Star of Season One of Donald Trump's *The Apprentice*, well known for helping entrepreneurs start and grow their businesses,
www.KristiFrank.com

W9-AYZ-395

"If you are finally ready to reach your financial goals with a safe and steady strategy, Pamela Yellen's *The Bank On Yourself Revolution* is what you've been searching for. You will no longer be held prisoner to the unpredictable dollar, the fickle stock market, or the confusing precious metals. After reading *The Bank On Yourself Revolution*, you will actually be able to sleep at night instead of worrying about your financial future."

—MaryEllen Tribby,
#1 Bestselling Author, *Reinventing the Entrepreneur:*
*Turning Your Dream Business into a Reality*,
www.MaryEllenTribby.com

———

"After reading Pamela's first book, *Bank On Yourself*, I implemented her strategy as part of my retirement plan. It allowed me to retire before age fifty and is working better than advertised. Pamela's latest book digs deeper into the strategy and is a perfect follow-up. Implementing this concept radically changed my view of financial planning and relieved me of hundreds of hours of worry. My family is relaxed when it comes to financial planning, which we now have in one solution that doesn't depend on chasing the latest investment fad. We are on financial auto-pilot and found financial independence with one product. Now *that* is *truly* revolutionary."

—Commander Bob Chambers,
U.S. Navy (Retired)

———

"The founder of our company, Martin Edelston, lived by this credo: 'The only things worth talking about are the things you can't talk about.' Thank goodness Pamela Yellen lives by that same credo and has given us one of the most important books I've read in many years. Pamela has made it her life's mission to buck conventional wisdom when it comes to the critical issues every consumer faces as they struggle to not outlive their money. In this book, she has laid out a unique blueprint that you won't find anywhere else, which delivers the game plan for a secure future. Pamela has been a hero to so many already...and with this book, she is now a superhero. *The Bank On Yourself Revolution* is a must read for anyone who values their money … and their future."

—BRIAN KURTZ,
Executive Vice President, Boardroom Inc.,
www.bottomlinepublications.com

———◦◦◦———

"Wow—this book makes so much sense it's bound to irritate the heck out of those that make a living telling you how to invest your money."

—JOHN JANTSCH,
Author of *Duct Tape Marketing*,
www.ducttapemarketing.com

———◦◦◦———

"Let's face it. We're a DIY nation. The time has come to have the courage to jump on opportunities, stand out, and be unique within the herd. In this book, Pamela Yellen has laid out the tools to successfully *bank on yourself* to survive this concrete jungle."

—MICHEAL BURT,
Nashville Fox Radio Host and author of *Zebras & Cheetahs: Look Different and Stay Agile to Survive the Business Jungle*

———◦◦◦———

"Pamela Yellen provides rock-solid, wealth-building strategies in *The Bank on Yourself Revolution*. A must read for anyone looking to protect and grow their assets while minimizing taxes and reducing risks."

—CHRISTINE FORAKIS, Esq.,
Senior Partner, The Forakis Law Firm, PLC

———◦◦◦———

"*The Bank On Yourself Revolution* is an absolute hit … I really enjoyed reading it. Wall Street is getting more and more corrupt and it's *not* the place to put our hard-earned money. I advise my clients to watch the movie *Margin Call* just to get an inside glimpse at what's really going on. Thanks to Pamela Yellen for everything she does and for her latest book."

—WOODY OAKES, DDS,
Founder of Excellence in Dentistry,
www.TheProfitableDentist.com

———◦◦◦———

"Everyone with money to invest should invest in this book before doing anything else. Smart, simple, right on point. A must read for investors who desire low risk, consistent results, and simplicity."

—DAN BENAMOZ,
CEO, Pharmacy Development Services,
www.pharmacyowners.com

———◦◦◦———

"In my experience getting rich, going broke, and getting rich again, I've found that the most profitable methods for success are also the least conventional. *The Bank On Yourself Revolution* lays out an unconventional route to achieve what so many Americans were denied during the most recent crash: Building and maintaining dependable and stable retirement savings, a nest egg that grows predictably, a college savings account that won't tank just before the kids are ready to fly the nest—and avoiding strangling debt all at the same time. Pamela Yellen is a rare woman of courage willing to thumb her nose at Wall Street and the financial pundits and advisors in order to help others find true financial security for themselves and their families. Read this book if you are ready to free yourself from the fear of recessions, bursting bubbles, and Wall Street fiascos."

—JIMMY HARDING,
CEO, Harding Enterprises, www.JimmyHarding.com

———◦◦◦———

"This book is a touchdown! It's a play-by-play for taking control of your own money and finances."

—JOSH A. JALINSKI,
Radio Host, Financial Quarterback, WOBM-FM,
New Jersey, and WOR 710 AM

———◦◦◦———

"*The Bank on Yourself Revolution* delivers a fresh and thought-provoking path to a lifetime of financial freedom. Pamela Yellen is audacious and deliberate in revitalizing the mind and giving you a wake-up call to propel your financial future."

—SUNDRA RYCE,
President & CEO, SLR Contracting & Service Company, Inc.

"So many of us go through life feeling everything would be better if we just knew the 'secrets' of the super successful. What do 'they' know that we don't? It's true that preparation, hard work, and good luck make most of the difference. BUT then a book like this comes along and you realize there actually *are* a few secrets to financial success."

—RICHARD ROSSI,
Founder of EnvisionEMI

"I have read and used Pamela Yellen's previous book introducing the creative concept to 'Bank on Yourself.' Her new book expands the 'how-to-do' of the process. We have used her advice for many of our clients who now have put away millions of dollars that are available for the generations of their family—all protected from estate taxes, probate involvement, and creditor lawsuits. I also like the availability of family money for convenient loans. This technique works many times better than conventional savings and retirement plans."

—JOHN F. GOODSON,
Goodson Law Group, President of the College of Preventive Law, and
Chairman of the Faculty of the College of Estate Planning Attorneys

"Pamela Yellen's *The Bank On Yourself Revolution* brings to the reader an updated plea to take charge of your finances and your future and to protect your loved ones. As a physician, the income I have earned over the years was somewhat diversified but still heavily weighted in stocks. To my dismay, my principal seemed to shrink more often than it grew, and all the returns that were predicted never materialized. That's why

I began my own Bank On Yourself plan. The Bank On Yourself system may not be the *only* way to invest your hard-earned money, but it is by far the *safest and surest* way to maintain your nest egg and grow it steadily. Keep yourself and your family safe from the greed of Wall Street and the banking system. Read and join *The Bank On Yourself Revolution* today."

—DR. TIMOTHY ZELKO,
Cosmetic Surgeon, www.ZBodySculpt.com

---

"What a refreshing read! Securing true wealth these days requires you be educated about every possible strategy there is—and if you're serious about securing your financial future, Pamela's book is a definite must read as part of your financial education."

—ROBIN ROBINS,
CEO of Technology Marketing Toolkit, Inc.,
www.TechnologyMarketingToolkit.com

---

"Don't wait another day. Seriously, buy everyone you know, respect, and care about a copy of *The Bank On Yourself Revolution* ASAP! It helped me work smart, invest even smarter, and show others how to easily do the same."

—Dr. BEN ALTADONNA,
Founder of The Practice Building Alliance™,
www.BenAltadonna.com

---

"As a baby boomer, when I first read about the Bank On Yourself plan, I was literally speechless. How could this have been around for as long as it has, and yet people still don't know about it? Then it occurred to me that there are those that would prefer as few people know about it as possible. Think of the effect it could have if average Americans really start to use this kind of plan that allows them to borrow from themselves to finance major items—cars, college, dream vacations, even businesses—and pay themselves back. That's why *you* need to educate yourself. Read this book and do what Pamela recommends."

—MICHELLE PRICE,
Co-Founder, National Association of Women Solo-preneurs,
www.NAWSConnect.com

"Pamela's latest book, *The Bank On Yourself Revolution*, expands upon the life-changing concepts that were so brilliantly introduced in her original Bank On Yourself book. I have recently implemented these concepts in my own life, and only wish I had learned about them 10 years ago. If you're tired of the banking nonsense and Wall Street volatility and want a better solution, this book is a must read!"

—DENISE GOSNELL,
CEO, ThrivingBusiness.com

"Most financial 'experts' make the simple complex; Pamela Yellen does just the opposite. Her advice to our readers always has been spot-on. Many people are many thousands of dollars richer thanks to her."

—WAYNE M. BARRETT,
Publisher and Editor-in-Chief, *USA Today Magazine*

"Pamela Yellen respects her readers. She knows they aren't stupid, nor are they looking for a get-rich-quick scheme. Through *The Bank On Yourself Revolution*, Pamela presents a real wealth-building alternative that just about anyone can use."

—MIKKI BANKS,
Philanthropist, Beauty Expert and Radio Host,
The Mahoghany Concept

"Traditional finance advice just doesn't work anymore. Things have changed, and Pamela Yellen is the first to find ways to teach others to secure their financial futures and become financially free in this new and confusing world."

—NICKY LAMARCO,
Writer and "The Review Mom"

"The strategies and concepts presented in this book are incredible. When compared with paying interest to the banks for so many things in both our business and personal lives, this is such a breath of fresh air. Who wouldn't want to put all that money in their own pocket, instead of giving it to the bank? This definitely is a message whose time has come."

—KEVIN THOMPSON,
Maximum Response Marketing,
www.AutomaticIncomeCoach.com/blog

"Pamela reveals a proven step-by-step plan for becoming your own source of financing and growing your wealth safely and predictably every single year —not a 'get-rich-quick' scheme, but having real wealth and financial security for as long as you live."

—DARBY DAVIS,
Editor, *Awareness Magazine*

# THE BANK ON YOURSELF
## REVOLUTION

# THE BANK ON YOURSELF

# REVOLUTION

*Fire Your Banker,
Bypass Wall Street,
and Take Control
of Your Own Financial Future*

## PAMELA YELLEN

BENBELLA BOOKS, INC.
*Dallas, TX*

Copyright © 2015 by The Hayward-Yellen 100 Ltd Partnership
First Hardcover Edition: 2014

BenBella Books, Inc.
10300 N. Central Expressway
Suite 530
Dallas, TX 75231
www.benbellabooks.com
Send feedback to feedback@benbellabooks.com

Printed in the United States of America
10 9 8 7 6 5 4 3 2 1
ISBN-13: 978-1-942952-10-7 (trade paper)

**The Library of Congress has catalogued the hardcover edition as follows:**
Yellen, Pamela G.
    The bank on yourself revolution : fire your banker, bypass wall street, and take control of your own financial future / Pamela Yellen.
        pages cm
    ISBN 978-1-939529-30-5 (hardback)—ISBN 978-1-939529-31-2 (electronic)
1. Finance, Personal. 2. Retirement income—Planning. 3. Investments. I. Title.
    HG179.Y452 2014
    332.024—dc23
                                                                2013032361

Editing by Glenn Yeffeth
Copyediting by Stacia Seaman
Proofreading by Cape Cod Compositors
    and Rainbow Graphics
Cover design by Hespenheide Design

Text design by John Reinhardt Book Design
Text composition by Integra Software Services Pvt. Ltd.
Printed by Lake Book Manufacturing
Distributed by Perseus Distribution

www.perseusdistribution.com
To place orders through Perseus Distribution:
Tel: (800) 343–4499
Fax: (800) 351–5073
E-mail: orderentry@perseusbooks.com

This book is dedicated to all the Bank On Yourself revolutionaries, the people who had the courage to question today's conventional financial wisdom, buck the system, and set out on a path less traveled.

In doing so, you created true financial security for yourselves and your families.

You are my heroes and my inspiration.

# Contents

# INTRODUCTION

# I Swore I'd Never Write Another Book

I absolutely did *not* want to write this book.

First of all, writing a book is a real pain in the you-know-what. It takes *months* of brain-numbing work and scads of helpers to do research, verify stats, and make it all readable. By the time I finished my last book (*Bank On Yourself: The Life-Changing Secret to Growing and Protecting Your Financial Future*), I swore to my husband Larry that I would never, *ever* again set myself up for the *stress* of looming deadlines, the *agony* of the editor's red pen, and the *loss* of so many weekends and so much sleep.

Nope. Never again.

Then the book hit the bestseller lists. (That was nice, and softened the pain a bit.) And we got a tremendous response from folks who were thrilled to have discovered Bank On Yourself. (That was even better.)

*Then* the backlash started. (Not fun at all.)

People who have a vested interest in keeping the same-old, same-old going (that would be many of your celebrity money gurus, financial advisors, stockbrokers, money managers, and bankers) went on *total* attack! I received vile letters and nasty e-mails that were unbelievably vitriolic and accusatory. (Honestly, who has that kind of time on their hands?)

I got attacked in blogs, in articles, and by talking heads both online and offline. Most of the attackers had not done their homework, and some were totally illogical and unreasonable in their arguments against the Bank On Yourself strategy. (Then again, I guess illogical and unreasonable is kinda the currency of the day, isn't it?) But I *still* had to step up and defend myself and the Bank On Yourself concept against them.

One article that I found particularly amusing was written by an investment advisor and blogger for a major news website. He wrote an "exposé" about how he'd discovered the *fatal flaw* in Bank On Yourself. Really? That I had to see. Turns out the only way he could punch a hole in the concept was to compare the cost of purchasing a car and financing it through Bank On Yourself to the cost of *not buying a car at all*. Well, duh. Of *course* you'll have more money if you don't buy a car! (Someone once told me that blogging isn't writing. It's graffiti with punctuation.) To read the point-by-point rebuttal we posted to that article, go to **www.BankOnYourself.com/rebuttal**.

If I had a dollar for every myth and misconception published online and offline about Bank On Yourself, I'd have more money than all the fat cats on Wall Street put together.

Does it sound like I took these attacks lightly? I didn't. The truth is that being attacked all the time—even if the attacks aren't valid—really hurts a lot and is exhausting.

So I told Larry, "That's it. I'm done."

It was a very hard time for me. Not only would I *never* write another book, but there were more than a few moments when I thought about completely giving up my mission to educate people about this proven wealth-building strategy. I'd just go back to the quiet life I had before all of this, where most people who know me actually like and respect me. That was in 2009.

## But Then...

By the end of 2010, the recession had *crushed* the net worth of most Americans. The median net worth of the middle class—who were hit the hardest—fell by so much, it erased eighteen years of gains.[1] Savers have been "rewarded" for their diligence with near-zero yields on their hard-earned life savings for five long years because the Federal Reserve deliberately kept interest rates as low as possible.

And soon the talking heads on Wall Street—whose advice got us into this mess in the first place!—were urging us to leap right back in and *take more risk*, as if it makes perfect sense to make up for your gambling losses by doubling down on your bets.

People who followed all the conventional financial wisdom got *clobbered* in the last recession, losing homes, college savings, and retirement funds. And they want us to do it *again*?

It makes me absolutely *furious* that the financial community is *bent* on getting us to walk down that same rosy garden path that has nothing at the end of it but quicksand! I *know* there's a way out, and I've *seen* so many people benefit from it. I *know* there's a safe way to grow your wealth and have access to the cash you need while guaranteeing a comfortable retirement and setting up a legacy to be left to those you love.

I couldn't just stand by and let people suffer when they don't have to.

So I said to Larry, "Maybe just one more book."

Prominently placed on my office wall is a quote from Dan Kennedy, one of my mentors:

*"If you don't offend somebody by noon each day, you're not doing much."*

And isn't that true? If I weren't stirring up the waters or getting any pushback, it would be because I was parroting the same old pap that clearly doesn't work.

But that's not what I'm doing.

I'm inciting a revolution.

# CHAPTER 1

# An Idea Whose Time Has Come

*The highest form of ignorance is to reject something*
*you know nothing about.*

—DR. WAYNE DYER

THIS BOOK may make you crazy angry.

It might make you feel uncomfortable, anxious, confused. It might make you question some of your long-held beliefs about money, the stock market, investing, how to get ahead, and how to build wealth. You may start doubting the very validity of the financial strategies and vehicles you've poured your blood, sweat, tears, and dollars into.

And if this painful truth hasn't dawned on you previously, you might feel more than a little squeamish to realize that *you've built your financial future on a house of cards* that can—or has—come tumbling down through no fault of your own.

Yep. I'm the bearer of bad tidings.

But if you can get through all the angst and anger and fear and sadness those bad tidings will cause you, I've got some good news for

> **INSIDE THIS CHAPTER . . .**
>
> - You Can't Predict the Future—But That's Okay
> - How I Figured Out What *Doesn't* Work
> - What's the Bank On Yourself Revolution All About?
> - Who Bank On Yourself Isn't Right For
> - Stop Losing Money to the Randomness of the Market and Create *Real* Wealth

you as well. And if you're willing to keep an open mind, I can show you a way out.

A way out of the constant worry about whether you'll ever be in a financial position to retire. Out of the stress of figuring out how you'll ever be able to afford your children's college education. Out of the crazy-making exercise of trying to second-guess a stock market whose strings are pulled by people whose greed is only outstripped by their ingenuity for coming up with complex smoke-and-mirrors financial schemes.

A way out of the discouragement you feel paying steep credit card fees, the panic you feel when unexpected and shockingly expensive emergencies strike, the sadness you might feel when you realize that you worked really, really hard for decades to end up with … not very much at all.

## Is It the Best of Times or the Worst of Times?

I have *no idea* what the economic climate will be as you read this book. Absolutely no clue. We could be in a screaming bull market, or in the throes of a financial crash and recession, or somewhere in between.

The critical question is: *How much does your financial security depend on things you can't predict or control?*

---

The critical question is: *How much does your financial security depend on things you can't predict or control?*

---

When my first book on Bank On Yourself came out in 2009, we were two years into what turned out to be the deepest and longest recession since the Great Depression. The stock market crashed, losing almost half its value—the second horrific crash in a decade. The housing market collapsed, ultimately wiping out a decade of home equity. Millions of people lost their homes, and many more homeowners found themselves owing more on their mortgages than their homes were worth. The government bailed out the too-big-to-fail companies, and all the little people like us were left to fend for ourselves.

It was the biggest financial crisis in decades, yet how many people saw it coming? As Nobel Prize–winning physicist Neils Bohr reminded us, "Prediction is very difficult, especially if it's about the future."

As I prepare to hand this off to my publisher today, it's the spring of 2013. The Federal Reserve and central banks around the world are still running their money printing presses 24/7, and government debt levels have hit unprecedented nosebleed territory. This is creating a level of debt that may mortgage our children's and grandchildren's future for decades. The Fed's easy-money policies are forcing money into riskier assets and creating new bubbles.

The stock market is reaching new highs and seems to break records on an almost daily basis (though not when adjusted for inflation and fees). Home values are recovering (though still well below their highs) and some real estate markets are even becoming hot again, with investors and home buyers swarming all over anything that hits the market (déjà vu all over again?).

Are things getting better? Or are we in the eye of the hurricane, the lull before the trailing edge of the storm whips through and lays us flat again? I don't know—*and neither does anyone else.* And *that's* the problem.

Economic growth is sluggish, unemployment is still too high, and many countries around the world are vulnerable to economic collapse. According to the EBRI, in 2013 60 percent of pre-retirees fifty-five and older (these are baby boomers, so there are *scads* of them) have less than $100,000 in savings and investments. The Center for Retirement Research at Boston College pointed out in 2012 that the typical pre-retiree's 401(k) and IRA will only provide $575/month, and for most, it's likely to be their *only* source of retirement income other than Social Security.

## Did They Fix What Was Broken in the Financial Markets?

Are they still rigging the system?

Banks were recently fined billions of dollars for rigging a key interest rate (Libor) to their favor, and regulators are now investigating them to determine if they've rigged another interest rate measure. The SEC filed *fifty-eight new actions* related to insider trading in 2012. One of the latest

*continued*

*continued from previous page*

discoveries is that high-speed traders are using a hidden facet of the Chicago Mercantile Exchange's computer system to get an edge before other traders get the same information.[1]

And in June 2013, it was revealed that some of the world's biggest banks manipulated foreign exchange rates and pocketed enormous profits by pushing through high-speed trades.

They've passed a passel of new regulations in the past few years, but has anything really changed?

Warren Buffett, who's considered to be one of the most successful investors of all time, told CNBC in May, 2013, "We will have a bubble, and it will burst. It won't be the same as the last one. That's been the history. You don't have one Internet bubble after another. You have [the] housing [bubble] after the Internet [bubble]."

Eye of the storm or economic recovery? I don't know (though I'd definitely land on the storm side of the debate because I just don't see that they fixed what was broken). But in many ways, *it just doesn't matter*.

It doesn't matter because the wealth-building strategy I'm writing about has survived and even thrived during *every* period of economic boom *and* bust for more than 160 years. Whether interest rates were high or low. During bull markets and crashes. Even during the Great Depression. Housing market that's tanked or steaming hot. Dow Jones up or Dow Jones down.

Whatever's going on, there *is* a way to secure your family's future, without being at the mercy of the economic climate that swirls around you, and without relying on banks and Wall Street.

---

Warren Buffett, one of the most successful investors of all time, told CNBC in May 2013 that "we will have [another] bubble, and it will burst."

---

## What I Know About You

Pardon me for being bold, but if you've picked up this book, I think I know a few things about you, things you and I have in common.

- **You're *not* stupid.** Your financial picture may not be as solid as you want it to be, but not because you didn't pay attention. You listened to the experts and did what they told you to do. You probably consult a financial advisor, have a CPA do your taxes, and follow trends in the economy. Maybe you've educated yourself by reading books on personal finance or taking classes. You don't just rely on hearsay, *you want the facts.* (Me, too.)

- **You're *not* lazy.** You work hard and earn every penny that comes your way. You're not looking for a free ride and wouldn't feel good if you got one. You're proud that, by working hard and using your talents, you can earn a good living. You will do almost *anything it takes* to provide for your family and secure their future. (Yep, me, too.)

- **You're *not* looking for a magic bullet.** Okay, it *would* be nice if there were some genie in a bottle to grant you the financial well-being you want. (If you find one, feel free to give me a call.) But you're not counting on it or even looking for it. (I'm not into fairy-tale finance either.)

### Did We Fix What Was Broken with Small Investors?

Having missed out on much of the recent rally on Wall Street, individual investors are now starting to pour in again—in *spite* of the fact that, in the history of the S&P 500, there have only been four times that the market gained a larger percentage than the current one.[3]

Small investors also have rediscovered margin debt (borrowing against their portfolios to buy more investments) at levels not seen since right before the last crash. Margin debt hit a peak right before the last two bear markets. "It's a warning sign that the Federal Reserve's easy-money policies are creating a bubble mentality among stock traders."[4]

- **You *are* misguided.** Say *what*? Yep, you're misguided. You've been following that same conventional financial wisdom that isn't working for *anyone*! You're pouring as much as possible into your 401(k) or IRA—and seeing its value decline or remain stagnant. You may be trying to pay off your mortgage early—only to see that the worth of your house is less than what you still owe on it. You're sinking money into a 529 college plan—only to worry that the market may tank again right when your child is ready to go to college.

    You've been misguided. (And so was I.) It sucks.

- **You *are* willing to see it differently.** Okay, here's where you either toss this book in the trash or you keep reading further. *Are* you willing to see it differently? Are you *willing* to absorb the stats, validate the research, do your homework, and see if maybe the conventional financial wisdom you've followed is flawed? Are you *willing* to entertain the possibility that there might be a solid, time-tested strategy that few financial gurus will acknowledge but that hundreds of thousands of people like you are using successfully? (I was willing, and so now I'm one of those hundreds of thousands!)

## I've Been There and Done That, Too

I'm not stupid. I'm not lazy. I wasn't looking for a magic bullet. But I was misguided. *And* I was willing to see it differently.

My husband Larry and I had invested in all sorts of financial products and vehicles starting in 1987, but we had never come close to getting the returns we were told we should be able to get.

At one point, we figured the problem must be *us*. You know how some people seem to be unlucky in love? Well, we seemed to be unlucky in investing. So we decided to hire an expert to manage our money for us. We ultimately hired three oh-so-pricey experts—and *all three of them* lost us money during what turned out to be the *longest-running bull market* in history!

We picked ourselves up, dusted ourselves off, and continued searching. Since 1990, I've coached tens of thousands of financial advisors on how to build their businesses, so I had access to a multitude of financial vehicles. I ended up investigating more than *450 different financial products, strategies, and vehicles*, and *only a few* passed my due diligence tests.

But even those few turned out to be disappointments. What sounded great in theory and looked seductive on paper simply didn't show up in reality.

---

### Did They Fix What Was Broken in Financial Products?

The financial products that played a role in the crisis are coming back. In just the first quarter of 2013, banks sold about $1 billion of synthetic collateralized debt obligations (CDOs)—the same stuff that caused the credit bubble to burst in 2008. The former head of the Troubled Asset Relief Program, which oversaw the $700 billion bailout, said, "History is repeating itself. Because banks profited from the credit bubble and then faced no jail time when it popped, there's little reason to think that [these instruments] are going to be significantly better this time around."[5]

---

Finally one of my financial advisor clients said, "Pamela, have you ever heard about this?" *This* turned out to be a *little-known twist* on a financial asset that's increased in value every single year for more than 160 years: **dividend-paying whole life insurance.**

Okay, so *now* you're ready to throw this book in the trash! But hold on. Don't tune me out, because this is *nothing* like the whole life insurance policies Suze Orman, Dave Ramsey, and most financial advisors love to hate.

Properly structured, the policies I'll show you grow cash value as much as forty times faster than the ones Suze and Dave, et al., talk about. They pay the advisor or insurance agent 50–70 percent *less* commission. And you can use them as a powerful financial-management tool right from the start to fire your banker, bypass Wall Street, and have financial security for life.

I'll explain it all in detail in this book.

# About the Bank On Yourself Revolution

This isn't a pitchforks-and-bayonets kind of revolution. It started quietly and without a lot of fanfare. People who were tired of doing "all the right things" financially and ending up with little or nothing to show for it simply decided that enough was enough. They didn't throw Molotov cocktails or storm the castle walls of the Federal Reserve. They just quietly stopped putting their money into financial vehicles that didn't deliver.

They put less money into their 401(k)s and IRAs, and some stopped funding them altogether. They pulled back on their mutual funds and stocks and bonds. They pulled the plug on some of their real estate investments. They stopped letting their futures be determined by the hysteria of Wall Street and the seductive advice of financial gurus.

They took back control.

For the first time in their lives they had a *solid* financial foundation to build their futures on. They could move forward without the stress, worry, and uncertainty they had lived with, in the past.

And even though everyone from Bloomberg to MSN to Yahoo Finance swore up and down that there was *no* place to hide from the recession that rocked the world, these quiet revolutionaries found one.

Hundreds of thousands of people embraced the Bank On Yourself method and saw their money grow *safely and predictably every single year—even when the markets tumbled.*

- Their plans never even skipped a beat when the stock and real estate markets crashed.
- They didn't have to gamble on Wall Street to accumulate a sizeable nest egg. They didn't have to worry about when the next crash would come and wipe out their life savings again.
- They could tell banks and finance and credit card companies to go take a hike and still have access to the money they needed, whenever and for whatever they needed it.
- They didn't need to depend on their employer or the government for their financial security.
- They finally had *control over their own financial futures.*

I wish I could take credit for this revolution, but I can't. It had started way before I was fortunate enough to learn about the financial tool and concept I now call "Bank On Yourself." Why did I name this strategy Bank On Yourself? Because I could see how people were using it to pull themselves out of economic bondage and move toward freedom and economic *sanity*. Where they had been seduced into banking on the government, Wall Street, and financial institutions to cover their backs, Bank On Yourself revolutionaries were now banking on *themselves*— their own effort, resources, and good sense—to keep their families safe and financially secure. They were no longer pawns being manipulated by faceless fat cats around the globe with self-serving agendas.

And I needed a phrase that I could use as a rallying cry, because when I realized the sheer power and potential of the Bank On Yourself method and how *few* people were aware of it, I knew I just *had* to spread the word. There really *is* a better way! It became my mission to help educate others about it so they, too, could break free of their economic chains and bank on themselves.

## Did They Fix What Was Broken in the Housing Market?

As of 2013, the same kind of subprime loans (high-rate mortgages for high-risk borrowers) that brought the housing market to its knees is making a comeback. The U.S. Federal Reserve has begun buying bonds composed of mortgage-backed securities—the same kind of "toxic assets" that drove the housing boom and fueled the housing bust.[6] In some cities, houses hit the market and receive multiple bids *above the asking price* on the first day, often accompanied by tearful letters from the hopeful buyers pleading to be given a chance (shades of 2007?).

In 2004, then president of the Federal Reserve Alan Greenspan claimed that *adjustable-rate* mortgages, rather than fixed-rate mortgages, could save homeowners tens of thousands of dollars. That speech came at a time Greenspan had been cutting or holding rates flat for years—but only a few months later, he proceeded to raise rates at every single Federal Open Market Committee meeting, more than quadrupling interest rates within two years.[7]

## How to Use this Book

My first book introduced many people to the Bank On Yourself concept. This book goes much further into debunking myths of conventional financial wisdom as well as explaining the nuts and bolts of the Bank On Yourself structure and how and why it works. I'll also show you how this vehicle can provide you with everything from liquidity to finance major purchases or a college education, to a safe, predictable way to grow your retirement fund, to how to leave a significant legacy while still having access to money when you need it.

What are *your* top concerns about money? Here's where I address them:

- Worried about having enough money to retire? Afraid that you've started too late? See Chapters 2, 5, and 10
- Anxious about how you'll pay for your children's college education? See Chapter 8
- Nervous about having too much of your nest egg on the roller coaster we call Wall Street? Disgusted with the poor results your investments are producing? See Chapter 2
- Uneasy about the economic landscape your children will be entering? Concerned about how they'll ever be able to make it financially? See Chapters 6 and 11
- Stressed about finding the capital you need to start your own business or keep your business going? See Chapter 9
- Feeling strangled by credit card debt? Or trying to avoid piling up debt in the first place? See Chapter 7
- Feeling strapped because you've retired but your nest egg isn't earning enough income for you, and you'd rather not take more risk with your money? See Chapter 10
- Fed up with feeling stressed about money in general? See Chapter 6—then read the whole book!

## How Almost Anyone from Age Zero to Eighty-Five Can Benefit

No matter what age you are, from zero to eighty-five, Bank On Yourself can be a powerful financial tool. To get the most benefit, I suggest you read the whole book, even sections that you don't think apply to you. But I also recommend that you focus on specific chapters depending on your age:

- **If you're in your twenties**: You may be struggling with student debt, a tough job market, and salaries that don't seem to leave room for savings. You may have seen your parents and grandparents struggle during the financial crisis and want to avoid making the mistakes they made. You need a strategy where you can start small and build it up. (See Chapter 6 for financial basics to get you started off on the right foot and Chapter 11 for an example of how starting small can end up being big.)

- **If you're in your thirties and forties**: You might be growing a family, maintaining a home, and starting to think about how to pay for college. You may have incurred a lot of debt and feel like it's all you can do to keep your head above water. You need a strategy that will help you turn the ship around and reduce your debt while growing money you'll need for the kids' college expenses and your own retirement. (Chapter 7 will show you how to become your own source of financing. See Chapter 8 for a smarter way to pay for college.)

And if you're starting to get serious about saving for retirement, don't miss Chapters 2 and 5.

- **If you're in your fifties and early sixties**: You may be in your peak earnings years, but you also may have parents and kids you're helping out financially. Yet it's time to make serious headway on your retirement savings, and you need to plan to cover the enormous health-care costs you know are looming. You need a strategy that will enhance your retirement savings yet remain liquid for potential emergencies. (See Chapter 5 for ways to build a healthy retirement fund that lets you access your money whenever you need or want to—while it continues growing as though you hadn't touched it.)

- **If you're in your late sixties, seventies, or eighties, or already retired**: Your nest egg may have taken a severe hit in recent years, leaving you less than you had planned for. If your money is in CDs, savings and money market accounts, you're probably concerned about the low returns you're getting. You may be worried about the forced distributions (RMDs) you're required to take from your retirement account. You also may be thinking about passing a financial legacy to your children and grandchildren. (See Chapter 10 for ways Bank On Yourself addresses the specific concerns of seniors.)

## Who Bank On Yourself *Isn't* Right For

Bank On Yourself is not a get-rich-quick scheme. It takes some patience and discipline. If you have those traits, it pays a lifetime of benefits. But if it takes pie-in-the-sky promises of 12 percent, 20 percent, or more in annual gains to get your attention, this book is not for you.

And if you regularly spend more than you make, wait until you've got that under control before looking at this strategy. (Chapter 6 has some helpful tips for gaining control of your money and spending.)

The Bank On Yourself strategy gives you a *rare combination of guarantees, safety, liquidity, and control.* Your money grows by a guaranteed and predictable amount every year, and that growth gets better every year you have it. Bank On Yourself is for those who want to grow their wealth consistently every day and have control of their money and finances.

This strategy is so safe and so consistent that it's actually really pretty boring. If you need something sexier, try your hand at pork bellies or gold futures on the commodity exchange. Trust me, Bank On Yourself is not the stuff that makes for titillating cocktail party conversation.

If you'd like to find a financial strategy that doesn't promise you the moon (but will deliver impressive results), and if you're more interested in truth and pragmatism than blue-sky fantasies, then let me introduce you to someone who now thinks *boring* is pretty darn *exciting.*

## When Boring Takes Your Breath Away

Dan Proskauer is vice president of technology engineering for a major health care company who holds three U.S. patents. He lives below his means and has significant savings discipline. Dan is a sophisticated investor, but after the two financial crashes of 2000 and 2008, he realized he had *nothing* to show for decades of saving and investing his hard-earned money and "doing all the right things."

Dan is very analytical and has spent literally *hundreds of hours* investigating Bank On Yourself and, as he puts it, "The more I look at this, the better it looks."

In late 2012, Dan sent me a chart showing how his family's net worth has grown since he started his first Bank On Yourself plan three and a half years earlier, and how that growth compared to the previous ten years of rolling the dice in the Wall Street Casino.

When Dan saw this chart on his financial tracking software program, he said his jaw dropped so hard it left a dent on his keyboard. He told me the story this way when I interviewed him for my Bank On Yourself blog: "One chart I track shows me our family's net worth, which is the value of our assets minus the value of any liabilities we have.

"I look at this chart every time I start up Quicken, or I at least glance at it, and I was thinking, 'Man, this chart just hasn't changed very much. It looks pretty much the same as it has for a long time.' I was expecting to see some difference as we embarked on our journey with Bank On Yourself.

"So, just two weeks ago, it was bothering me so much I opened up the chart and took a closer look at it." It turns out that two years previously, Dan had set the chart for a specific date range and forgot that he'd done that. So for two years it was just showing him the same data over and over again.

"When I removed that date restriction and saw the data from my whole record, I was stunned!

"When I compared what happened to the left of that arrow to the time we started to implement the Bank On Yourself method, the picture

## NET WORTH OVER TIME: EXCLUDING HOME/REAL ESTATE

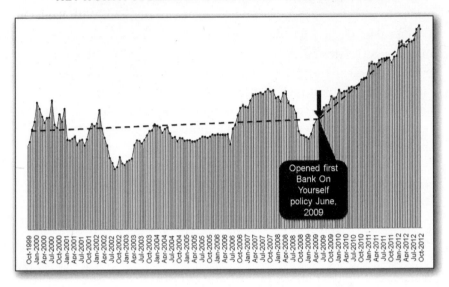

was completely different. After starting our Bank On Yourself plans, the volatility is largely gone. It's a very smooth slope, and the slope is tremendously steeper—in a *good* way—than I ever expected. That just floored me."

## High Expectations Exceeded

Dan continued, "When I saw this chart, I realized that my high expectations had been really exceeded. I felt a tremendous sense of accomplishment that I made this decision. Frankly, it's working out far better than I could have expected. I feel really good about it, and I want to shout it from the rooftops!

"The other thing is, I go to sleep every night knowing I don't have to worry about 'What's going to be the news out of Europe when I wake up in the morning? What's going to be the news out of Asia?' Or when I get up and go to work, 'What's going to happen during the day in the U.S.?' I just don't really worry about any of that. I know that our family has a solid and predictable financial future, with this as a foundation.

"The Bank On Yourself method offers something you truly deserve, but may not have—financial security and peace of mind. With Bank On Yourself, you can sleep well knowing your savings can only grow, never shrink. With Bank On Yourself, you *know*, rather than hope."

## Eliminate Volatility and Create *Real* Wealth

"The reduced volatility you see in the chart is completely expected, obviously, because we're out of the stock market. We're not having those ups and downs, so I'm not surprised to see the volatility be lower. But the growth! That just blew me away."

Here's a more detailed version of Dan's net-worth chart that makes it clear how market volatility was affecting his wealth:

**NET WORTH OVER TIME: EXCLUDING HOME/REAL ESTATE (WITH ANNOTATIONS)**

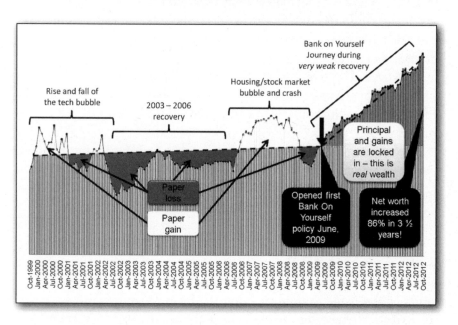

Because all of your principal and growth is *locked in* when you use the Bank On Yourself method to grow your nest egg, you have *real*

rather than paper wealth. The numbers you see on your annual statements represent the *real* values of your plan. They don't go backward when the markets crash. And that makes *all* the difference in the world. The next chapter shows you why.

Dan noted that his income has increased some in the last four years, as has the amount he saves each year. But the significant difference is that he now has a great place to put that income—his Bank On Yourself plans—where he no longer loses any of it to the randomness of the market. Dan's convinced that the picture of his net worth wouldn't look nearly this good if he hadn't discovered Bank On Yourself.

That's the kind of story I consistently hear from folks who use the Bank On Yourself wealth-building method. Because you can *see* the growth and you have access to your money in the plan, you're actually more *motivated* to save. You don't have to worry about losing your hard-earned dollars due to the events of the day in the U.S. or in some faraway place. And that gives you the confidence to save more.

Why would someone be willing to discuss something as personal as his net worth for the whole world to see? Because, in Dan's words, *"If I can help a few people start Bank On Yourself this year, instead of next year or instead of never, then it's well worth it."*

But Dan did even more than banish volatility and gain financial peace of mind by creating *real* wealth instead of paper wealth. He also uses the *living benefits* of his policies to live a fuller lifestyle today. Here's one of his examples:

"I'm fortunate that my mother has a home in New Hampshire, and we spend some time there in the summer. My brother has four children, and I have three children, and we have a boat that we put on the lake. This boat holds eight people. When the kids were younger, we could squeeze the four adults plus my mother and all seven kids into the boat. Twelve people into an eight-person boat, but it wasn't too bad.

"However, the kids have gotten older and bigger. My oldest is sixteen and drives the boat, but we can no longer squeeze everybody in. This summer, everyone wanted to go on the lake, so we had to take turns. That really bothered me because we enjoy boating so much. We're only all together up there a couple weeks a year. So after my brother's family left, I started dragging my wife around to used-boat stores. We found a twelve-person boat that we really liked. And we were able to make a decision on the spot to buy that boat.

"I called my Bank On Yourself Authorized Advisor and said I needed a policy loan. We got the money within days, and we bought the boat. I set up a repayment schedule to pay off the policy loan. It was an easy decision to make, given that we knew the money we spent on the boat was still continuing to grow." (Learn how this unique feature of the Bank On Yourself method works and how to fire your banker and become your own source of financing in Chapter 7.)

---

To listen to or read the full interview
I did with Dan Proskauer, go to
**www.BankOnYourself.com/dans-interview**

---

## Is Bank On Yourself for You?

I would need to write a book the size of the New York City phone book to tell you all the inspiring stories I've heard from Bank On Yourself revolutionaries like Dan Proskauer. My commitment to spreading the word about this concept deepens every time I hear a new story of success from these quiet revolutionaries. I would love everyone to take a serious look at Bank On Yourself!

But I can't coerce you into taking that look and investigating this. Heck, I can't even make you finish reading this book! (But I hope I've intrigued you enough to keep reading.)

Is the Bank On Yourself Revolution right for you? Perhaps it all comes down to how you answer these questions:

- Are you determined to *never again* tolerate another go-nowhere-for-more-than-a-decade level of performance in your financial plan?
- Are you tired of pinning your financial future on things you can't predict or control?

- Are you concerned about another market crash in the next five or ten years—or even tomorrow?
- Are you sick of being held hostage to high interest rates on your credit cards, and fed up with begging for money from bankers who hold all the cards?
- As you think about your future retirement, is it looking pretty bleak—unless you hit the lottery jackpot?
- Are you tired of the hope-and-pray method of financial and retirement planning?

Don't be concerned if at the moment you don't know where you'll find the funds to begin with Bank On Yourself. Don't worry about any health challenges you may have that have made you ineligible for other types of insurance. Don't worry that you may be too old to take advantage of this. You'll discover that those concerns are often irrelevant.

Your financial success is up to *you*. There's no bailout coming for us. There's no financial silver bullet coming from the government. Banks and Wall Street will continue to line their own pockets at your expense—but only if you let them. You *can* opt out of the system where the odds are stacked against you.

It's up to you. But I believe you would do yourself and your family a disservice if you didn't at least investigate this option. I encourage you to keep an open mind and keep reading. As John F. Kennedy said in his address to the 1962 graduates of Yale University:

*"The great enemy of the truth is very often not the lie—deliberate, contrived, and dishonest—but the myth, persistent, persuasive, and unrealistic…. We enjoy the comfort of opinion without the discomfort of thought."*

I invite you to turn the page, release the "comfort of opinion," and really investigate and consider this. There are conventional wisdom myths that are sabotaging your financial peace of mind—and there's another way.

**Note:** This book is *not* a training manual for financial advisors who want to help their clients implement this strategy. It will show you the basics, but if you want to learn to become an expert at it, expect it to take a year of study—even if you're an experienced financial advisor. (To find out how you can get the training you need, turn to "Bank On Yourself Is Looking for a Few Good Men and Women" near the end of the book, or visit **www.BankOnYourself.com/authorized-advisors**.)

## CHAPTER 2

# You Can't Eat Paper Profits

*Just 'cause you're following a well-marked trail doesn't mean that*
*whoever made it knew where they were goin'.*

—TEXAS BIX BENDER

I JUST KEPT STARING at it: *minus* $62,734.06. That's the "unrealized loss" we had in one of the mutual funds in our retirement account. It said so in the statement we'd just received.

*A $62,734.06 unrealized loss!*

I guess I thought I could stare that number down. After all, it was 2010, and we'd just had a nice run-up in the stock market. That particular mutual fund had one of the best long-term track records of any fund! And I'd already been waiting ten long years for my losses in that fund to recover. I kept staring, hoping that number would magically somehow turn positive. It didn't.

A $62,734 *unrealized* loss. Is that an oxymoron, like *Great Depression, small* fortune, *accurate* forecast, and *quick* reboot? There was nothing *unrealized* about it because I fully *realized* I had lost a whole bunch of money.

---

**INSIDE THIS CHAPTER . . .**

- Paper Wealth Versus Real Wealth
- Thirteen Losing Years on Wall Street
- Why Investors Will Never Win
- What Has Wall Street Done to Our Retirement Plans?
- Where the Smart Money Goes

---

19

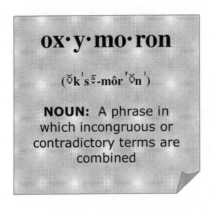

**ox·y·mo·ron**

(Ŏk'sē-môr'ŏn')

**NOUN:** A phrase in which incongruous or contradictory terms are combined

And I definitely remember working my butt off to make that money.

I don't know if *unrealized loss* qualifies as an oxymoron. But I do know it's moronic that we keep pinning our hopes and plans for our financial security and retirement on investment strategies we can't predict or control. Looking at the stock market's ups and downs since 1997 makes a day on the roller coasters at Six Flags look tame.

At the time, my husband was sixty-one and theoretically four years away from retirement. Larry probably won't retire at sixty-five because he says he'd get bored. But if we were relying *only* on the conventional financial planning wisdom, retirement wouldn't even be an option for either of us.

At least Larry and I *have* options, thanks to our Bank On Yourself plans. That's not the case for far too many people.

As I continued to review our retirement account statement, to my relief, another mutual fund showed an unrealized *gain* of $8,012.16. But I couldn't get too excited, because I knew the word *unrealized* hides a bleak reality:

*You don't actually lock in a profit (or loss) until you sell an investment.*

---

**You don't actually lock in a profit (or loss)
until you sell an investment.**

---

(Are you wondering why we still own any mutual funds at all? We hold on to them for one reason only: to prove that even if you buy and hold your investments and avoid acting emotionally, the stock market is still a crapshoot where the odds are stacked against you.)

The Federal Reserve's widely publicized *2010 Survey of Consumer Finances* showed that between 2007 and 2010, Americans' wealth plunged by *nearly 40 percent* due to the collapse in home values and the stock market. It revealed that the net worth of U.S. families had been reduced to a level not seen since 1992. Yet there's another side to this story that the report completely missed:

*You can't eat a number on paper.*

---

You can't eat a number on paper.

---

## Paper Wealth Versus Real Wealth

Those glowing reports about how much Americans' wealth had ballooned *prior* to the financial crash were pure fiction. Until you sell your assets and lock in your (hopefully) gains, you have nothing more than a bunch of eye-popping numbers on paper. Those numbers repeatedly sucker many of us into believing we have *real* wealth and financial security when we do *not*.

It's true that during the bull markets we had some exceptional growth. Then, of course, we lost those gains when the market inevitably crashed. There's a *big* difference between paper wealth and real wealth. During the go-go years of the dot-com bubble, Larry and I got into checking our retirement account almost every day because it was growing that fast. Yahoo! Some weeks we'd see such an enormous jump that we'd high-five each other shouting, "We're rich! We're rich!"

Didn't we all feel like we were sitting real pretty again right *before* the financial crash of 2008? Then we discovered for the zillionth time that what goes up fast usually comes down fast, too. The stock and real estate markets did just that with a resounding thud. These collapses took the retirement security of millions of Americans with them. All our prosperity went *unrealized*.

We see the same principle in our home values: The rise in a home's value is only an unrealized or paper gain—and it may vanish just when you really need the money. During the real estate boom years, we got some astonishing appraisals. We'd hear that a neighbor sold their home and get all excited: "Oh my gosh! Look how much money they sold their home for!" Our home value seemed to be jumping up every month. But soon we'd figure out that the high sales price of our neighbor's home meant little to us. It was nothing more than a number on paper unless we were ready to sell our home and lock in our gains. But then we'd have to find another place to live. Uh-oh. The inflated profit we could get from the sale of our old home would end up disappearing in the inflated price we had to pay for the next one.

Paper wealth is really meaningless when it comes to having financial security and knowing the value of your retirement nest egg on the day you plan to tap into it. *Real* wealth and financial security come from having a strategy that guarantees steady, predictable growth—no matter what the economic climate is. That's what Larry and I set out to find.

## What's Your Money IQ?

**Q:** If you have a $20 stock and it goes up by 40 percent, how much money did you make on that stock? (Hint: This is about a key financial principle, *not* a math question.)

**A:** Most people don't get the answer, and the talking heads on Wall Street hope the truth never dawns on you: You don't make *any* money unless you actually sell your stock and lock in your gains—assuming there *are* any gains to lock in. The same principle applies to the value of your home and any other investments.

## The Wall Street Casino

We've been told again and again that to get our money to "work" for us, to build a comfortable retirement and get a rate of return that will outpace inflation, we must invest in the stock market and be willing to accept its inherent risks. How many times have you heard that the stock market is the best place to grow your nest egg?

I'm going to prove that this is a myth Wall Street has brainwashed us into believing! Wall Street grudgingly admits there are no guarantees that your investment account won't lose some value in any given year. But let's look beyond that seemingly benign statement to the heart-stopping reality:

- Many people saw their investment accounts *plunge by 50 percent or more* when the dot-com bubble burst. Many investors—myself included—had moved their money into NASDAQ technology stocks, which plunged 78 percent from March 10, 2000, to October 9, 2002. More than a decade later, the NASDAQ is still *well* below its 2000 high.

- Investors who were diversified beyond tech stocks didn't fare much better. The S&P 500, which is a broader measure of the market, *lost 49 percent* in that same two-and-a-half-year period.
- After the S&P 500 peaked at 1565 in October 2007, it proceeded to *lose 57 percent* by March 2009. *That's two heart-stopping losses over 49 percent in one decade.*

Then, as the market began to pick up steam in March 2009, Wall Street urged us to jump back into the market with both feet. By the spring of 2013, they were boasting that both the S&P 500 and the Dow had hit new all-time highs.

But there's a tiny detail Wall Street forgot to mention: Our 36 percent inflation rate from 2000 to 2013 took an enormous bite out of the purchasing power of your dollars. And even when you look at the total return of the S&P 500 (including reinvested dividends), the real (inflation-adjusted) purchasing power of your investment remains *negative* after thirteen years. This assumes you have *no* fees, commissions, or taxes—not gonna happen!

A picture is worth a thousand words:

**YOUR RETIREMENT "PLAN" POWERED BY WALL STREET:
13 YEARS OF THE S&P 500 INDEX**

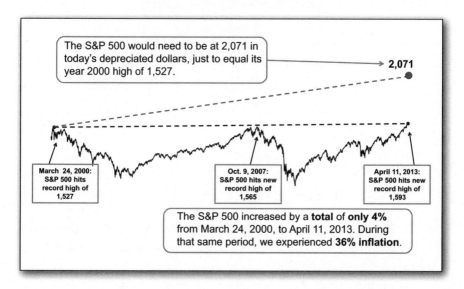

The S&P 500 would need to be at 2,071 in today's depreciated dollars, just to equal its year 2000 high of 1,527.

2,071

March 24, 2000:
S&P 500 hits
record high of
1,527

Oct. 9, 2007:
S&P 500 hits new
record high of
1,565

April 11, 2013:
S&P 500 hits new
record high of
1,593

The S&P 500 increased by a **total** of **only 4%** from March 24, 2000, to April 11, 2013. During that same period, we experienced **36% inflation**.

The end of 2012 marked the thirteenth year of a go-nowhere market. But how can you be sure it's all behind us now? Unless you have a crystal ball, you can't. Only time will tell. Most people don't realize or remember how long it can take the stock market to recover after a crash.

## How Long Does It Take the Stock Market to Recover?

Since 1929 we've had three market crashes where the Dow took *between sixteen and twenty-five years to return to pre-crash levels.*

After the stock market crashed in 1929, there was a six-month sucker rally, then the Dow continued tanking. Ultimately the Dow took three years to bottom out—dropping a staggering 89 percent! Then it took *twenty-five years* just to return to its pre-crash level.

Could something like that happen again? I don't know and neither does anyone else, including all the talking heads on TV and in magazines and newspapers. That's the problem. Too many of us have pinned our hopes for financial security on things we can't predict or count on— and we never could and never will be able to.

So the big question to ask yourself is (in the immortal words of Dirty Harry): "Are ya feelin' lucky?"

Can you even imagine the impact on your own retirement plans and current lifestyle if you had to wait *twenty-five years* for the market to recover?

---

Can you even imagine the impact on your own retirement
plans and current lifestyle if you had to wait
*twenty-five years* for the market to recover?

---

Here's a revealing way to gauge your tolerance for market risk: What is the minimum acceptable annual return you'd want to get that would make you willing to stomach the nerve-wracking volatility of the stock market? 7 percent? 10 percent? Maybe even more? I've surveyed thousands of people, and almost *everyone* says they wouldn't go through the agony if they got only 5 percent. But even if you only insisted on a 5 percent annual return, the Dow would have to be *over 32,000* right now—*today*—to have given you that return, after adjusting for inflation. No, that's not a typo. For proof, go to **www.BankOnYourself.com/Dow-32000**.

How long do you think it will take for the Dow to go to 32,000?

## Investors Are Predictably Irrational

What will happen in the stock market isn't predictable. But one thing is absolutely for sure and for certain: Investors are predictably *irrational*. We're not talking smart or stupid, sophisticated or naïve. We're talking across-the-board irrational.

So maybe you're thinking you can handle the volatility of the market by just gritting your teeth and praying everything turns out all right as you roll the dice in the Wall Street Casino. Or maybe you think that at the first sign of trouble, you'll be able to bail out of stocks and into bonds or money market funds to lock in your gains.

Unfortunately, that's not what's happening. History shows that most of us are far more successful at locking in our *losses* than our gains. Since 1994, DALBAR, Inc., the leading independent, unbiased investment performance rating firm, has studied the *actual* long-term results investors get in the market. In the 2015 Quantitative Analysis of Investor Behavior, they concluded:

- Over the last *three decades*, the average equity mutual fund investor has earned *only 3.79 percent per year*, or about *one-third* of the return of the S&P 500—beating inflation by only 1 percent per year. (Was that worth the roller-coaster ride and sleepless nights?)
- Investors in asset allocation funds (which spread your money among a variety of asset classes) earned *only 1.76 percent per year*, and fixed-income fund investors (like those in conservative bond funds) earned *less than 1 percent per year for the past thirty years*!

Shocking, isn't it? But if you've noticed your investment accounts aren't rising at the rate of the market, you recognize the truth of those numbers. How is it even possible for so many people to underperform the market indexes like that?

The verdict is in: DALBAR, Morningstar, and the behavioral finance experts confirm that the majority of investors *consistently buy and sell at the wrong times.* Sound irrational? Well, we're human, and we humans make emotional decisions driven by fear (survival) and greed. But as financial writer Brett Arends warns us, "You can't buy low and sell high if you buy high." And that's exactly what too many of us do.

---

The verdict is in: DALBAR, Morningstar, and the behavioral finance experts confirm that the majority of investors *consistently buy and sell at the wrong times.*

---

## What's Your Money IQ?

**Q:** What percentage of mutual funds, financial advisors, and investment advisory services *underperform* the overall market? And why?

**A:** 80 percent, according to the Hulbert Financial Digest. And it's not just because of the fees they charge. It's because all the experts are human, too, and are predictably irrational like all the rest of us, buying and selling at the wrong times.

In his book *Predictably Irrational*, behavioral economist Dan Ariely talks about how we human investors typically forget about our losses and mentally exaggerate our successes. (You gotta love the name of the institute Ariely co-founded: the Center for Advanced Hindsight.)

## Are You the Dumb Money?

How many times have you sworn you're *done* with the stock market *forever*? But then the market starts to rise. The Wall Street jocks tell you nonstop what you're missing out on. Your friends talk about how much their investments are going up—and you jump back in because you can't stand the pain of watching it rise day after day without you!

---

*"In investing, the majority is always wrong."*
—Wall Street adage

---

I heard a well-respected investment analyst interviewed about why he believed the stock market rally still had legs in spite of the fact that it had recently nearly doubled. (By the way, students of history will tell you how *rare* it is for a market to continue rising after such an extraordinary rally—only a handful of bull markets in S&P 500 history have gained more than 100 percent.) He said, "People who missed out on the rally will jump in and propel the market higher." Really? Have you heard that old saying, "If you're sitting at a poker table and you can't figure out who the sucker is, it's *you*"?

The investing world has a specific technical term for that kind of investing: **dumb money**. When the dumb money is piling into the market, you know it's about to reach a top. And when the dumb money is fleeing the market, a bottom isn't very far away. Dumb money, which is a heck of a lot of investors, misses the mark on both sides.

### What's Your Money IQ?

**Q:** According to Morningstar, Inc., the top-performing mutual fund for the decade ending December 31, 2009, enjoyed an 18 percent annual return. However, the typical *investor* in that fund wasn't so fortunate. What annual return did the typical *investor* get in that top-performing fund and why was their return so different?

**A:** The typical investor in the best-performing mutual fund of the last decade *lost an average of 11 percent per year, every year for ten years, even though the fund's prospectus boasted an 18 percent annual gain.* That's because mutual funds are legally required to advertise only the results of "buy-and-hold" investors. So when a fund advertises returns for any given period—in this case, a decade—it assumes investors bought the fund on the first day of the period and held it until the last day of the period—no matter how wild the ride got. Not gonna happen in real life. In fact, on average, investors hold mutual funds for less than five years.[8]

For more financial IQ quizzes, money tips, and
straight-talking special reports,
check out the free resources available at
**www.BankOnYourselfNation.com**

## What Has Wall Street Done to Our Retirement Plans?

I'll discuss retirement more thoroughly in Chapter 5. But according to a recent study by the Employee Benefit Research Institute, two-thirds of all workers say they're behind schedule in saving for retirement and plan to continue working to support themselves.[9] Even many of those who carefully did "all the right things" ended up with only sleepless nights and broken retirement dreams to show for it. Instead of achieving the financial peace of mind they hoped for, they've dug themselves into a financial hole so deep they may never be able to retire.

The stock market will continue on its endless roller-coaster ride, but you have only a limited amount of time to take control of your financial future. It seems that almost every week, a new Wall Street scandal gets exposed, doesn't it? Insider trading, high-speed computerized trading that stacks the deck against you, corporations cooking the books, giving investors the shaft. And as soon as the government cracks down on one scheme, Wall Street invents a new, obscure way to separate us from our money that nobody can figure out until it's too late.

### Play the Tortoise and Hare Savings Race Game

Wall Street has conditioned us to believe that the *only* way to get inflation-beating returns is to risk your money in the market. To find out if that's really true, we created a fascinating little game for you to play.

You can give the tortoise and the hare whatever amount of money you choose. The tortoise will put that money in a savings vehicle earning a steady 5 percent interest, year after year. The hare will put the money in an investment account earning a more exciting 8 percent return every

*continued*

year…except one. In the one year you select, the investment account will suffer a 30 percent loss.

I figure a one-time 30 percent loss is pretty realistic, when you consider the typical investor lost 49 percent or more in the market *twice* since 2000.

Which "loss year" will let the hare be ahead of the tortoise ten years from now? The first year? The tenth year? Or somewhere in between? Here's a clue: If the 30 percent loss happens in the fifth year, the tortoise wins by more than 16 percent. But will the hare win if the loss is in the second or eighth year? You can choose different years and different starting amounts by going to **www.BankOnYourself.com/race** and playing the game yourself.

## Is Your 401(k) on Life Support?

Government and industry statistics tell us that about 50 million Americans participate in employer-sponsored retirement plans. On the face of it, 401(k)s have it all—matching employer contributions, tax deferment, and professional administration and fund management. Workers are led to believe they can simply choose a fund, decide on a contribution amount, and then forget about it. Don't give it a second thought. Just let the money grow over time.

Why wrestle with the time-consuming, risk-prone task of managing your own retirement financial planning when you can simply push the autopilot button and check back again in two or three decades to see how large your financial stockpile has grown? A Greek chorus of government regulators, Wall Street executives, financial planners, and media commentators regularly advises us that only *professional* retirement investment planners can hope to get the best long-term outcome for our nest egg.

Because Americans can't possibly successfully grow their own retirement funds themselves, the government has instructed employers to offer their workers a variety of retirement plans, most commonly 401(k)s. And most of us assume that because the government gives its blessing to these plans, and employers offer them, they must be good for us, right? After all, they were "designed to make it easier for investors" to avoid the headaches and inherent risks of managing our own retirement accounts.

Easier? Yes. But wiser and less risky? *Often not.* The problem is that getting good returns depends on picking the right stocks, funds, or money managers. As we just learned, 80 percent of all mutual funds and 80 percent of all investment newsletters and advisors *underperform* the market over the long term.

But what wage earners don't yet understand is that many of those personal retirement accounts we've been paying into will *bleed tens, even hundreds of thousands of dollars in taxes, fees, and commissions—regardless of how the markets perform over the coming decades.*

John Bogle, the founder of Vanguard, the world's largest mutual fund company, has stated, "No mutual fund has yet reported on the returns that it actually earned for its investors." Why? He explains, "Fund investors do not earn the full market return … because fund investors incur costs, and costs are subtracted directly from the *gross* returns funds earn." Bogle also notes that during the 1990s bull market, "the 6.5 percent annual return earned by fund *investors* was 3.3 percent behind the 9.8 percent annual return reported by the funds themselves."[10] Wow! Investors received *one-third less* than what the funds advertised.

---

During the 1990s bull market, investors earned
only a 6.5 percent annual return—*one-third less* than
what the mutual funds advertised, according to John
Bogle, founder of Vanguard.

---

And the 401(k) fee creep is hidden. *Few people realize the compounded costs of high fees paid out over decades.* These charges, paired with taxes and inflation, can *all but consume a retiree's capital appreciation.*

Doesn't it seem like the government ought to step in and fix this?

Well, it has—sort of. In 2006, Congress approved legislation to provide protection. But Congress didn't protect *you!* Instead, Congress approved legislation *that protects your employer and their 401(k) administrators,* just in case you wake up one day and finally realize how much you have lost. The legislation says you can't sue for damages as long as your employer *automatically* invests your 401(k) money in certain types of mutual funds!

---

As long as your employer automatically invests your 401(k) money in certain types of mutual funds, you can't hold them liable for your losses, thanks to a law Congress passed in 2006.

---

Would it surprise you to learn that these "automatically invested" mutual funds impose some of the *highest* fees while underperforming the overall market (often *significantly*), and that the mutual fund industry heavily lobbied Congress to ensure *their* best interests won out? Didn't think so. Just one more example of how the deck is stacked against you.

I'll get into more detail on the problems of 401(k)s in Chapter 5.

## CDs and Other "Safe" Investments

In recent years, the Federal Reserve Board threw seniors and savers under the bus by keeping interest rates at historic lows, and returns on CDs, savings, and money market accounts have been so low you need a magnifying glass to see them. Those who sought safety in these vehicles have a *negative* yield after taking inflation into account.

But you've got options. Throughout this book, I'll show you a better alternative to traditional savings vehicles and unreliable conventional investments. And if you've had enough, you can join the hundreds of thousands who have already opted out of a system where the odds are stacked against you.

## The "Home Sweet Home" Investment Plan

The stock market gives you no guarantees or predictability, and savings accounts and CDs typically don't keep up with inflation. Are you ready to take a look at another bit of conventional financial wisdom that has been turned on its head?

We were taught we could count on the equity in our homes to be a major part of our retirement and wealth-building plan. Not long ago, home equity was the biggest chunk of most nest eggs. Many of us even made extra mortgage payments or refinanced into fifteen-year loans so we could have the security of knowing our homes would be paid off in full when we retired. Here's a snapshot of how well the strategy of plowing money we could have put into our savings into our homes instead has worked out in recent years:

SOURCE: *Standard & Poor's Case-Shiller Home Price Index.*

Starting in January 2002 to the peak of the housing market bubble in June 2006, home values skyrocketed by 71 percent. But by March 2012, they had plunged to a level barely 10 percent above where they were a decade earlier.

From January 2002 to January 2013, housing prices increased by less than a measly 2 percent per year. However, we had 30 percent inflation during that period, which more than wiped out any real gains in home values. And that ignores the pain and suffering experienced by millions of people who lost their homes or are underwater on their mortgages.

The real estate bubble laid bare the fiction that housing prices only go *up*. Real estate is subject to the same volatility and unpredictability as any other investment. Even seasoned home buyers who regularly purchase properties to improve them and flip them for profit were caught short in this latest real estate crash.

Real estate investments *can* be part of a well-diversified financial plan. Real estate enjoys some tax advantages and has the potential for income and appreciation. But you have no way of predicting real estate values, whether residential or commercial. You also can't predict how much rent you'll be able to charge for your property, how long it will take to find a tenant, or what maintenance costs you'll incur.

And the financial crisis and credit lockdown have made it painfully clear how little control you have over the equity in your home and other real estate. Home equity lines of credit have been slashed or frozen without warning, and refinancing options dried up even for people with good credit.

Many people were unpleasantly surprised to discover how difficult it can be to *sell* your real estate to get at your equity. Much like trying to predict the stock market, you can't guarantee the real estate market will be up when you're ready (or need) to sell, and you have no way of knowing how long it will take to sell.

## How an Experienced Real Estate Investor Got Caught Short

Eric Greene proudly bought his first home forty years ago when he was only twenty-three years old. Since then he's bought and sold a dozen homes and investment properties, making a profit each time. As the owner of a successful retail business, he accumulated a nice nest egg by saving diligently and investing the money in the stock market. He planned to retire around age sixty-five.

Eric built his last dream house in 2004. As the value increased rapidly over the next few years, he refinanced several times, investing the cash in home improvements. He felt confident that this real estate investment, like all his others, would continue to increase in value. "Heck," Eric says, "even the government and Congress told us real estate was just going to continue to rise."

When the bubble burst in 2007, Eric found himself underwater on his mortgage by hundreds of thousands of dollars. And with the slowdown in his business, he could no longer afford to make the payments and make repairs to his home. After Eric negotiated fruitlessly with the bank for more than a year, his dream home was sold on the courthouse steps. His retirement account was totally decimated by the stock market crash. Now at age sixty-three, Eric is facing the unimaginable prospect of having to build a retirement fund from scratch. Fortunately, Eric found Bank On Yourself and says he now has the peace of mind of knowing the Bank On Yourself plan he started four years ago will give him the predictability and guarantees that were missing from his previous financial plan.

Even if a crash of the magnitude of 2007 proves to be a one-time disaster, is owning real estate a reliable wealth-building strategy? According to Robert Shiller, co-creator of the widely used Case-Shiller Home Price Index, periods of rapid increases have consistently been followed by declines. As a result, home values in the U.S. have outpaced inflation by only about 1 percent per year over the long term. That's not even close to the growth rate you really need for your nest egg, is it? And the days of using a house as a piggy bank or an ATM are gone.

---

**U.S. home values have only outpaced inflation by about
1 percent per year over the long term.**

---

In the April 13, 2013, article, "Why Home Prices Change (or Don't)" in the *New York Times*, Shiller wrote, "Booms are typically followed by busts, usually in far less than ten years. In a decade, an entire housing boom, if there is one in inflation-corrected terms, is likely to have been reversed and completely washed away." As a 2011 opinion piece titled "The Housing Illusion" in the *Wall Street Journal* noted, "A home's main economic purpose is—or should be—shelter. During the mania of the last decade, housing too often became an investment out of proportion to any sensible contributions to national wealth and well-being."

## How Precious Are Metals?

Now let's take a look at the promise of gold and other precious metals. I've found most people who are buying gold today have no clue about the volatile history of that metal. And as the saying goes, those who forget or are ignorant of the past are condemned to repeat it.

Again, a picture is worth a thousand words:

**INFLATION-ADJUSTED PRICE OF GOLD**

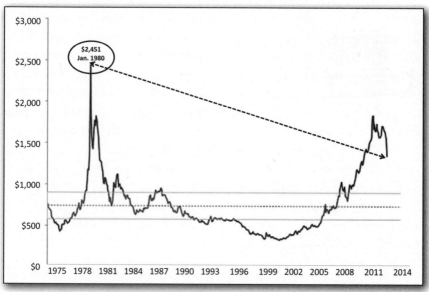

An ounce of gold would have had to be worth $2,451 in May 2013 to have same purchasing power it had in 1980.

In September 2011, gold hit a record high of $1,920 per ounce. Anyone who bought gold at its low of $608 in 2007 and sold it at or near its high enjoyed a most impressive gain. What I haven't been able to find are any flesh-and-blood individual investors who timed their gold purchases to actually cash in on these theoretical returns. I'm sure some such lucky souls did make a killing. They are, however, far more rare than the precious metal itself.

By June 2013, gold had plunged by 38 percent. On April 15 alone, gold fell a whopping $115 per ounce—it's like bungee jumping *without* the bungee cord!

On an inflation-adjusted basis, the price of gold would have to be *around $2,500 per ounce* today to have the same purchasing power it did *thirty-three years ago*. In spite of gold's recent meteoric rise, that's around $1,300 per ounce *more* than gold's price as I write this in June 2013.

For those of us who don't have the Midas touch when it comes to investment timing, gold remains a leaden financial vessel.

In *Common Sense on Mutual Funds*, John Bogle points out that "Gold provides no internal rate of return. It provides none of the intrinsic value that's created for stocks by earnings growth and dividend yields, and none of the value provided for bonds by interest payments. For the more than two centuries between 1802 and 2008, an initial investment of $10,000 [in gold] grew to barely $26,000 in *real* returns."

Gold pays no dividends and generates no income, so your only way to profit from a gold investment is to actually sell it for a higher price than you paid for it. Until you do sell, your paper profits do you little good, since you can't take that pretty number on paper to the grocery store.

And what about taxes? Most people don't realize that you will pay one of the *highest* federal tax rates on any profits you might make with gold whether you've got gold coins or bars or an exchange-traded fund that invests in gold bullion. That's because precious metals are considered a *collectible*, which is *taxed at nearly double the rate* of stocks and real estate capital gains.

## What About Silver?

Like gold, silver gains popularity during times of economic and stock market volatility. However, the returns on silver are among the lowest of all commodities, compared to the long-term risk. Through the spring of 2013, silver lost an incredible 56 percent of its value since its high in April 2011. That's a big decline for a so-called safe asset, and it's a reminder of the dangers of commodities.

In sum, gold and silver provide zero certainty, especially for individual investors hoping to shield their savings from volatility and risk. History has proven that chasing rising gold prices is a fool's errand. Folks rush to metals when times are tough as a predictable savings vehicle, yet gold is one of the most volatile investments of all. To really build your nest egg safely, you need a strategy that allows you to chart exactly how much your money will appreciate year after year, no matter what. That's truly the gold standard of building wealth.

## Pundits Tell Us Not to Worry

From articles and columns in the *Wall Street Journal* and *Financial Times* to the madcap commentary and analyses of CNBC's Jim Cramer, talking heads and financial "gurus" keep spouting the same old platitudes to reassure investors—*despite* all evidence to the contrary. Consider these widely accepted beliefs about personal finance:

1. Over time, the stock market has consistently proven the best and most reliable investment vehicle for the vast majority of Americans. (Not.)

2. You won't require as much income when you retire as you do while working.

(Hey, old age isn't a prison sentence! After working and sacrificing for most of your adult life, retirement should be a reward. With *proper* planning, the vast majority of people *can* live wealthy lives in their golden years.)

3. You'll retire in a lower tax bracket. (Does anybody believe tax rates are going to go *down* over the long term?)

4. No worthwhile investment is free of volatility and uncertainty. (Keep reading!)

I can personally attest that many hundreds of thousands of people— folks just like you and me—have beaten the system by shunning uncertainty and volatility in exchange for guaranteed annual growth of their financial portfolio. These savvy savers have never had a losing year *or even a single losing day*.

Yet the financial gurus—whose advice got us into this mess in the first place!—are telling us to "take more risk," "keep working until you drop," and "plan on living on a lot less in retirement."

To which I say, "Phooey!" Join the Bank On Yourself Revolution, and see that disastrous conventional wisdom turned on its head!

## Where the Smart Money Goes

Many people have bought into Wall Street's mantra that "investing pays off over the long haul" and try to just shrug off their losses. Wall Street has been very successful in brainwashing us into accepting the dubious insight that the market will experience ups and some downs, "but if you just hang in there, it'll all work out in the end." Really? Hey, I'm sixty now, and I no longer have *decades* to wait around for my investments to recover!

The chart on the next page shows the growth pattern of one of my Bank On Yourself–type policies. It displays the growth I've had so far, along with the growth I'll have if I continue paying the level premium and the dividends stay where they are today. Right now dividends, like interest rates, are at historic lows. If they increase, the growth will be even greater.

(Keep in mind that no two plans are alike, so your plan won't look like mine. Yours would be custom-tailored to *your* unique situation and your short-term and long-term goals. But unlike traditional investing and saving strategies, you can actually know the bottom-line guaranteed amount you'll have in your plan at every point along the way, *before* you decide if you want to move forward with Bank On Yourself. To find out what *your* numbers and results could be if you added Bank On Yourself to your financial plan, request a free Analysis at **www.BankOnYourselfFreeAnalysis.com** or by completing and submitting the form on page 265.)

If you want a growth curve that just keeps increasing at a steeper pace—no luck, skill, or guesswork required—take a look at Bank On Yourself. That's how these policies are engineered to grow.

## GROWTH CHART

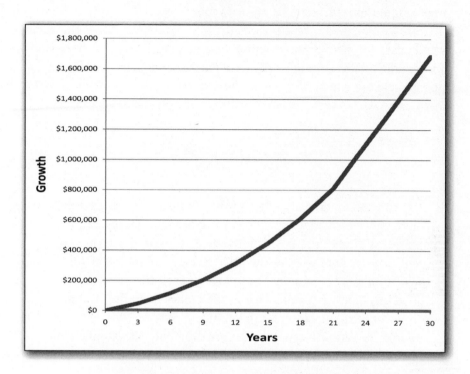

Growth Pattern of Cash Value in a Properly Structured
Dividend-Paying Policy Over Thirty Years

And that's why Larry and I have built our financial foundation on Bank On Yourself. After researching over 450 financial products and strategies, I found only one that allows people to bypass Wall Street, fire their bankers, and take back control of their own financial futures. In the next chapter we will look at exactly what Bank On Yourself is and how it works. That's your first step toward joining the Revolution and growing your wealth safely and predictably.

On the other hand, if you still believe that Wall Street holds the key to your financial security and that the economic challenges that have caused the volatility in the markets are over, keep doing what you've been doing. Cross your fingers and hope that, against all odds, it will still work out.

But ask yourself: "Will continuing to invest the same way I've been investing get me the financial peace of mind I want?"

Once you've made the decision to stop wandering down the same blind alley, you need to take action. You need to take the proper steps and use the financial vehicles that will give you a solid financial foundation and ensure you *never* again suffer a "lost decade"—or even another lost year.

# KEY TAKE-AWAYS

1. **You can't count on paper profits.** We've been seduced into believing we have real wealth by eye-popping numbers on pieces of paper. Whether that's your brokerage account or 401(k) statement, a home appraisal, or the price today of an ounce of gold, those numbers are *meaningless* unless you sell the asset and (hopefully) lock in a gain. That's called **market timing**, and most people and experts fail miserably at it.

Bank On Yourself–type policies are different. The numbers on your annual statement represent *real* wealth that doesn't disappear when the markets crash.

2. **What the stock market gives, it takes away.** The wild swings we've witnessed in this age of electronic trading prove that Wall Street is *not* the smart choice for the twenty-first century. Your bets are not going to regularly beat the market. In fact, the only thing Wall Street guarantees is that they, the money managers and brokers, get paid, *whether you win or lose.* Can you really afford to risk your financial nest egg? Would you plunk it all down in Vegas? If you might need that money in the next twenty years for *any* purpose, you can't afford to entrust it to the Wall Street Casino either.

3. **Nothing in life is free.** When you entrust your nest egg to financial professionals, the fees you pay for their services are compounded year after year and can take an enormous bite out of your savings. But with Bank On Yourself, *all* of the fees and costs have *already* been taken into account in the bottom-line

results you are guaranteed *before* you even begin your plan. There are *no* nasty surprises.

**4. CDs, savings, and money market accounts have trouble just beating inflation.** Being conservative by keeping your money in cash keeps you at the mercy of a bank, and banks are not in the habit of being generous.

**5. The sobering lesson of the Great Recession is that real estate prices do *not* only go up.** Over the long term, home values have appreciated by only 1 percent more than inflation. Live in your home, enjoy your home, but don't expect to cash out big when you sell it.

**6. There is no pot of gold at the end of the rainbow.** With their wild price gyrations and high tax rates, you'd have to have a magical Midas touch to get your pots of gold and silver to really pan out.

**7. Bank On Yourself has important advantages not offered by traditional investments.** Your money will grow predictably. It doesn't go backward or suffer a lost decade, and you will know right from the start the guaranteed amount it will grow every year. You can go to sleep at night confident that, on the day you need it, your money will be waiting for you.

# CHAPTER 3

# The Engine Behind Bank On Yourself

*An invasion of armies can be resisted, but not*
*an idea whose time has come.*
—VICTOR HUGO

BASED ON what I shared in the last chapter, can you see why doing the same-old, same-old is *not* going to get you where you want to go? Painful, isn't it? Crazy-making?

When I came to that same realization, I was ready to ditch Wall Street, fire my banker, and take back control of my financial future from those yahoos who had threatened it! But how? As a business-building consultant to more than 40,000 financial advisors over two decades, I've investigated hundreds of different financial vehicles, products, and strategies in my search for a safe, simple, and predictable way to grow wealth—no matter what happens in the stock and real estate markets. Most turned out to be not even worth the paper they were printed on; some were actually dangerous to your financial health. My husband and I put the best of the bunch into practice in

---

**INSIDE THIS CHAPTER . . .**

- What the Experts Got Wrong
- Using Dividend-Paying Whole Life Insurance to Build Wealth
- How the Economy Affects Bank On Yourself
- The Big Lie: Buy Term and Invest the Difference
- Why Whole Life Beats Term
- Not a Good Bet: Equity Indexed Universal Life

our own financial plan, and most of those turned out to be disappointments, too. We lost every penny of the six figures we put into just one supposedly "safe" investment.

Fortunately, my investigation uncovered *one* financial product that gives you an *unbeatable* combination of safety, guarantees, flexibility, liquidity, control, and tax advantages. I'm so confident of that statement that I'm offering a $100,000 cash reward to the first person who uses a different strategy that can match or beat it. My challenge has been out there since 2008, and no one's won it yet. But feel free to give it a shot! And in the immortal words of Dr. Phil, "Good luck with that." (To see if you can win that $100,000 Challenge, go to **www.BankOnYourself.com/challenge**.)

As I mentioned briefly in Chapter 1, this financial vehicle is a little-known variation of an asset that has increased in value *every single year for more than 160 years*, and it's the basis of Bank On Yourself: **dividend-paying whole life insurance**.

## It's Not *That* Whole Life Policy!

You're thinking, "She must be kidding, right?" If you have a knee-jerk negative reaction to whole life insurance, you're not alone. After all, well-known financial advisors such as Suze Orman and Dave Ramsey, among others, will tell you to avoid whole life insurance like the plague. But the whole life policies used for the Bank On Yourself method are *dramatically* different from the ones these experts have criticized in *three key ways*. Their objections simply don't apply to the Bank On Yourself–type policies. For example:

> **1. Financial pundits say that the money you can access in the plan, your cash value, grows much too slowly in a whole life policy.** They claim that you typically won't have *any* cash value at all in the first couple of years.
>
> True for some whole life policies. However, a Bank On Yourself–type policy incorporates little-known riders that dramatically accelerate the growth of your money in the policy so you have up to *forty times more cash value* than the policies most experts talk about, especially in the early years of the policy.

Adding these riders, or options, allows you to use your policy as a powerful financial management tool from day one. (I'll show you exactly how these riders speed up the growth of your cash value in the next chapter.)

Celebrity financial gurus say one reason for the slow growth in cash value in a traditional whole life policy is the high commissions paid to the insurance advisors who sell them. Again, true in some other policies. But when a qualified advisor structures a Bank On Yourself–type policy for you, they receive *50–70 percent less* commission because much of your premium is directed into the riders that make your cash value grow significantly faster.

## Ⓜ Ⓨ Ⓣ Ⓗ Ⓑ Ⓤ Ⓢ Ⓣ Ⓔ Ⓡ
### The Commissions Are High

Who complains the loudest that Bank On Yourself–type policies pay too much commission? Often stockbrokers and financial planners. They claim that high commissions are the only reason agents sell these policies.

Nope. The reality is that those whining money managers are actually making up to *ten times as much* off your business as Bank On Yourself Advisors! Let's compare: Assume you put $10,000 per year for thirty years into a Bank On Yourself–type policy and the very same amount into an investment account.

According to those financial planners and experts, the agent who sold you the policy would earn about $10,000 commission in the first year and a small commission each year after that.

That would be true of the policies most advisors talk about. But because a Bank On Yourself Authorized Advisor will direct much of your $10,000 annual premium into the riders that make your cash value grow a lot faster, that advisor will only make between $3,000 and $5,000 in the first year, *not* $10,000. They'll receive a small renewal commission during the remaining years, bringing the *total commission paid* over thirty years to about $8,500.

Meanwhile, the planner who's complaining that this is *way too much* commission will earn a management fee every year of *at least* 1 percent of your account value (and often it's 1.5 percent or even 2 percent) which, if the market has moderate returns over the same thirty years, means he'll earn *$100,000—or more!* You don't need your calculator to figure who's getting paid *way too much*.

*continued*

continued from previous page

Add to that, the investment account manager will *not* be able to tell you how much your account is going to grow over that thirty years *because he has no clue.* (Wanna try a fun experiment? Ask your broker or money manager if he'll guarantee that you'll have a specific amount in your account in ten or thirty years, and if he'll give you a money-back guarantee if he misses the mark!)

On the other hand, before you even initiate a Bank On Yourself plan, you'll know the *minimum guaranteed value of your plan in any given year.*

So let me ask you: Would you rather pay $100,000 to the money manager who has no idea how it will all turn out in the end? Or $8,500 to the Bank On Yourself Advisor who can tell you your guaranteed result? By the way, unlike fees you pay a money manager, all fees and expenses, including the Bank On Yourself Advisor's commissions and the cost of insurance, have *already* been deducted from your guaranteed bottom-line numbers

**2. Most financial experts and advisors only discuss whole life policies in which the death benefit stays level for the life of the policy.** Let's ignore the fact that we researched over forty life insurance companies and couldn't find *any* that still offer that kind of whole life policy. (I'm thinkin' Suze and Dave just might want to update their talking points.)

In dividend-paying whole life policies (as in Bank On Yourself–type plans), dividends can be left in the policy to purchase additional coverage while at the same time growing your cash value in the most efficient way possible. I've posted one of my own policy statements on my website that shows you how the death benefit can keep growing. In this case, it increased by more than $8,000, or 3.5 percent, by the end of the first year. (You can see my statement at **www.BankOnYourself.com/policy1.**)

Over time, the death benefit can increase many times over, as you'll see in the next chapter.

**3. The financial experts often complain that the insurance company "only pays you the death benefit and keeps your cash value" when the policy owner dies.**

Really? Then how do you explain this: In another one of my policy statements posted at the link above, you can see that if I'd died on the date the statement was issued, my family would have received a check for $381,776, which is a few thousand dollars *more* than the original $250,000 death benefit *and* current total cash value ($128,361) *combined.*

It's amazing to me that so many people—and so many experts—hold whole life insurance to a totally different standard than other financial vehicles. For example, if you have $100,000 of equity in your home and you sell it for $250,000, do you expect to end up receiving *both* amounts, for a total of $350,000? Of course not.

However, as I just demonstrated, a Bank On Yourself–type policy *can* deliver that advantage!

## Whole Life as a Wealth-Building Vehicle

How can I explain the difference between whole life as a wealth-building vehicle and most other products and strategies the financial gurus favor? On the freeway, can you spot the difference between a teenage boy putting daddy's hot sports car through its paces, and a young suburban mother in her minivan taking two kids to play soccer, with a toddler buckled in a car seat? One driver is trying to get some-where *fast*, while the other is getting to her destination while doing everything possible to protect those who are near and dear to her. If you can understand that difference, then maybe you can sense the difference between the Wall Street Casino and the life insurance industry.

As Jesús Huerta de Soto noted in his book *Money, Bank Credit and Economic Cycles*:

> The institution of life insurance … is based on a series of technical, actu-arial, financial and juridical [relating to the law and its administration] principles of business behavior which have enabled it to perform its mis-sion perfectly and survive economic crises and recessions which other institutions, especially banking, have been unable to overcome. Therefore the high 'financial death rate' of banks, which systematically suspend payments and fail without the support of the central bank, has histori-cally contrasted with the health and technical solvency of life insurance companies. (In the last two hundred years, a negligible number of life insurance companies have disappeared due to financial difficulties.)[11]

With Bank On Yourself–type policies, you receive a guaranteed and predictable cash value increase *every single year*—in both good times *and* bad. In addition, you have the potential to receive dividends. While not guaranteed, the companies preferred by Bank On Yourself Authorized Advisors have paid dividends every year for more than 100 years, including during the Great Depression.

The growth in a whole life insurance policy is not only guaranteed, it's *exponential*. It's designed to become more efficient every single year, simply because you stick with it rather than jumping from one investment to another. This gives you some *built-in protection* against inflation.

## Corporate Accountant Fires Wall Street

Derek Logan is a textbook poster boy for someone who did all the right things financially that we've been taught to do. He's been working since he had a newspaper route at age ten. He diligently set his goals and used a budget system. He maxed out contributions to his 401(k) and had his home paid off by the age of forty-five. As a corporate accountant for more than thirty years, Derek realized he had achieved all of the goals he set for himself—*except* for the goal of being able to retire at a specific age with a specific amount of money.

As he closed in on his hoped-for retirement age, he became disheartened and frustrated because the value of his retirement account had been slashed several times over the years. After doing his due diligence like any good accountant, Derek started a Bank On Yourself–type policy. And he's thrilled that he no longer throws his hard-earned dollars down on the tables of the Wall Street Casino!

When the market recently experienced volatility as it so often does, Derek sent me this grateful note: "As the market went down, I smiled. Not at the anguish so many must have been feeling, but at the joy of knowing I wasn't being affected—this time, or ever again. I printed Thursday's headline—*512 Point Plunge on the Dow!*—and included it in my Bank On Yourself portfolio notebook as a reminder of the best financial decision I've ever made!" (Read or listen to my interview with Derek at **www.BankOnYourself.com/derek**.)

For most of us, the whole life insurance scorned by financial pundits actually proves to be a lot safer and smarter—*if* you pick the right policy. Be warned: Not all cash-value life insurance policies are created equal. In fact, some of them, such as universal and indexed universal life, should be avoided. (See why at the end of this chapter.) Do your own investigation and don't jump from the frying pan into the fire.

## Dentist Achieves Financial Security

"I've used the Bank On Yourself method since 2004 and now have several policies. We've used them to finance our RV, home renovations, vacations, and unexpected expenses. In the process, we're growing wealth safely and securely for retirement that we can access when and how we want—no taxes due on it."
—Thomas Hesch, DDS

By doing your research, you'll find that Bank On Yourself–type policies build a guaranteed and predictable cash value—*and* they build it much faster than policies most financial advisors talk about. Both your cash value and your death benefit grow more efficiently every year, and your cash value is guaranteed to equal your death benefit when the policy matures.

This is *true* wealth creation with none of the volatility and risk associated with the stock and real estate markets. You know the minimum guaranteed value of your policy in any given year, as well as the minimum guaranteed income you could take from the plan and for how long you could take it. "I tell my clients about it every day. Simply put: peace of mind," says Patricia Smith, a hair salon owner in New England. "I've just gotten started, but already I feel more confident about my future than I have in my entire life riding the Wall Street roller coaster. I love knowing that if I'm ever in a place where I need money unexpectedly, it will be there."

## Is This a Safe and Secure Place to Put Your Money?

The companies recommended by Bank On Yourself Authorized Advisors are among the financially strongest life insurance groups in the country. In essence, they're owned by the policy owners (you!), which means these companies focus on the long-term best interests of the policy owners rather than the short-term demands of Wall Street.

Many people don't realize that life insurance companies are strictly regulated via four layers of protection:

1. They're audited regularly by the state insurance commissioner's office (sometimes by dozens of different states) to ensure they maintain sufficient reserves to pay future claims and that they are on solid financial ground.

2. If a company gets into financial difficulty, the state insurance commissioner's office can take over and run the company in the interests of policyholders. Historically, a failed insurer's business is then taken over by another company, according to the National Organization of Life and Health Insurance Guaranty Associations.

3. Most insurance companies are audited regularly by several independent rating companies.

4. Additional policy owner protections are available on a state-by-state basis. For example, in one annual policy statement I received, there was a notice regarding the various protections provided by the Insurance Guaranty Association of New Mexico, the state where I live.

In addition to these layers of protection, life insurance companies are simply run *differently*. Remember that mom driving in the minivan versus the kid in the hot sports car? Life insurance companies aren't trying to grab short-term profits wherever they can. Their mission is to get you and your family to your destination *safely*.

## ⓂⓎⓉⒽⒷⓊⓈⓉⒺⓇ

### The Truth About AIG

Is AIG an example of a big, bad insurance company? When AIG captured head-lines during the financial crisis and received a bailout, many people assumed their life insurance operations were at fault.

According to a 2009 posting on the National Association of Insurance Commissioners (NAIC) website, they weren't. They "did not receive a bailout; they are financially solvent." The NAIC also stated that AIG's insurance subsidiaries did *not* cause the problem and would, in fact, be part of the solution. It was the company's *non-insurance* operations that wreaked all the havoc.

## Facts of Life (Insurance)

- **Drivers of the economy:** Life insurers have $4.3 trillion invested in the U.S. economy, making them one of the largest sources of capital in the nation.[12] They paid more than $19 billion in federal, state, and local taxes in one recent year.

- **Meets safe capital requirements:** I've said that life insurance is safe, but don't just take my word for it. Banks are legally required to have a foundation of very safe liquid assets, known as Tier 1 capital. Life insurance is considered to be so safe that bank regulators allow life insurance policies owned by banks to meet their Tier 1 capital requirements. In fact, as of June 2011, the nation's banks owned guaranteed, high-cash-value permanent life insurance with a surrender value of approximately $135 billion.[13]

- **Blessed by the Oracle of Omaha:** Warren Buffett, widely considered to be the most successful investor of our time, owns several life insurance companies. (Buffett can't legally own the kind of insurance companies used for the Bank On Yourself concept because they are owned by policy owners rather than stockholders.)

- **Diversified low-risk investments:** As for the companies recommended by Bank On Yourself Authorized Advisors specifically, the bulk of their portfolios is invested in investment-grade fixed-income assets. Their bond portfolios are highly diversified across many industries and companies, and typically no investment represents more than 1 percent of assets. Less than 1 percent to 2 percent is invested in U.S. Treasury or other government debt. These companies had virtually no exposure to the risky investments that caused the market meltdown of 2008.

  Due to their financial strength and reserves, these companies have the ability to hold on to any assets that may decline in value for many years until those assets recover.

- **Source of capital, even in tough times:** Life insurance cash values serve as a source of available capital to individuals, families, and businesses, even when credit is difficult to obtain. At the end of 2011, there were $129 billion in life insurance policy loans outstanding.[14]

### The Pillar in Retired Navy Commander's Financial Plan

"I almost didn't call the Bank On Yourself Authorized Advisor I was referred to. When I first heard about Bank On Yourself, I thought it was another investment scheme and almost didn't look into it. I'm glad I overcame my concerns—it's now a major pillar in our financial plan."
—Commander Robert Chambers, Jr., U.S. Navy, Retired

- **Bedrock of our grandparents' savings plans:** Back in 1900, *half* of all Americans' savings was held in life insurance and annuities.[15] And fully one-third of families owned whole life insurance policies in 1950.[16]

- **Help great businesses succeed:** Many famous people have used life insurance policy loans to start or grow their businesses when no banker would lend them a dime. Following the 1929 stock market crash, famous retailer J. C. **Penney** borrowed against his life insurance policies to help meet the company payroll. Had he not had this ready access to capital, the company probably would have been forced to close its doors.

**Walt Disney** borrowed from his life insurance policy in 1953 to help fund Disneyland when no banker would lend him the money.

**McDonald's** might have only served a few hundred thousand burgers had it not been for Ray Kroc's whole life insurance policies. Kroc had constant cash flow problems during the early years and borrowed from his policies to help cover salaries of key employees and to create the initial Ronald McDonald advertising campaign.

In 2002, Doris Christopher sold her kitchen tool company, the **Pampered Chef**, to Warren Buffett for a reported $1.5 billion. She had started the company in her suburban Chicago home in 1980 with $3,000 she borrowed from her life insurance policy to purchase inventory.

**Foster Farms** was founded in 1939 when Max and Verda Foster borrowed $1,000 against their life insurance policy to buy an eighty-acre farm near Modesto, CA.

All of these fully documented stories and more can be found in the article *Six Famous Brands Started or Saved by Life Insurance* on **www. LifeHealthPro.com**.

Of course, you don't have to be famous to take advantage of the financing opportunities these policies offer. Suzi Hersey, a real estate investor in Virginia, reported, "I was able to take a loan with no questions asked and no credit check. I'm the one who determines when and how I'll pay the loan back. I *want* to pay the loan back because I'm recouping interest I would have paid to a credit card company or bank. And by paying it back the way my Authorized Advisor showed me, my plan value increases. I feel so fortunate to have found Bank On Yourself."

## How the Economy Affects Whole Life Policies

Over the years I've been asked a number of questions about how Bank On Yourself policies might fare in different economic situations. I hear from people every day who tell me they want to add Bank On Yourself to their financial plan, but they haven't quite been able to make the leap yet. They worry about what direction the economy is going. They want to see what the political climate will be. They want certainty in an uncertain world.

I don't have a crystal ball, but let's take a look at the potential impact various economic conditions might have on Bank On Yourself policies:

- **A decline in the dollar:** No one knows for sure what direction the dollar will go. The current economic environment can change at any time, and it can turn on a dime, as it has in the past. We're a global economy, and the actions of other nations impact us and our own economy.

  An article from MSN.com's MoneyCentral on October 13, 2009, reported that when the dollar was taking a beating in 2009, central banks in numerous Asian countries were "actively buying dollars to check its fall against their currencies." Why would they do that? Because their nation's exporters "can't handle a drop in profitability and competitiveness" if the dollar drops too far.

  As Bloomberg.com reported on August 24, 2011, "A weak dollar may be one of the bright spots in the U.S. economy, and it could be the gift that keeps giving." The article spelled out several ways the U.S. benefits from a declining dollar.

  The point is that the effect on the economy of the value of the U.S. dollar is not a black-and-white issue, and no one can accurately predict what will happen. But the dividend-paying whole life policies used for the Bank On Yourself concept *have survived and thrived for over 160 years while the dollar was strong, while the dollar was weak, and in virtually every economic situation imaginable.* Since you must park your money *someplace*, you would be hard-pressed to find a safer, more advantageous place to put your dollars in good times *or* bad.

- **High inflation:** Insurance companies recommended by Bank On Yourself Authorized Advisors have much of their assets in long-term investment-grade fixed-income assets like corporate bonds. When inflation drives up interest rates, the rates on new bonds typically follow suit, which can increase policy dividends as well. This helps offset the increase in inflation for policyholders. This is precisely what has happened during high-inflation periods in the past.

It's interesting to note that since 1920, according to Federal Reserve Economic Data, *corporate bond yields have been higher than inflation*, except for a couple points during the 1970s when inflation was skyrocketing. However, corporate bond yields *did* catch up and surpass the inflation rate and have held a positive spread above inflation since then.

Life insurance companies don't trade in and out of bonds. They have the reserves to hold bonds until maturity, if necessary, so they can avoid taking losses. And they can invest new premiums at higher rates.

Plus, Bank On Yourself policies are designed to grow more efficiently every single year. Because the growth of both your cash value and your death benefit is guaranteed and exponential, but your premium never increases, *you receive some built-in protection against inflation on both accounts.*

- **Deflation:** In a deflationary environment, income is king. In that scenario, investors struggle to find safe, dependable sources of income. Top-quality bonds that provide that income—and that make up a major portion of an insurer's portfolio—typically boom in that environment. Bonds do well because as interest rates decline, the higher interest that is credited on existing bonds become more valuable.

Again, insurance companies generally hold bonds until maturity. So in a deflationary period, older bonds with higher interest rates help offset new bonds that are purchased at lower interest rates.

- **A booming stock or real estate market:** If you crave the adrenaline rush you get from the whipsawing roller-coaster ride of stocks and other investments, the safe and predictable growth of Bank On Yourself will bore you silly. We live in an instant-gratification society of quick fixes and magic bullets. Wouldn't it be great to put something under your pillow at night and *know* you'll wake up rich in the morning?

Well, other than a winning lottery ticket, for most of us, it ain't gonna happen. (By the way, if you find that magic something, enter my $100,000 Challenge!) How many more investment bubbles have to burst before we really learn that lesson?

Take a look at this chart of the S&P 500 over the past thirty-eight years:

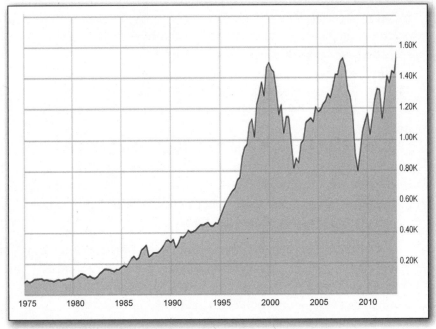

The S&P 500 Over the Past Thirty-Eight Years (1975–2013)

It might be fun if it were a roller coaster. Not so much when it's your hard-earned dollars whipsawing up and down. Now take another look at the chart of the typical growth pattern of a Bank On Yourself policy that I showed you in the last chapter:

Recall that once credited to your plan, both your guaranteed annual increase and any dividends you received are *locked in*. They don't vanish due to a market correction. Your principal is locked in, too.

On the other hand, the chart of the S&P 500 over the past thirty-eight years reveals a lengthy period of extreme volatility. The market can (and does) tank when you least expect it, ruining your best-laid plans for a comfortable retirement and a secure financial future.

When you Bank On Yourself, you may feel left out of the fun at times. You know, those times when your friends start bragging about the killing they're making in the latest hot investment everyone's jumping on—real estate, tech or oil stocks, commodities,

## GROWTH CHART

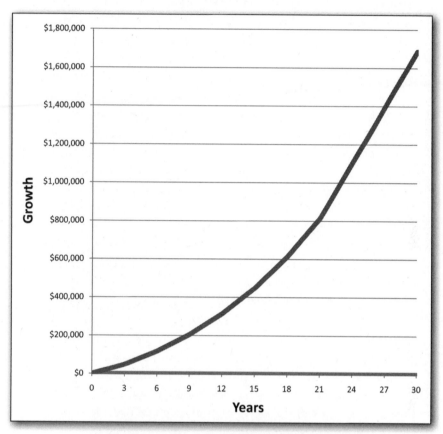

Growth Pattern of Cash Value in a Properly Structured
Dividend-Paying Policy Over Thirty Years

currency, gold, or ostrich farms. But Bank On Yourself is all about
building a *solid* financial foundation and a *secure* future, not chasing returns. You're not going to experience thrilling spikes—but
you're also not going to get hit with those *unpredictable, heart-
stopping losses* that inevitably follow! And that's when you'll thank
your lucky stars for your Bank On Yourself plan.

---

Bank On Yourself is all about building a *solid* financial
foundation and a *secure* future, *not* chasing returns.

---

Remember corporate accountant Derek Logan earlier in this chapter? When the Dow hit a record high in the spring of 2013, I asked him if he felt like he was missing out on it. He replied, *"The only thing I'm going to miss out on is the next crash."*

With Bank On Yourself, it's not an either/or proposition. If you own a Bank On Yourself–type policy and you want to take advantage of an investment opportunity that comes up, you can do it by using the equity (cash value) from your policy. You'll get the same guaranteed annual increase and dividends on the money you borrowed, which means your money can be working for you in two places at once. (However, if your investment doesn't work out and you can't pay back the loan, or at least the loan interest, and you *also* find yourself unable to pay the premium, it's possible for your policy to lapse. So be cautious before using your safe money for risky investments!)

As I've mentioned, not all companies offer a whole life policy with the feature that pays you the exact same guaranteed increases and dividends even on the money you borrowed. That's why I always recommend that you work with a Bank On Yourself Authorized Advisor who knows how to properly structure your plan for maximum growth *and* knows which companies offer the policies that let you take *full* advantage of this concept.

To get a referral to one of only 200 Advisors in the U.S. and Canada who have met the rigorous requirements to be Authorized Advisors, and who can provide you with a free Analysis and recommendations, go to **www. BankOnYourselfFreeAnalysis.com** or complete and submit the form on page 265.

• **Personal financial difficulties or job loss:** Of course, the overall economy might negatively impact your personal economy. When you sign an insurance contract, you are obligated by its terms. So what happens if you lose your job and can't pay the premiums specified in the whole life insurance contract?

The design of a Bank On Yourself–type policy gives you great flexibility and built in options that enable you to make adjustments to keep pace with your changing financial situation.

For starters, typically at least 50 percent of your premium will be directed into a Paid-Up Additions Rider (PUAR), with the rest going toward your base premium. The PUAR is the little-known option that significantly supercharges the growth of your cash value. (More on this in the next chapter.)

Because paying the premium that goes into your PUAR is *optional*, in a pinch you can cut back on or stop paying that premium. Some companies will even allow you to catch up on some or all of that premium later as your financial situation improves. You can also use your cash value and dividends to pay your base premium when cash flow is tight. You can borrow against your policy and then put it right back in as a premium payment.

(However, you should be aware that in the first couple of years, if you are unable to pay your *base* premium and you don't have enough cash value to cover it, your policy could lapse, and you wouldn't get back every dollar you put in.)

There is also an option available to you of making your policy **"reduced paid-up,"** which means no more premiums will be due and the death benefit will be reduced. This is one of the many options that your Bank On Yourself Authorized Advisor can discuss with you should your financial situation change for a prolonged period of time.

• **Other economic conditions:** Are there other economic conditions that I haven't covered? Probably. But the bottom line is that dividend-paying whole life insurance companies have a 160-year track record. They have already been through virtually *every* economic scenario imaginable and *still* delivered on their promises—even during the Great Depression.

## Does Having Money Safe and Available Take Away Any of Your Options?

You are *not* putting your money in a straitjacket! When you store your savings in a Bank On Yourself policy, you have safety, liquidity, and control. Having money you can access when and how you want—and having it continue growing, even on the money you're using—gives you *more* options and flexibility, not less. Make sense? (Chapter 7 explains how this works.)

---

Dividend-paying whole life insurance companies
have been through virtually *every* economic scenario
imaginable over the last 160 years—and *still* delivered
on their promises.

---

Picture that mother driving her kids to soccer practice.

## If It's So Good, Why Isn't Everyone Doing It?

Okay, but if Bank On Yourself is so good, why isn't everyone already doing it? And why aren't those financial gurus on board? Just browse the personal finance section of any bookstore, turn on the TV, or open a magazine on finance. You'll see that 99 out of 100 financial gurus *insist* that whole life insurance is a lousy place to put your money.

Sigh.... As we just saw, these financial experts know nothing about the specially designed type of dividend-paying whole life policy used for the Bank On Yourself method. It's not totally their fault (though they could have done a bit more research before spouting off!). Out of 1,000 major life insurance companies, our research shows only a handful offer policies that have all the features required to maximize the power of the Bank On Yourself concept, and the strategy isn't even mentioned in the standard industry training programs.

Plus as I explained, an advisor who helps a client implement a Bank On Yourself–type policy takes a 50–70 percent cut in commission. Though I like to think it's not the case, that fact *could* be another reason why your advisors haven't mentioned this possibility to you.

In any event, they're more likely to advise you to follow another course, which is …

## Buy Term and Invest the Difference

How common is this advice? "Experts"—from your in-laws to your barber to your preacher and your kid's kindergarten teacher—all parrot the same gospel: Buy cheaper term insurance and invest the money you save in the stock market. (Wait! Do they mean the stock market that hasn't even beaten inflation since 2000? Yep. *That's* where they want you to put your money?)

This strategy, they all say, promises to carry young Americans to their old age, to safeguard their loved ones and to build a large retirement portfolio along the way. Problem is, the promise differs markedly from reality, and it's all based on a faulty assumption that, as the years pass, *we'll all be rich enough to self-insure!*

Based on this, Orman, Ramsey, and others advise their followers to *always* buy term life (which is cheaper than whole life) and invest the difference in the stock market, where it can grow unfettered for decades. Ramsey tells his believers they can expect to make 12 percent annually on their mutual funds. (Really? Starting when?)

This "surefire strategy" claims that by the time term policyholders reach their fifties and sixties, they'll *no longer need* their policies because their investment portfolios will have ballooned to such a massive size that they will be wealthy enough to self-insure in the event of their death. In other words, we won't need life insurance because our estates will be large enough without it.

Then they bolster their argument by saying that by the time policyholders retire, they will be empty nesters and will no longer be responsible for the financial well-being of their children, much less their elderly parents. Yippee!

## How "Buy Term and Invest the Rest" Became Unhappily Ever After

But wait—the story didn't actually turn out like that, did it? At least not for millions of our friends, neighbors, and family members. Many of us who bought term life policies in our twenties and thirties are now in our fifties and sixties, and our stock market portfolio didn't grow at the 12 percent annual rate that Ramsey claims it would. In fact, many of us have yet to regain the dramatic losses we suffered when the stock and real estate markets crashed in 2008. Uh-oh.

And many of our kids grew up, then had to move back home due to a difficult job market and housing they couldn't afford. Add to that, grandma and granddad are living longer and longer, beyond what they'd ever thought, and beyond what their own retirement funds can cover. In fact, 58 percent of boomers are providing financial assistance to their aging parents, according to an Ameriprise Financial survey in late 2011, and almost all boomers (93 percent) say they've given their grown kids assistance.

The Employee Benefit Research Institute reported in their *2013 Retirement Confidence Survey* that a whopping 69 percent of workers plan to work for pay in retirement due to their savings shortfall. (Hey, isn't "work for pay in retirement" another one of those oxymorons?) In addition, data from the Federal Reserve's Survey of Consumer Finances indicates the typical pre-retiree has only saved enough in their 401(k) to be able to withdraw a paltry $260 a month. Many of us can't afford to retire yet, and we certainly can't afford to die. And we definitely can't afford to self-insure. If we drop dead today without insurance in place, many of us will leave our loved ones in the poorhouse. The happily-ever-after promised by "buy term and invest the difference" simply ain't happening.

## Is Term Insurance a Good *Insurance* Vehicle?

Millions of Americans who've religiously paid their term life insurance premiums for decades have grown older. They aren't in a position to self-insure, so they must now confront an agonizing decision as their term policies come up for renewal: Do we continue to shovel larger and larger barrelfuls of cash into our term policies to get the death benefits our families will someday need? Or do we drop our insurance now, exposing loved ones to potential financial disaster in the event of our death? Quite a choice, huh?

But isn't there an easy fix to that? Just continue to pay a buck or two a day to maintain your term policy? Nope.

Our cheap insurance isn't so cheap when we get older. When policyholders are young and healthy, term life insurance is very inexpensive. Young and healthy policyholders can purchase hundreds of thousands of dollars of coverage for less than $50 a month. This appears a wise and easy choice for young adults, who often are early in their careers, may be starting a family, and still have student loans to pay off. Using cheap term life policies, young adults can afford to purchase more death benefit for less than if they used whole life insurance. So far so good, right?

Problem is, those low monthly rates for term insurance apply only when policyholders are *young and healthy*. As you age, your rates rise and ultimately become astronomical.

---

## M Y T H B U S T E R

### You Should Be Able to Self-Insure

Even if your story is different and you're somehow, some way, on track to save enough money to self-insure by the time you retire, an ill-timed economic crisis, boomerang kids, or aging parents who need assistance can ruin your best-laid plans. So why not have a Plan B, just in case?

Think of it this way: How often has a family complained they were left too much money when the breadwinner passed away? (And if it's truly more money than a family can use, there are *many* deserving charities and causes that could benefit.)

---

And what if you develop health problems as you age? It will be extremely expensive—if not *impossible*—for you to obtain additional or replacement death benefits. So if you're a responsible adult with a health challenge, the choice now boils down to dropping your life insurance altogether or paying a king's ransom to renew the term insurance you have. (Wouldn't you rather have a choice between something that is good and something that is better, rather than the least horrible of two choices? Me, too.)

Case in point: I own a fifteen-year term life policy that will expire in two years. I just checked the policy to see how much more it would cost me to continue that policy in case I am unable to qualify for a new policy for health reasons two years from now. I *could* continue paying to keep that policy in force—*if* I wanted to pay a premium that's *fifteen times higher* than what I'm paying now. And ten years later, that premium will be almost *forty times higher* than I'm paying—a 4,000 percent increase. No problem! I'll just go and pluck some dollars off the money tree growing in our back yard!

> Even the financial advisors who recommend buying term
> life insurance instead of whole life agree the policies are
> designed to terminate *before* you do.

Studies show people who put money into a term life policy likely will have nothing to show for it because *99 percent of all term policies never pay out a claim*, according to a Penn State University study. Even advisors who recommend term insurance point out that term policies are designed to terminate *before* you do. In *The Road to Wealth*, Suze Orman wrote: "These policies are not very expensive...because the insurance company knows you have relatively little chance of dying while the policy is in force."

Is there anything more *expensive* than paying for something you *most likely* won't get any benefit from?

## Term Insurance Is Renting, Not Owning

Buying term life insurance is like renting a home. No matter how many years or decades you pay rent for a home, you receive no credit for prior payments if you can't pay this month's rent. With term life insurance, if you stop paying your premium this month or this quarter, the term insurance company will cancel your coverage in thirty-one days. The thousands of dollars you paid over the years will buy you *zero* mercy.

What stings even more is that the term life policies many of us purchased decades ago are worth far less today in inflation-adjusted dollars. Most term policies recommended by the financial gurus have a level death benefit for the term of the policy. If you buy a $250,000 twenty-year term policy, and inflation averages 4 percent per year, *your policy will lose 56 percent of its value* over its twenty-year term. Yikes!

And what about the part of the assumption that people will actually *invest* the difference between what they pay for term insurance and what they might pay for a whole life policy? Although much lip service has been given to that notion, I've *never* met anyone who actually bought a term policy, priced the cost of a permanent policy with an equivalent death benefit, and then put the difference into an investment account every month. It just doesn't happen. For *most* people, "buy term insurance and invest the difference" ends up being "buy term and *spend* the difference."

---

*"Most people's egos prefer THEIR facts to THE facts."*
—Dan Kennedy, marketing guru and author

---

## Advantages of Whole Life Over Term Policies

Whole life has scads of advantages over term insurance as an insurance vehicle. True, in their early years these policies require more out-of-pocket cash than term life policies. But fast-forward a decade or two, and an entirely different scenario presents itself. At that point, dividend-paying whole life policyholders have a *great deal* to show for their patience. And because they *own* their policies, not just rent them, their premiums are being converted into safe and liquid savings, and their rates don't ratchet upward—*ever*.

Inflation also works to the benefit of whole life policyholders. Huh? Premiums on these policies are set at a fixed rate. As policyholders age, they pay the *same amount*, only they're now paying in *inflation-diminished dollars*. While out-of-pocket costs for *term* policyholders soar over time, the cost for *whole* life policyholders effectively *shrinks* with age.

---

While out-of-pocket costs for *term* policyholders soar over time, the cost for *whole* life policyholders effectively *shrinks* with age.

---

Most whole life policyholders eventually reach the point that they no longer need to contribute any further premiums out of their pockets to keep their insurance in force. The dividends and cash value in the policy can be used to cover the premiums. And you also have the option of converting the policy into one that is paid up with no more premiums due, as I mentioned earlier in this chapter.

Death benefits offered by Bank On Yourself–type whole life policies actually grow at an ever-increasing rate and can significantly surpass those of fixed term life policies over time. And the premiums you pay as a whole life insurance policy owner generate a cash value that can be used whenever and however you wish, and can provide you income in retirement that is predictable and secure.

By the time holders of these supercharged policies near retirement, many of them have built an impressive nest egg that they've been able to draw upon as needed, the whole time. *It's their money, and they don't need to die in order to benefit from it.* With Bank On Yourself, you benefit if you live a normal or extended life—and your loved ones benefit (income tax-free) if you don't.

The recommendations Suze Orman, Dave Ramsey, and others make about term life are certainly popular and often entertaining. But they're also dead wrong. It's a lesson that too many of those who followed their advice have learned all too well—and painfully.

---

Want to be a fly on the wall as Suze and Dave discuss Bank On Yourself? Our hidden camera captured it all at **www.BankOnYourself.com/fly-on-wall**.

---

## Is Equity Indexed Universal Life the Magic Pill?

Is a Bank On Yourself–type policy the only life insurance option available for building wealth? Nope.

What if I told you there was a relatively new life insurance product that lets you share in a portion of the gains of the stock market in those years it goes up, but protects you from losses when the market goes down? Sounds pretty enticing, doesn't it?

And what if I sweetened the deal so you'd profit in the years the market increases, but in those years when the market is flat or tanks, you'd still get a guaranteed increase of 1, 2, or even 3 percent?

You'd probably say, "Wow! That's a no-brainer! Where do I sign up?"

I've just described one of the "hottest" and most *overhyped* life insurance products around today: Equity Indexed Universal Life (EIUL), also known as Indexed Universal Life (IUL).

An equity indexed universal life policy is essentially an annually renewing **term** policy with a cash account on the side. Remember the term insurance we just talked about? The policies that get more expensive as you get older, until they ultimately become so costly most people are forced to drop them? In an EIUL policy, the term insurance *automatically renews every year at a higher rate.* You do the math!

EIUL policies are ticking time bombs for many reasons. Here are *seven reasons to be wary*—that advisors who tout these policies often neglect to point out.

**1. Illustrated Values:** EIUL policies' illustrated interest rate predictions are based on the past performance of various stock market indexes—often focusing on a recent twenty- to thirty-year period that included the longest bull market in history. (Do you want to bet your life savings that history will repeat itself?)

Agents who sell these policies will tell you the policies have a proven track record. But they've only been around for fifteen years! So, because they don't *really* have a lengthy track record, agents who sell EIUL policies will tell you they've been "back-tested" to "increase accuracy."

Back-testing *assumes* that what happened in the past *will* happen again in the future. Whatever happened to the disclaimer "past performance is no predictor of future performance?"

The illustrated returns are further skewed by using an average annual rate of return and assuming you will get *that* return every year. (Not gonna happen!)

Actual results can vary widely from what's shown on the illustration—even by 100 percent or more!—depending on which indexing method is used.

And the company can change how much of the market's increase you'll be allowed to share in, at its discretion.

In contrast, whole life policy illustrations are required by law to predict future growth *no higher* than the rate based on the *current* dividend. In essence, a Bank On Yourself Advisor will show you results based on what the company is *actually* paying right now, while a promoter of indexed universal life policies can dangle pie-in-the-sky numbers in front of you and tell you, "These are the returns I bet we can get for you!"

Furthermore, your cash value in a dividend-paying whole life policy is guaranteed to increase by a larger dollar amount each year that the premium is paid.

**2. Costs:** Costs for insurance and administrative charges are deducted from the policy every month. These can include cost of insurance charges, monthly policy charges, transaction charges, policy issue charges, premium charges, and additional rider costs.

Furthermore, the contract states that the insurance company can increase those costs each year for *any* reason (up to a guaranteed maximum).

All insurance policies have costs that the policy owner pays. But an EIUL insurance contract states that when those costs go up for the company, *they can pass them on to you,* the policy owner, up to some maximum limit. Bank On Yourself-type policies can *never* pass more costs on to you.

EIUL agents will typically show you projections that are based on the current charges (the ones the company can increase every year for *any* reason) and using interest crediting rates of 8 percent or more each year—which, if it actually ever happened, would be pretty darn good. Do I really need to mention that just because you're shown an illustration with a projected 8 percent return every year, that doesn't mean you will get 8 percent in *any* year?

On one typical EIUL illustration I reviewed recently, the insurance company credited a very generous *3 percent annual guarantee* and assumed the charges were the maximum allowed. The cash or surrender value of the policy as shown was *guaranteed* to go to *zero* in the fifteenth year! Heck, I can make my money disappear *today* by handing my wallet over to my fourteen-year-old niece at the mall. Why wait fifteen years?

But what if the assumptions were a little less drastic? What if mid-point variables were used instead—say, an annual interest rate credit of 5.72 percent per year and middle-of-the-road allowed charges? That forecast came out better: It took until the twentieth year for the policy to have *zero* cash value! (Would you like my niece's address so you can just send her the cash instead?)

It's true that *if* an EIUL policy is consistently funded to the highest allowable premium level, the costs typically won't increase dramatically. However, you *still* won't have any idea what your cash values will be!

**3. Guarantees:** Some policies come with an interest rate guarantee of 1 percent, 2 percent, or even 3 percent per year to offset years where the market goes down or is flat, and the illustrations from companies offering these policies reflect that. However, most companies do *not* credit this to your policy *every* year. They may do it only every five to ten years or, very commonly, *only when the policy is terminated. The illustration is pure fiction.*

Meanwhile, all the costs are still coming out each month, which means your policy will *lose* value in years the market goes down or sideways. And it *may* even lose value in the years *when the market goes up only a little.* You then need even *higher* future returns to make up for that negative return. I have yet to find an agent promoting EIUL who will warn you about that!

It's possible that you could pay premiums every year and end up with *no cash value* and *no death benefit* if the stock market indexes used do not perform as projected.

With a dividend-paying whole life policy, *everything* except the dividend is **guaranteed** and determined in advance. Your cash value is guaranteed to equal your death benefit when the policy matures. There are *no* unpleasant surprises.

**4. Death Benefit:** The death benefit of an EIUL policy, like the premium, is flexible and not guaranteed unless you have a **no-lapse guarantee.** That guarantee (*if* your policy has it) means you'll have a death benefit. However, you may have no cash value, which means you'll have to continue to pay premiums out of your pocket to keep the death benefit in force. Agents promoting this product don't usually mention that either.

Premiums and loan repayments that are missed or delayed can reduce how long your death benefit guarantee stays in effect and can void it altogether.

Unlike a whole life policy, there is also *no* option to turn an

EIUL policy into one which is fully paid up with no more premiums due. This means that, depending on many factors outside your control, you may have to continue paying premiums out of your pocket for the *rest of your life* to keep the policy in force.

**5. Risk:** EIUL policies shift all the burden and risk of managing the policy from the insurance company to *you*, the policy *owner*. The insurance company gets its money but you don't necessarily get yours. You might very well find yourself having to pay skyrocketing premiums just to keep the policy from lapsing—*or* risk losing everything you've paid into the policy over the years. Again, contrast that with a whole life policy where your costs, premium, cash value, *and* death benefit are *all* guaranteed and predetermined.

---

EIUL policies shift all the burden and risk of managing the policy from the insurance company to *you*, the policy *owner*.

---

The carrot they hold out with EIUL policies is that the return *might* exceed the return of a whole life policy. Do we *really* need more hope-and-pray vehicles in our financial plans?

**6. Policy Loan Risk:** Advisors selling EIUL like to tout a loan feature available in some policies that could allow you to actually *make* money by taking a policy loan.

For example, the illustration may show a 6 percent *loan interest rate* and an 8 percent *annual gain*, which means (theoretically) you'd have a 2 percent gain on the amount you borrowed. Woo-hoo! If that's the case, you'd come out ahead to take every dime out of the policy at 6 percent and earn 8 percent on it.

There's just one problem with that: In most EIUL policies, in years when there is no gain in the stock market index, there is little or no credit to the policy. Meanwhile, the *costs* are continuing to be taken out, and *now you have a recipe for disaster.*

Since one of the most popular and valuable features of the Bank On Yourself method is using your cash values for financing things, can you see why using an EIUL policy for this purpose can be dangerous to your wealth? (Check out Chapter 7 to learn more about how Bank On Yourself policy loans work. They have *none* of these downsides.)

7. **Lawsuits:** Why would any advisor sell a policy that has as many pitfalls as EIUL? I suspect it's because we all want to believe that there's a "magic pill" answer to the volatility of the stock market—and, until you dig deep, EIUL appears to have it all. (But there are *no* magic pills, and it's time for all of us to stop the endless, fruitless search for them.)

The lawsuits have already begun. One lawsuit claims that ...

- "Any policyholder who purchases one of these policies is in a precarious situation."
- The EIUL marketing brochures "conceal material risks that the policies will not perform as illustrated, but will, instead, lapse."
- "The guaranteed values used in the illustration are *misrepresented* as annual guarantees, when in fact they are calculated upon policy **termination** on the basis of *average* annual guarantees."
- "The costs *significantly* diminish the accumulation of value in the policies, *regardless* of whether the projected gains are realized."

So for these seven reasons, when it comes to EIUL, buyer beware! Whole life insurance comes with more guarantees than *any* other life insurance product and has stood the test of time. It is the *only* form of life insurance recommended for the Bank On Yourself concept.

With a Bank On Yourself–type whole life insurance policy ...

1. Your *premium* is fixed and can never increase
2. Your costs are guaranteed, and the company *cannot* increase them for any reason
3. Your *cash value* is guaranteed to grow each and *every* year
4. And your *death benefit* is also guaranteed

## Taking Charge and Taking Action

It's important to do your own investigation, but please don't get stuck in the paralysis-by-analysis trap. There are some things you simply can't control. *Not* taking action is actually deciding to let chaos and uncertainty rule your life. There may never be a *perfect* time to move forward and take back control of your financial future. But there *is* a good time. And that time is *now*.

Bank On Yourself isn't a magic pill. I don't believe there *are* any magic pills. But what I do know is that Bank On Yourself provides a long-term solution to a number of long-term challenges. The Bank On Yourself Revolution is not radical. Rather, it is a wise application of an idea whose soundness has been proven over time.

And the only regret expressed by most people who use it is that they didn't know about it sooner. Check out some of their stories and testimonials at **www.BankOnYourself.com/reviews**.

## KEY TAKE-AWAYS

1. **The whole life policies the talking heads love to hate are *not* the ones used for Bank On Yourself.** Bank On Yourself policies have accelerated growth and pay much lower commissions.

2. **"Buy Term and Invest the Difference" is built on a false assumption.** It assumes that the stock market will make us so rich as we age that we'll be able to self-insure. It's not happening.

3. **Term insurance may be cheap in the beginning, but it will nail you in the end.** Premiums for these policies go through the roof as you age, but the benefit stays flat and doesn't keep up with inflation. And if your health takes a turn for the worse, you may have to pay much more to renew your policy, or you may not even qualify for coverage at *any* price.

4. **Equity Indexed Universal Life lacks guarantees and predictability.** The illustrations agents show you are misleading. The product shifts *all* the risk from the insurance company to *you*,

the policy *owner*. Building your financial plan on something that offers neither predictability nor control isn't a financial plan. It's a financial mirage.

**5. You don't have to die to benefit from Bank On Yourself.** The premiums you pay into a Bank On Yourself policy grow your cash value by a guaranteed and predictable amount, and the growth curve of each steepens every year. You can build a sizeable nest egg without the risk of stocks and other volatile investments. One of the great *living benefits* of the policy is that you can use your cash value whenever and however you want.

# CHAPTER 4

# The Genius of Good Structure

*It is not the beauty of the building you should look at. It's the*
*construction of the foundation that will stand the test of time.*
—DAVID ALLAN COE, MUSICIAN

O KAY, you've gotten this far, and you're probably thinking, "Hmmm. Sounds like this Bank On Yourself thing really *could* give me predictable growth and protect my nest egg. But how the heck does it actually work? Dividend-paying whole life policies? Additional riders to supercharge growth? How does all of that come together? It sounds complicated!"

It's sophisticated but *not* complicated! It's like a sleek sailboat. A no-frills dividend-paying whole life insurance policy is the hull of the sail boat, and Bank On Yourself builds on that foundation. Let's put this boat together so you can see how it works.

But first, let me give you the CliffsNotes version of what whole life is. **Whole life insurance** is a permanent, or **cash value**, life insurance policy that provides benefits for the *whole* of your life (versus term insurance, which only lasts for a specific period of time). Whole life policies increase in cash

| INSIDE THIS CHAPTER . . . |
|---|
| • Powerful Advantages of Building Wealth with Whole Life |
| • How to Supercharge the Growth of Your Cash Value |
| • Chart Comparing the Growth Speeds of Three Policies |
| • Your Reward for Patience |
| • How to Have More Death Benefit *and* More Cash Value |

value each and every year, by a guaranteed and pre-set amount that's specified in the contract. The cash value is guaranteed to equal the policy's death benefit in some specific future year. That future date is called the policy's **maturity date**, and it's typically the year the insured reaches 121 years of age. (Some *very* optimistic actuary must have come up with that number!)

Insurance companies are owned either by stockholders or by policy owners. In a company owned by stockholders (a stock company), the stockholders receive the profits of the company. But if your company is owned by the policy owners (known as a mutual company), guess who shares in the profits? You do! These companies are also called **participating** companies, because the policyholders participate in the profits. These profits are given in the form of dividends. Although dividends are *not* guaranteed, some participating companies have paid dividends consistently every year for over 100 years, including during the Great Depression. These are the companies Bank On Yourself Authorized Advisors recommend.

How are dividends determined? The company does an annual accounting of its income and expenses. If it performed better than its worst-case projection, the directors may declare a dividend, which goes to the policy owners in participating companies.

## Benefits and Guarantees of Whole Life Insurance:

- Level premium guaranteed to *never* increase, giving you some protection from inflation
- Cash value that grows by a guaranteed, predictable amount every year
- Guaranteed death benefit
- Allows you to borrow against your cash value. You can become your own source of financing and bypass banks, credit card companies, and finance companies—as well as their nosey, time-consuming paperwork and requirements!
- Provides a predictable income in retirement, without the risk or volatility of stocks, real estate, and other investments

A typical Bank On Yourself–type policy starts with a dividend-paying whole life policy, issued by a company that is financially very strong and has an unblemished history of paying dividends for 100 years or more. In our sailboat analogy, this is the hull of the Bank On Yourself boat.

But a hull is just a large rowboat with no oars. It may float with the current or get stuck in the reeds. If it goes anywhere at all, it won't go very fast! So Bank On Yourself Advisors add a mast and a big sail in the form of **riders** (options) that can grow your cash value up to forty times faster than the plain-vanilla policies most financial experts love to hate, especially in the early years of the policy. With these riders in place, you have cash value in your policy from the very first *month*. And you can potentially use that cash value as a powerful financial management tool right from the start.

## A *Total* Return of Only 5% After Sixteen Roller-Coaster Years in the Stock Market

Ed Ingle, a former teacher from Ohio, started his first Bank On Yourself policy in December 2009. He was very cautious at the start and said, "I read all I could about Bank On Yourself on the Internet from both critics and supporters. We wanted to be sure that we weren't doing something that would jeopardize our finances."

After Ed left teaching in 1994, he withdrew all of the money in his retirement fund and put it into seemingly solid mutual funds. After learning about Bank On Yourself and seeing the guaranteed returns it provides, Ed decided to check on his mutual fund account. He figured that since nothing had been added to it and nothing had been taken out from it, it would be an excellent comparison.

But Ed had an unpleasant surprise waiting. He discovered that from 1994 through 2009, "The *total* gain on that mutual fund was only 5 percent! Through all the ups and downs, that's it!" A 5 percent *total* return after sixteen years of roller-coaster ups and downs. And that's not even factoring in inflation.

*continued*

*continued from previous page*

Ed says, "The difference is that with our Bank On Yourself plan, we have the security of *guaranteed* growth, and we *know* the money will be there when we retire. I also can take out loans to make purchases, I get tax benefits, and I have a death benefit, so I know my wife will be cared for if something happens to me."

## Secrets of a Sleek Sailboat

Bank On Yourself Authorized Advisors are trained on the proper way to add a mast and sail that will turn your rowboat into a sleek sailboat. Let's see how that's done.

A key goal of the Bank On Yourself strategy is to *maximize the growth of your cash value without increasing your premium*. The cash value in the policy is the storehouse of money you'll use to bypass banks, credit card companies, and finance companies and become your own source of financing. Use the money in your storehouse wisely, and you might eventually be able to finance your entire lifestyle from it!

Properly designed, your Bank On Yourself policy will perform like a sleek and agile racing sailboat.

**The Hull:** Everything is built upon the hull. Picture a big rowboat with no source of power. It simply floats with the current. The hull represents your basic no-frills dividend-paying whole life policy *before* the riders that supercharge the growth of the policy are added.

In insurance lingo, this basic policy is called the **base policy**. It's important to select a base policy that's seaworthy, which translates into a policy that pays dividends and has all the features needed to maximize the power of the concept. Unfortunately, most insurance agents and financial planners only know about hulls, which leaves you with a clunky rowboat without oars.

**The Sail:** A sailboat can drift listlessly without a sail. But a boat with a properly sized sail to fully catch the wind and propel the sailboat forward has real power. That sail is a Paid-Up Additions Rider (PUAR) into which you can pour a significant portion of your annual premium. This rider is the most efficient way to build cash value because it channels most of your premium directly into the cash value portion of the policy, while purchasing a small death benefit.

Paid-Up Additions are essentially mini-life insurance policies that require a one-time-only premium.

 **The Mast:** You can't use your sail unless it's attached to a mast. In a Bank On Yourself plan, the mast is a term insurance rider. This rider is added so you can fill your insurance policy with even *more* cash value than you otherwise could. (I'll give you more detail about this in a moment.)

 **The Rudder:** You *can* buy a sailboat and set sail with no rudder to guide you. Bad idea. You'll end up foundering and may even capsize. A Bank On Yourself policy is a financial management tool you'll use throughout your lifetime. The *way* you use it can make a *big* difference in how much cash value you'll ultimately have. The rudder is your Bank On Yourself Authorized Advisor, who will offer you ongoing coaching and support and show you the most effective ways to use your policy.

Each of these parts of our Bank On Yourself sailboat is critical. Without any one of them, the boat floats—but loses much of its power.

## Compare the Boats

Table A compares three different dividend-paying whole life insurance policies, all created for the same thirty-five-year-old man. The annual premium in each policy is set at $12,000, but *how* the premium is being allocated varies. (Don't get hung up on this specific premium. It's just an example. Your policy would be custom-tailored to your personal situation, so you start at whatever level works for you. Plans can be designed for newborns and for folks up to age eighty-five.)

---

### Quick Highlights: Cash Value Comparison (Table A)

• Although all three comparison policies had *identical* premiums, Policy 3—which has both a Paid-Up Additions Rider *and* a term rider—had *eight times* the cash value of Policy 1 at the end of the *very first year*.

• By adding a Paid-Up Additions Rider (Policy 2), the annual cash value increase began exceeding the annual premium in Year 5—*two years earlier* than without such a rider.

• By adding *both* a Paid-Up Additions Rider *and* a term rider (Policy 3), the annual cash value increase exceeded the annual premium even sooner—in the fourth year in this example.

• In Year 20, in Policy 3 the cash value increased by more than *twice* the premium paid.

*continued*

- And beginning in Year 30, Policy 3's cash value increased by *more than three times* the annual premium.

- Finally, in Policy 3, Year 40 was the last year *any* premiums were paid. But the cash value continued to grow *every* year—no luck, skill, or guesswork required. For example, in Year 50 the premium paid was *zero*, but the cash value *grew by $59,425*.

**TABLE A: Cash Value Growth***

| Policy Year | Age | Net Annual Premium | Policy 1 Designed for Maximum Death Benefit All Base | | Policy 2 Designed for Accelerated Cash Value Growth Base + Paid Up Additions | | Policy 3 Designed for Maximum Cash Value Growth Base + Paid Up Additions + Term | |
|---|---|---|---|---|---|---|---|---|
| | | | Annual Cash Value Increase* | Total Cash Value* | Annual Cash Value Increase* | Total Cash Value* | Annual Cash Value Increase* | Total Cash Value* |
| 1 | 36 | $12,000 | $1,107 | $1,107 | $6,745 | $6,745 | $8,495 | $8,495 |
| 4 | 39 | $12,000 | $10,070 | $29,098 | $11,869 | $40,360 | $12,337 | $43,608 |
| 5 | 40 | $12,000 | $10,855 | $39,953 | $12,572 | $52,932 | $13,007 | $56,616 |
| 7 | 42 | $12,000 | $12,405 | $64,004 | $14,016 | $80,241 | $14,404 | $84,719 |
| 10 | 45 | $12,000 | $14,721 | $105,912 | $16,287 | $126,826 | $16,748 | $132,688 |
| 15 | 50 | $12,000 | $19,191 | $193,314 | $20,741 | $221,570 | $21,183 | $229,535 |
| 20 | 55 | $12,000 | $23,048 | $301,009 | $25,390 | $339,131 | $26,077 | $349,956 |
| 25 | 60 | $12,000 | $26,432 | $424,647 | $30,366 | $479,907 | $31,558 | $495,901 |
| 30 | 65 | $12,000 | $30,903 | $570,082 | $36,331 | $649,384 | $37,994 | $672,718 |
| 40 | 75 | $12,000 | $42,490 | $940,366 | $51,546 | $1,093,442 | $54,351 | $1,139,545 |
| 50 | 85 | $0 | $49,038 | $1,377,040 | $57,021 | $1,601,199 | $59,425 | $1,668,710 |
| 60 | 95 | $0 | $59,917 | $1,926,446 | $69,671 | $2,240,039 | $72,608 | $2,334,486 |

* Annual Cash Value Increase, Total Cash Value, and Death Benefits in the charts in this chapter are based on the dividend scale as of March 2013. Dividends can change and are not guaranteed; however, the companies generally recommended by Bank On Yourself Authorized Advisors have consistently paid dividends every year for more than 100 years.

## Policy 1: The Hull—All Base

Policy 1 is a traditional dividend-paying whole life insurance policy for a healthy thirty-five-year-old we've called Martin for no particular reason. *All* of Martin's premium is allocated to the base policy, and *no* riders are added. This policy is like a sailboat without a mast, sail, or rudder. It will move with the current, but not very quickly. Many people are only aware of a life insurance policy's *death* benefit, so they choose a policy structured for maximum death benefit with the lowest premium possible. That sounds reasonable, but it doesn't work out very well if you want to enjoy the most *living* benefits of a policy.

See the circled amount on the line for Policy Year 7? This is significant because beginning in this year, Martin's annual cash value increase is more than the premium he pays each year. (His $12,405 cash value increase is greater than his $12,000 premium.) That makes Martin a happy camper.

## Policy 2: Hull with a Sail—Base + Paid-Up Additions Rider

In Policy 2, only 40 percent of each year's premium goes toward building the base policy. The remainder goes into the Paid-Up Additions Rider—the sail for this boat. These additions accelerate the growth of his cash value—which is what Martin wants—while providing a smaller death benefit. See the circled amount on the line for Policy Year 5? With much of his premium purchasing Paid-Up Additions, Martin's annual cash value increase begins exceeding his annual premium *two years earlier* than in Policy 1. (His $12,572 cash value increase is greater than his $12,000 premium.) Woo-hoo!

Well over 90 percent of every PUAR premium dollar goes directly to building cash value, very little goes to the cost of the death benefit, and only a miniscule amount goes to the advisor as a commission. (An advisor who wants to help you build your cash value by adding a significant PUAR *must* be willing to take a huge cut in commissions.)

Note: The premium you pay into your Paid-Up Additions Rider is an *optional* premium. You don't need to pay it to keep the policy in force. So in a pinch, you can cut back on it, and some companies will even let you catch up on some or all of it later, as your situation allows. That gives you greater flexibility than a traditional no-frills whole life policy has.

## "Does My Whole Life Policy Have a Paid-Up Additions Rider?"

That's a question we're asked from time to time. If you look on your annual policy statement, you may see a column labeled "Paid-Up Additions" or "Cash Value of Additional Life Insurance Purchased by Dividends." That's *not* the same as a Paid-Up Additions *Rider*. It simply means the dividends the company gave you were left in your policy and used to purchase additional life insurance. For you to have a policy that truly maximizes the cash value, your annual statement and/or policy must indicate that a portion of your *premium* is being *directed* into a Paid-Up Additions Rider and not into the base policy.

If you didn't request that your policy be designed that way, or weren't informed it was being structured that way, it's *very* unlikely that you have a Bank On Yourself–type policy.

## Policy 3: Hull with a Sail *and* a Mast—Base + PUAR + Term Rider

In Policy 3, only 30 percent of Martin's premium is used to pay for the base policy. The remainder purchases Paid-Up Additions (our sail) *and* a term insurance rider (the mast for our sail).

Why add a term rider to a whole life policy? Isn't term insurance a bad idea? As a *substitute* for permanent life insurance, generally yes, for all the reasons discussed in Chapter 3. But term coverage has a valuable place as a *rider* to a permanent policy. Here, the term rider allows you to pay more into your PUAR, and thus build cash value faster, without running afoul of IRS guidelines.

How do those guidelines work? The IRS places a limit on the percentage of premium that can be channeled into the *cash value* rather than the death benefit of a life insurance policy without jeopardizing its tax benefits. If the policy exceeds this limit, it becomes a modified endowment contract (MEC) and loses a key tax advantage. The limit is based on a complicated formula that compares the cash value to the death benefit. The higher the death benefit, the more money can be channeled into the cash value.

Because the term rider *raises* the death benefit, the IRS formula allows Martin to plow *more money* into his cash value, without turning the policy into a MEC. In other words, a taller mast lets you use a bigger sail—at least to a certain point. If the sail is *too big*, the policy becomes an MEC and the boat capsizes, losing a tax advantage. The term rider is designed so that it can be jettisoned sometime between the end of the seventh and the twentieth policy years. (The first seven years of a policy are the most critical years in determining whether or not a policy will become a MEC.)

Note: It's important to understand that *it's not always possible to structure a policy so that only 30 percent goes toward the base policy.*

Every policy is different based on many variables such as age, need for insurance, how soon you plan to take retirement income, etc. But when you work with a Bank On Yourself Authorized Advisor, they will structure your policy to direct the lowest percentage of premium to your base policy that will let you achieve the goals you set for your plan—without turning the policy into a MEC.

## Eight Times More Cash Value at the End of the First Year

Getting back to Policy 3, you'll notice several interesting items. First, look at the circled amounts on the line for Policy Year 1. At the end of the *very first year*, Policy 3 has almost *eight times more cash value* than Policy 1 (the policy with no riders at all). Now we're talking! See what a strong mast and sail can do for a boat? A properly applied Paid-Up Additions Rider and term rider provide that powerful supercharging effect.

What about the circled amount on the line for Year 4? The PUAR and the term rider have caused Martin's annual cash value increase to exceed his annual premium beginning in the fourth year—*one year earlier* than Policy 2, and *three years earlier* than Policy 1. (His $12,337 cash value increase is greater than his $12,000 premium.) Go Martin!

## Your Reward for Patience

As I've stressed, these policies are not get-rich-quick magic pills. Even the supercharged variations used for the Bank On Yourself concept grow more slowly in the early years than in later years. It takes a while for your cash value to equal the premiums you paid, though of course from day one, your premiums are *immediately* providing you with the *full* death benefit of your policy and the peace of mind this brings. And your reward for patience is the growth curve that gets steeper every year you keep the policy.

Go back to the chart and look at the line for Year 20 in Policy 3. Beginning this year, Martin's cash value increases by more than *twice* the amount of premium he pays ($26,077 cash value increase, compared to $12,000 premium paid). And beginning in Year 30, his cash value increases by *more than three times* his premium ($37,994 cash value increase, compared to $12,000 premium paid). Martin is spiking the ball in the end zone and doing his happy dance!

Even more exciting: Look at the line for Year 40. That's the last year Martin is scheduled to pay *any* premium at all. The policy keeps on growing, but without any premium payments. See the line for Policy Year 50? The premium paid was *zero*, but the cash value *grew by $59,425*—no luck, skill, or guesswork required.

---

The premium paid in Policy Year 50 was *zero*,
but the cash value *grew by $59,425*—no luck,
skill, or guesswork required.

---

One more thing to keep in mind: It's possible to have even *more* cash value than shown in this chart, depending on how you use your policy for financing major purchases. That's another reason it's important to work with a Bank On Yourself Authorized Advisor who can show you ways to maximize the value of your plan.

Each policy is custom-tailored. There are no cookie-cutter plans, so your plan won't look like Martin's. However, you can find out what a plan designed for your unique situation, goals, and dreams can look like when you request a free Analysis at **www.BankOnYourselfFreeAnalysis.com** or by completing and submitting the form on page 265. When you do, you'll get a referral to one of the Authorized Advisors who can answer your questions and help you find the money to fund your plan.

---

## Ⓜ Ⓨ Ⓣ Ⓗ Ⓑ Ⓤ Ⓢ Ⓣ Ⓔ Ⓡ

### Dividends Are Just a Return of Premium You Overpaid

One of the objections you may hear about dividend-paying whole life insurance is, "What's the big deal about dividends? They're just a return of premium the company overcharged you." Recall that dividends are paid when the company's income less its expenses exceeds its projected worst-case scenario. Technically, the IRS defines dividends as a return of excess premium and therefore *not* taxable. (Sounds good to me!)

Over time, *those dividends can exceed the premium you paid in by a significant amount.* And in the example we just saw, in Year 50, Martin paid zero premium, but the cash value grew that year by $59,425. If that's the result of "overcharging," I say, "Bring it on!"

Life insurance companies are consistently good at under-promising and over-delivering. I'll take that any day over Wall Street promising the moon and stars, then handing me a night-light with a dim bulb year after year!

Wouldn't you?

---

## Your Financial Security Blanket

In 2008, a year that was abysmal for stocks and real estate, one of my dividend-paying whole life insurance policies grew by nearly two and a half times the annual premium I paid. All of the premium I put in during that turbulent year was still in my policy after the markets crashed, as was *all* of my principal and *all* of my previous growth. (View that annual statement for my policy at **www.BankOnYourself.com/policy2**.) Can you say the same about money you put into your stock portfolio during that time? I'm guessing not.

In your Bank On Yourself policy, as soon as your guaranteed annual cash value increase and any dividends are credited, they're *locked in*. You don't go backward. The cash value of a whole life policy can never decline due to market fluctuations, and it is not subject to the volatility of the stock or real estate markets.

Compare that to the experiences of most folks who followed the conventional financial wisdom. They lost half or more of both their principal *and* their gains in their retirement and investment accounts—twice in just one decade! They would need close to a 100 percent gain *after each crash* just to get back to even!

That's why I believe Ban°k On Yourself may be the ultimate financial security blanket in both good times *and bad*. Imagine looking forward to opening your policy statements because they always have good news and never have ugly surprises!

## More Death Benefit *Plus* More Cash Value?

But what about the death benefits of the three policies in our comparison? If we've kept the premium at $12,000 per year and used much of that premium to grow the cash value faster, are these policies building up much death benefit? That's a good question, and Table B shows you the answer.

## Quick Highlights: Death Benefit Comparison (Table B)

- Although all three comparison policies had *identical* premiums, Policy 3 built the *largest* death benefit over time, because it contained *both* a Paid-Up Additions Rider and a term rider in the proper proportions.
- In Year 40, the premiums stopped. But both the death benefit *and* the cash value continued to grow each year.
- By Policy Year 50, the death benefit in Policy 3 grew by about $380,000 in the ten years since Year 40, even though *no* premiums were paid during those years.
- If the insured passed away at age seventy-five, Policy 3 gave him a legacy of $1,646,123 for his family or favorite charities. And that gift can pass income tax-free under current tax law, and without going through probate.
- Should the insured live until age eighty-five, that legacy would have grown to more than $2 million, and at age ninety-five, it would have grown to more than $2.5 million.

As you see in that table, all three policies build solid death benefits. But over time, Policy 3 (with its basic hull, properly sized mast, and billowing sail) actually builds the *largest* death benefit of them all.

Let's compare the death benefits in Year 1. In the early years of Policy 1, the cash value was relatively small while the death benefit was relatively large, right? In the first year, the death benefit in Policy 3 is a little more than half of the death benefit in Policy 1. For Martin, this is a good thing, because the growth of his cash value is very important to him. He's paying for roughly half the death benefit, but he's building almost *eight times more* cash value, with all the financing power, control, and tax benefits that a whole life insurance policy offers him.

Something significant happens in Policy 3 in Year 7. The death benefit drops from $580,440 to $506,010 the following year. Huh? This happens because the term rider is jettisoned, and the money that was paying for the term rider can now buy more Paid-Up Additions. So now Martin's policy is positioned for maximum cash value growth, and the death benefit in Policy 3 is growing *even faster*

## TABLE B: Death Benefit Growth†

| | | | Policy 1 Designed for Maximum Death Benefit | Policy 2 Designed for Accelerated Cash Value Growth | Policy 3 Designed for Maximum Cash Value Growth |
|---|---|---|---|---|---|
| | | | All Base | Base + Paid Up Additions | Base + Paid Up Additions + Term |
| Policy Year | Age | Net Annual Premium | Death Benefit* | Death Benefit* | Death Benefit* |
| 1 | 36 | $12,000 | $692,188 | $353,378 | $352,704 |
| 5 | 40 | $12,000 | $726,227 | $478,468 | $505,915 |
| 7 | 42 | $12,000 | $751,463 | $541,440 | $580,440 |
| 8 | 43 | $12,000 | $765,688 | $572,942 | $506,010 |
| 10 | 45 | $12,000 | $796,446 | $635,741 | $579,227 |
| 15 | 50 | $12,000 | $881,289 | $790,221 | $756,297 |
| 20 | 55 | $12,000 | $968,626 | $939,377 | $925,454 |
| 24 | 59 | $12,000 | $1,038,696 | $1,057,438 | $1,059,008 |
| 30 | 65 | $12,000 | $1,148,637 | $1,239,339 | $1,264,082 |
| 40 | 75 | $12,000 | $1,358,401 | $1,579,525 | $1,646,123 |
| 50 | 85 | $0 | $1,673,053 | $1,945,398 | $2,027,422 |
| 60 | 95 | $0 | $2,135,300 | $2,482,891 | $2,587,577 |

---

† Annual Cash Value Increase, Total Cash Value, and Death Benefits in the charts in this chapter are based on the dividend scale as of March 2013. Dividends can change and are not guaranteed; however, the companies generally recommended by Bank On Yourself Authorized Advisors have consistently paid dividends every year for more than 100 years.

than in either Policy 1 or Policy 2. In fact, by Year 24, Martin's death benefit in Policy 3 *exceeds* what he would have had in *either* Policy 1 or Policy 2.

Recall from Table A that Policy 3 also has more cash value than either Policy 1 or 2. So Policy 3 ends up with *both* more cash value *and* more death benefit. *That's* what a master boat builder can do with a sleek hull, a sturdy mast, and just the right sail.

In Year 40 in each of these policies, Martin's premiums will stop because the policies are designed to be fully paid up at age seventy-five. Both his death benefit *and* his cash value will continue to grow each year. By Policy Year 50, the death benefit in Policy 3 tops $2,000,000, even though he didn't pay any more premiums after Year 40. If Martin passes away at age seventy-five, Policy 3 could allow him to leave a legacy of $1,646,123 for his family or favorite charities. And that gift can pass income tax-free under current tax law, and without going through probate.

Should he live until age eighty-five, Martin's legacy could grow to more than $2 million, and should he live to ninety-five, it could grow to more than $2.5 million.

---

### Lifetime Benefit of Policy 3

Premium paid (40 years x $12,000/year): $480,000

~~~~~~~~~~~~~~~~~~~~~~~

Cash value at age 75: $1,139,545
Death benefit at age 75: $1,646,123

~~~~~~~~~~~~~~~~~~~~~~~

Cash value at age 95: $2,334,486
Death benefit at age 95: $2,587,577

~~~~~~~~~~~~~~~~~~~~~~~

*The lifetime benefit to you and your family could be substantial!*

---

## Summing It Up

To sum up how Bank On Yourself works, all three policies have identical annual premiums—$12,000. Look at the bottom line in both Table

A and Table B. In both cash value *and* death benefit, Policy 3 (a Bank On Yourself–type plan) *outperforms* either of the other two policies. Greater cash value equals greater financing power and control and more passive retirement income. A bigger death benefit means a bigger legacy for your family or favorite charity.

Isn't it a shame most insurance agents and financial planners don't understand how to build this sleek sailing vessel? So much benefit can be created by creatively and skillfully building additional value and *living* benefits into a whole life insurance policy! Too bad most agents only know how to build hulls.

## KEY TAKE-AWAYS

1. **A dividend-paying whole life insurance policy is only the starting point for a Bank On Yourself plan.** Your Authorized Advisor can make sure that your plan is structured to meet your specific goals and requirements.

2. When structured correctly, your policy will typically have two important riders: **The first is a Paid-Up Additions Rider** into which you can pour a significant portion of your annual premium. This rider is the most efficient way to build cash value because it channels most of your premium directly into the cash value portion of the policy while purchasing a small death benefit.

3. **The second rider is a term rider**, which, by increasing your death benefit, allows you to grow your cash value even faster, without turning the policy into a modified endowment contract and losing a key tax advantage.

4. **A policy that has both of these riders can ultimately have more cash value *and* more death benefit** than a no-frills policy that does not include these riders.

# CHAPTER 5

# Retirement: Fantasy Versus Reality

*Errors of human judgment can infect even the smartest people, thanks to overconfidence, lack of attention to details, and excessive trust in the judgments of others, stemming from a failure to understand that others are not making independent judgments, but are themselves following still others—the blind leading the blind.*

—ROBERT J. SHILLER, PROFESSOR OF ECONOMICS, YALE UNIVERSITY

ACCORDING to the 2012 AARP survey, *Boomers' "Anxiety Index" High*, 72 percent of baby boomers believe they'll be forced to postpone retirement, and half have little confidence they'll *ever* be able to retire. How can this be? To me, it's obvious: so many of us blindly followed the conventional investing and retirement planning advice. And more than *half* of all boomers won't have enough money to cover even basic living expenses, like food and medical care, during retirement.[17] How wise does conventional wisdom look to you now?

> **INSIDE THIS CHAPTER ...**
> - Will You Have to Work Till You Drop?
> - The 401(k) Fiasco
> - A Retirement Fund You Can Use *Before* You Retire
> - Putting Money in a Government-Controlled Retirement Plan Is Putting It in Prison
> - The Pitfalls of Deferring Taxes
> - How Fees Are Devouring Your Nest Egg
> - Retirement Plans Comparison Chart

If you've been doing "all the right things" financially, but have been disappointed again and again, do you think continuing along the same path will suddenly start bringing you a different outcome? (By the way, isn't that a definition of insanity? Doing the same thing over and over and expecting different results?)

## Dismal Stats

Too many of us are just beginning to wake up to how much we may need to save. The Employee Benefit Research Institute's 2013 Retirement Confidence Survey reports that the percentage of workers confident about having enough money for a comfortable retirement is at record lows, *in spite* of an uptick in the economy and a rallying stock market in the spring of 2013.

The stats reported in the survey are bleak: More than *half* of workers report *less* than $25,000 in total household savings and investments (excluding the value of their primary home and any company plan promising a lifetime income). Only 24 percent reported savings of $100,000 or more.

When you hit retirement, what kind of lifestyle do you think you'll have on $25,000 or even $100,000 spread over several decades? That greeter job at Wal-Mart? (I'm not against smiling, I'd just prefer to do it for fun rather than $8.47 per hour.) Living off your kids (who have their own children and retirements to worry about)? Sharing Tabby's food while waiting for the monthly pittance from Social Security to arrive?

One wit really hit it on the head when he observed, "I have enough money to live comfortably for the rest of my life—*if I die by next Tuesday!*"

## Work Till We Drop?

Remember the scene from the 1983 movie classic *The Big Chill*? Michael Gold (played by Jeff Goldblum) is arguing that rationalization is more addictive than sex and makes his point by asking, "Have you ever gone a week without a rationalization?" (Okay, maybe you had to be there.)

When faced with the dismal statistics about retirement, many of us simply try to rationalize away the fact that we won't be able to retire when and how we had planned. "Hey, I enjoy my career. Why would I retire? I'll just keep working." But according to the Employee Benefit Research Institute, almost *half* of all retirees were *forced* out of work earlier than they planned due to layoffs, poor health, or the need to take care of a loved one. So "working forever" may not be an option you can count on, even if you *were* okay with saying, "And would you like fries with that?" a hundred times a day.

Here's a sobering fact from the U.S. Senate Committee on Health, Education, Labor, and Pensions:

"After a lifetime of hard work, many seniors will find themselves forced to choose between putting food on the table and buying their medication."[18]

---

After a lifetime of hard work, many seniors will find themselves forced to choose between putting food on the table and buying their medication.

---

How the heck did it come to this?

(By the way, if the stats above describe you and your situation, take heart! By the end of this chapter, you'll know there's a way out.)

## The Fix That's Broken

A funny thing happened on the way to retirement. In 1978, Congress added Section 401(k) to the tax code, creating a tax-deferred way for employees to *augment* their pensions.

These plans were never intended to *replace* company retirement plans, but that's what's happened. Nearly 75 percent of all company retirement plans *disappeared* between 1980 and 2012. Companies figured out that it's cheaper to offer a small matching contribution to an employee's 401(k) plan than to fund and pay for the management of a company pension plan. So they transferred the burden of funding employees' retirement to the employees themselves.

But before this recent trend, your grandfather's or great-grandfather's employer promised him a certain amount of money every month in retirement. Those plans are called pension plans. The technical name is **defined benefit plans**. But clearly pension plans are flying out of existence along with the dodo bird.

If you are an employee today, most likely your company offers a 401(k) or similar plan. That plan depends on the Wall Street Casino and since 2000, we've all witnessed how well *that's* worked out. Technically, these plans are called **defined contribution plans**, but the more accurate name is *hope and pray plans*.

## Why the Father of the 401(k) Has Disowned It

Well, I hate to dash those hopes and disappoint those prayers, but you should know that *even the man who's considered to be the Father of the 401(k) now despises the whole system!* Ted Benna, who three decades ago seized on an IRS loophole to transform American retirement savings, thinks he's created a monster. He says that the 401(k) "monster is out of control.... It is far beyond what most participants were able to deal with.... We're throwing tons of money away trying to teach participants how to become skilled investors ... but it just hasn't worked.... I would blow up the system and restart with something totally different."[19]

Wait a minute! We've been told again and again that these plans are the *best* way to save for a comfortable retirement. Heck, the government legislates and blesses those plans and lets you defer paying taxes on your contributions—at least under current tax law. Your employer offers them and will even give you matching funds when you contribute. What's not to like about that? So what's the problem?

That employer match is almost irresistible, isn't it? But it's the same marketing ploy that hot Vegas casinos use: They'll give you $20 in free chips *after* you plunk down $100 from your own pocket. Great! So now you get to lose $120 rather than $100! You're *still* gambling.

In 401(k) plans, your company administers the plan, makes its match (when times are good), then washes its hands regarding the outcome.

Your employer offers you a plan and—thanks to the law Congress passed—often even invests your retirement funds without your permission. Then, if the investments flop, your employer can't be held responsible. Wow!

Today's government-approved retirement plans offer absolutely *no* guarantees—except the guarantee that brokers and plan administrators are going to make money, no matter how much money *you* lose! For many retirees, these plans have been *worse* than nothing.

According to the U.S. Census Bureau, the average value of 401(k) accounts of *pre-retirees* between the ages of fifty-five and sixty-four is only $170,645, and the average value of their IRAs is only $147,345. And *half* of all those close to retirement age have *less than $50,000* in these plans.[20]

---

Half of people nearing retirement have less than $50,000 in their 401(k) or IRA, according to the U.S. Census Bureau.

---

A 2012 study by the Center for Retirement Research at Boston College found that "Even if households work to age sixty-five—which is above the current average retirement age—and annuitize all their financial assets, including the receipts from reverse mortgages on their homes, *more than half* are at risk of being unable to maintain their standard of living in retirement."

I want you to realize that you *do* have another option, and you *can* take charge of your retirement planning. You can take back control of your finances and your future retirement by simply understanding the five essential issues: **predictability, control, liquidity, tax consequences, and fees and expenses**.

So let's get educated about these five areas.

## Predictable or Unpredictable?

Here's the million-dollar question: Is your money safe, guaranteed to grow, and protected from market volatility? (Hint: If your retirement money is in a conventional plan, unless you've parked your cash in a CD, money market account, or fixed annuity, the answer is "no.")

Before 1978, speculating in stocks was a pastime of the wealthy. Today, thanks to the explosive growth of 401(k) plans, mutual funds, and the Internet, the typical working person has bet his financial future on a roll of the dice in the Wall Street Casino.

In the next chapter, we'll talk about the critical differences between saving and investing. For now, let's quickly define these two terms: *Saving* is what you do with money you *can't afford to lose*, so you know *for sure* that the money will be there when you need it. *Investing* is what you can do with money you *can* afford to lose. You throw it onto the Wall Street roulette wheel or speculate in Florida swampland. You're taking a risk, with the *hope* of making a gain.

Now let me ask you: Is money in your retirement account money you can afford to lose? Nope, didn't think so. And if you can't afford to lose it, should you be *investing* that money or *saving* it?

## Conventional Plan Unpredictability

Despite the fact that we can't afford to lose the money we'll need for retirement, we've been told that the best way to grow a substantial retirement nest egg is to put our money in the market, especially through tax-deferred, government-approved market-based retirement accounts like 401(k)s, 403(b)s, IRAs, SEP-IRAs, and Keogh Plans.

But if your money is invested in the market, you could lose some or even *all* of it! You have *no* way of predicting what the value of your plan will be when you want to tap into it. In fact, if you bet your money on Wall Street since the year 2000, you most likely have little to show for it, other than a pile of pocket lint—and a lot of sleepless nights.

Pension plans of prior generations weren't based on speculation and risk. Most were funded with life insurance and annuities. But today's government-sponsored plans are much different. Barry Dyke, author of *The Pirates of Manhattan*, writes:

> The 401(k), without any guaranteed returns, is a recipe for disaster. The 401(k) is a speculation bonfire—over 77 percent of the savings in these

plans are invested in volatile equities and mutual funds—which dumps all of the investment risk on uninformed retirement savers. Tying all of retirement income to the stock market is insane.[21]

What about **target date funds (TDFs)**? These are mutual funds that invest in a mix of assets, shifting from higher-risk to lower-risk investments as participants approach their target retirement date. Under provisions of the Pension Protection Act of 2006, eligible workers can be automatically enrolled in 401(k) plans unless they explicitly choose to opt out of participation, and TDFs have emerged as by far the most popular **default** investment—the one your employer automatically chooses for you. And 90 percent (!) of all new hires let their plan administrator choose where their money will be invested *for* them, according to Towers Watson, a global financial consulting firm.

It sounds good in theory, doesn't it? Take more risks when you're young, and dial back the risk as you get older. But in practice, it's been a disaster! A 2011 report from the federal government's General Accountability Office (GAO) revealed that between 2005 and 2009, investors in the largest TDF funds lost as much as 31 percent of their money.[22] That 31 percent loss is outrageous, especially considering that the Dow Jones Industrial Average lost only 1.61 percent during that very same time period!

It gets worse. The GAO report also states, "As a result of the severe financial market turbulence of 2008, some TDFs designed for participants retiring in 2010 lost considerable value, just over *forty percent* in one case. Further, according to some experts, many participants were unaware of the risks associated with these investments and that such losses were possible so close to the retirement date."

Can you imagine being just months from retirement, only to see your nest egg take a 40 percent hit? Would you be stunned? Devastated? "[M]any participants were unaware ... that such losses were possible so close to the retirement date." Ouch!

It'd be like putting all your cash in one of those fancy steel wallets for safety—only to find out the metal ate the ink off 40 percent of your currency!

But when your employer follows the law and automatically puts your money into TDFs, you have no recourse if you lose your shirt! The

Pension Protection Act of 2006 gave your employer protection from liability, as I mentioned earlier.

---

**Bank On Yourself Beats Twenty Years of Wall Street**

Dan Olson, a retail store manager from Minnesota, noted, "I have more money in my Bank On Yourself policy in six years than from funding my 401(k) for twenty years." (See more testimonials and reviews at **www. BankOnYourself.com/reviews**)

---

In too many companies, the important decisions about your 401(k) are made by someone with no training or education. Ninety percent of the country's employees' 401(k) plans are watched over by people who "need no special qualifications and no investing expertise or experience," according to *SmartMoney* magazine.[23] Really? Whose great idea was that?

### Your 401(k) Plan Administrator Picks Good Funds

A study from the Center for Retirement Research at Boston College in June 2013 found that plan administrators choose mutual funds that lag comparable indexes. Just like the rest of us humans, they routinely chase returns. About the best thing the study would say was that, even though employers choose funds that lag the indexes, at least their choices were better than randomly selected funds. (Translation: Their choices were marginally better than a monkey throwing darts, or a random-name generator.)

## Bank On Yourself Lets You Sleep at Night

The money you put into your Bank On Yourself policy, and the growth you receive on it, are simply *not* going to disappear. You're not going to open your statement to find that 40 percent or more of the money you'll need for retirement somehow drifted off into space based on the machinations of some greedy investment bankers whose latest Frankenstein topples the market.

Nope. Not only does the money you put into it remain secure, but also the growth of your money in a Bank On Yourself policy is both predictable and guaranteed. You receive a guaranteed annual increase, *plus* you have the potential for dividends. Dividends, while not guaranteed, have been paid every single year for more than 100 years by the companies recommended by Bank On Yourself Authorized Advisors. Their track record is so good because life insurance companies are masters at under-promising and over-delivering—unlike our friends on Wall Street.

As Jesús Huerta de Soto wrote in *Money, Bank Credit and Economic Cycles*:

> Life insurance companies tend to underestimate their assets, overestimate their liabilities, and reach a high level of static and dynamic solvency which makes them immune to the deepest stages of the recessions that recur with economic cycles. In fact when the value of financial assets and capital goods plunges in the most serious stages of recession in every cycle, life insurance companies are not usually affected.

Back to the tortoise and the hare. These tortoises know that "slow and steady wins the race." Always. Every time. (See Chapter 3 for more about the safety and long-term track record of the life insurance companies used for the Bank On Yourself concept.)

## A 2% TOTAL Return During the *Bull* Market?

Bank On Yourself "kept us safe and sane during the stock market crash," reported Debbie Wilder. "We started our first four Bank On Yourself policies seven years ago—one for me, one for my husband, and one each for our two kids—and now have thirteen policies. When we were maxing out our 401(k)s and IRAs, we were only up 2 percent *total* over a fourteen-year period which included the bull market! Our Bank On Yourself policies never go backward, and the increases are guaranteed and predictable. We're excited to watch our policies grow."

## Maximum Growth When You Need It Most

As people get older, they are usually advised to take less risk with their money to avoid losing significant amounts right before or during retirement. Following the conventional wisdom, that means accepting very low growth in exchange for more stability.

But Bank On Yourself plans turn that entire notion upside down. The dollar amount by which your plan increases is guaranteed to increase every year—and it does so *without your taking on more risk*. In the Bank On Yourself Revolution, the growth is *greatest* at the time people usually need it most—in retirement.

## Who Controls the Money in Your 401(k)?

I don't consider myself a control freak (though my husband might tell a different story!). But I think all of us should have some control over our *own money*, right? Whatever your current retirement plan, ask yourself these critical questions:

- Can you even make your own decisions regarding the money in your plan?
- Can you put in as much as you want and take out what you want when you want it?
- Do you have *accurate* projections about the value of your retirement fund so you can make intelligent decisions about your future?

If, like most Americans, you followed conventional wisdom and have a conventional retirement plan, the answer to each of these questions is "no." But it's created a nice retirement plan for your broker or money manager!

Your company can also change your 401(k) plan's rules and participation rates with little or no notice, throwing years of your careful financial planning into chaos.

For example, in 2013, IBM decided to no longer give employees their 401(k) match during each pay cycle. Instead, IBM will make one lump-sum payment to employee accounts on the last day of each year, December 31. Employees will lose an entire year of growth on the match money—and if an employee is fired in November, he won't get *any* match for the year.[24]

Is your company next in line to change or scale back its 401(k) plan?

## It's Like Putting Your Money in Prison

Government-approved retirement plans have more strings attached than Pinocchio before he became a real boy. It's like your money is locked up in a maximum-security prison where someone else calls the shots—and you barely get visitation! In most of these plans, you will be told *how much* you may put in your plan, what you *can and cannot invest in*, how much you can borrow and how you *must* pay it back, *how long* you must wait before you can access your money, when you *must* access your money, and how much you *must* withdraw (and pay taxes on) at that time. Penalties for running afoul of these regulations can be huge.

Withdrawal rules are very restrictive: You'll pay *penalties* for taking most distributions before you're 59½, and you're *forced* to start taking distributions when you reach 70½—whether or not you want to or need to. A big complaint I'm hearing today from seniors who've managed to accumulate some money is that they're being forced to take Required Minimum Distributions (RMDs) from their retirement plans once they turn age 70½. It's one of the many strings attached to those government-blessed plans. That's because the government can't afford to wait any longer to start collecting those taxes they let you defer all those years.

Roth plans have one less restriction than most other retirement plans: While there are no requirements to begin withdrawing from a Roth plan at a certain age, there are still restrictions about 1) *how much* you can put in each year, 2) *how soon* you may withdraw your earnings, and 3) *where* you can invest it.

Don't get suckered into believing *you* control the money in your 401(k) or IRA, or any similar plan. The *government* controls it and can—and does!—change the rules any time they want! The prison warden has your money under lock and key, and while your money's in the slammer, he can arbitrarily impose any new restrictions or regulations he comes up with—and you have *no* recourse.

---

**No Permission Needed to Use Your Money**

"I didn't want to have to ask for permission to use my money," remarked David Shelton, a healthcare V.P. in Texas. "I had very limited control of my money in my 401(k). I couldn't put in as much as I wanted, and I needed permission to borrow my own money if necessary. Bank On Yourself gives me control over my money. We're also using it to pay for our two sons' private school education in one installment to take advantage of a discount."

---

## Will the Government Take Over Your Retirement Account?

In February 2013, *American Thinker* published an article titled "The Feds Want Your Retirement Accounts." The article states, "Quietly, behind the scenes, the groundwork is being laid for federal government confiscation of tax-deferred retirement accounts such as IRAs. Slowly, the cat is being let out of the bag. Last January 18, in a little-noticed interview with Richard Cordray, acting head of the Consumer Financial Protection Bureau, Bloomberg reported, '[t]he U.S. Consumer Financial Protection Bureau is weighing whether it should take on a role in helping Americans manage the $19.4 trillion they have put into retirement savings.'"

And in the spring of 2013, the Obama administration proposed a budget plan that would limit how much a person can accumulate in IRAs, 401(k)s, 403(b)s, and other qualified plans. According to a White House statement, that proposal would generate $9 billion in revenue for the Treasury over the next decade. The government's rationale for such a move? "Some wealthy individuals are able to accumulate ... more than is needed to fund reasonable levels of retirement saving."[25]

*So now they're even telling us how much money is "too much"!*

Why are government-approved retirement plans such an attractive target for government control and ownership? For the same reason notorious holdup man Willie Sutton gave when he was asked why he robbed banks. "That's where the money is!"

Because the government created these plans, they know where your money is and how much you have there.

## Who Controls Your Money in a Bank On Yourself Plan?

Life insurance policies are private, unilateral contracts. That means the company can't change the rules unless you agree to it. That's the law.

The *policy owner* controls the money in a Bank On Yourself plan. There are no government-imposed limits on how much you can put in each year. (The upper limit is determined by your income, assets, and life insurance needs.) You can borrow against your cash value any time you want, without qualifying or begging for a loan. And there are no rules requiring you to pay it back on a certain schedule or face stiff penalties.

In addition to being able to tap your cash value at any time and for any reason, your plan can provide retirement income when and how you want it, with *no* government restrictions or penalties for "early" withdrawal or waiting "too long." There are *no* penalties for taking "too little" each year, and *none* of the mandatory minimum annual withdrawal requirements that are common to qualified retirement plans.

## Are Self-Directed IRAs Better?

What about self-directed IRAs? People have the mistaken impression that *self-directed* means you don't have to operate within the same government controls and restrictions. Not so. Self-directed IRAs receive the same tax treatment as traditional IRAs and they're subject to the same fees and expenses. You can determine what investments to place in the plan, but even that is within limits the government sets. A self-directed plan operates under the same rules and restrictions as a traditional IRA, and you must avoid the myriad of transactions the government prohibits.

And now the Securities and Exchange Commission has gotten into the act because there have been so many abuses and scams by those who promote self-directed IRAs: "According to a 2011 report by the Investment Company Institute, U.S. investors held approximately ... $94 billion of IRA retirement funds in self-directed IRAs. The large amount of money held in self-directed IRAs makes them attractive targets for fraud promoters ... because they permit investors to hold unregistered securities and the custodians or trustees of these accounts likely have not investigated the securities or the background of the promoter."[26]

## How Liquid Is Your Retirement Fund?

Here's the key question: How quickly and easily can you get your hands on the money in your retirement account when you need or want it?

With 401(k)s, IRAs, and similar plans, you typically have to *sell* the investment that you were counting on for growth if you want to get your money out. If it's a bad time to sell, you're out of luck. You have to bite the bullet and take a loss.

If you need access to your money in a 401(k), you may or may not be able to borrow money from it, depending on how the plan was set up. But even if your plan *permits* borrowing, there are government-imposed limits on *how much* you can borrow, *how long* you can borrow it for, and *how often* and in *what amounts* you must make loan payments. If, during this loan period, you lose your job or leave your company for any reason (and you haven't reached the magic age of 59½), in most cases you're required to pay your loan *back in full with interest in thirty to sixty days*, or you'll have to pay income taxes on the money you borrowed *plus* a 10 percent penalty.

Wait! Wasn't this *your* money in the first place? But if your money's locked up in the pen, it can't even get out on parole without major hassles and penalties!

In addition, some plans don't even allow workers to make *any* contributions while making payments on loans. Others require workers to wait a set time before contributing again after taking a withdrawal. If your employer matches contributions, you'd be taking a double hit.

Aside from the penalties and taxes you may owe by borrowing from your 401(k), one study reported in the *New York Times* calculated that a thirty-five-year-old with a $20,000 plan balance who takes out two loans in fifteen years ends up with about $38,000 less at age sixty-five than someone who never borrows, *even if the loans are repaid without penalty.*[27]

## How Likely Are You to Default on a 401(k) Loan?

It's worse if you default on your loan.

"But I would *never* default on a 401(k) loan!" Really? Dr. Brigitte Madrian, a Harvard University economist, estimates that 15 percent of 401(k) loan balances go into default, and at least 75 percent of workers who leave their jobs with a loan outstanding end up defaulting and getting stuck paying penalties and taxes.

Oh, and by the way, borrowing from your IRA is a no-no. The plan custodian will tell the IRS, and the value of your *entire* IRA immediately becomes taxable. Even using your IRA as collateral for a loan triggers taxes.

Borrowing from your Roth plan or using it as collateral for a loan is also prohibited. But with a Roth plan you can withdraw contributions you made to the plan at any time without any taxes or penalties. You can also withdraw your growth or earnings after five years under current tax law. Yahoo! But of course any money you withdraw will no longer earn you any interest or investment income. Boo hiss!

## Bank On Yourself Gives Your Money a "Get Out of Jail Free" Card

Bank On Yourself gives you complete control over the equity (cash value) in your policy. You can borrow your equity whenever you want, for whatever you want, with no government restrictions. There are *no* penalties for early withdrawals, late withdrawals, or *no* withdrawals.

With Bank On Yourself–type plans, you have full access to 85 percent or more of the cash value of your policy *beginning the very first month*, without selling your assets to do it. In fact—and this is one of the hardest things for people to grasp—if your policy is administered by one of the handful of companies that offer this feature, when you borrow money, your policy can *continue growing*, just as if you hadn't touched a dime of it. I'll show you exactly how that works in Chapter 7.

But understand this: With a Bank On Yourself–type policy, you can literally get your hands on the money you need from your account *within days*. You aren't selling off assets. Your money is still growing like you never touched it. You aren't running afoul of government regulations. And you aren't subject to penalties.

It still really is *your money*.

## Liquidity, Control, and Predictability with Bank On Yourself

Here's an example that shows what can happen when you use the Bank On Yourself method for two of its most popular benefits—retirement planning *and* becoming your own source of financing.

We're going to call this guy John. John starts his Bank On Yourself policy when he turns thirty-five, and he decides to fund his policy with $12,000 a year. (Keep in mind you can start at whatever level is comfortable for you.)

Now, watch closely. Here comes the part where John tells banks to go take a hike, accesses the liquidity built into his policy, and becomes his own source of financing. In Year 4, John starts borrowing against his policy to finance a new $30,000 car every four years. He pays the loans back. And because it's a Bank On Yourself–type policy, his policy grows at the same rate, even though he's taken out a loan. The growth continues as if he never touched a dime of it. Nice, huh?

Now, from the very same policy, when John turns seventy-one, he starts taking $55,000 for retirement every year (tax-free under current law).

*continued*

And here's the big payoff. The bottom line for John and his family? His total retirement income over thirty years is $1.65 million (Yep, John lives to be 101!). And he still has a death benefit of $220,000 remaining to leave a legacy for his family and/or favorite charity.

That's a total benefit to John and his family of $1.87 million—and he did it all on just $420,000 in premiums.

*That's* why Bank On Yourself may be the *ultimate* wealth-building and retirement strategy.

Would you like to find out how big *your* nest egg could grow—guaranteed and predictably? It's easy to find out when you request a free Analysis at **www.BankOnYourselfFreeAnalysis.com** or by completing and submitting the Request Form on page 265.

## What If You're in Your Fifties and Not Your Thirties When You Start?

We just saw an example of what can happen when you start a Bank On Yourself plan when you're in your thirties. But you may be wondering how it might play out if you're starting a plan when you're in your fifties. So let me introduce you to Stuart and Mary Kay, who just started a Bank On Yourself policy for each of themselves to supplement their retirement income.

Stuart is fifty-eight and plans to retire when he's seventy, and his plan was designed to fund the policy with $2,000 a month for ten years, plus a one-time initial lump-sum deposit of $66,000 from a 1035 Exchange on an old underperforming insurance policy. (Learn more about tax-free 1035 Exchanges in Chapter 9.) His initial death benefit is just over $305,000.

When Stuart turns age sixty-nine, his policy is projected to have a cash value of over $394,000 and a death benefit of over $650,000, based on the current dividend scale.

(I should point out that at the time this book went to press, dividends—like interest rates—were as low as they had *ever* been. Historically, as interest rates have risen and fallen, dividends have followed suit.)

*continued*

*continued from previous page*

Stuart plans to start taking $25,500 per year of retirement income from age seventy through age ninety, for a total of $535,500 (tax-free, under current tax law). At age ninety, Stuart's plan could still have over $32,000 of cash value and a death benefit of $81,000 to leave a financial legacy to his family.

Stuart's wife, Mary Kay, is four years younger and started her policy at age fifty-four. She is funding it with $1,000 a month for ten years and made a one-time initial deposit into the plan of $22,000 from the exchange of an old policy.

When Mary Kay is sixty-six, her plan is projected to have almost $185,000 in cash value and a death benefit of almost $370,000. Mary Kay could take $11,000 of retirement income per year (with no taxes due on it) from age sixty-seven to ninety, for a total of $264,000. At age ninety, she could still have $20,000 in cash value and a financial legacy of nearly $60,000 to leave to her loved ones.

Meanwhile, Stuart and Mary Kay plan to use their cash values for financing major purchases.

As you can see, there are *many* ways to design a Bank On Yourself plan, depending on your age, resources, situation and goals!

## The Tax Man Cometh

Let's cut to the chase: Do you know what surprises the tax man has in store for you when you take money out of your conventional retirement plan? Let me answer that for you: No.

With the exception of Roth plans, money you put in a government-sponsored retirement plan isn't taxed now. But it *will* be taxed later. Deferred taxes might sound good today, but deferring your taxes is like putting off a visit to the dentist. The problem will only get worse. Unfortunately, as you've been trying to build your secure nest egg through conventional plans, the deferred-taxes strategy has created massive financial *insecurity* because it doesn't address two critical questions:

- What will your retirement account be worth on the day you plan to tap into it?
- What will the tax rates be during your retirement?

(And because you can't answer these questions with certainty, you don't have a financial plan. It's a crapshoot—pure and simple.)

So how does this work? The money you put into a conventional tax-deferred retirement plan is money you haven't paid taxes on. Over time, you hope that money grows. Later, you'll pay tax on *everything* you withdraw from the plan. *Everything* means *every single penny* you take out.

In our immediate-gratification society, deferring taxes sounds good when you're putting money into your plan. But keep in mind, when the tax man eventually comes calling, he won't ask you what your tax liability *would have been* if you'd been paying taxes all along. He'll tell you what your tax liability is *at the time the taxes are due.*

## Are You Sitting on a Tax Time Bomb?

The reality is that you're sitting on a tax time bomb. Here's why:

• What direction do you think tax rates are headed over the long term? Just check out the news and notice the changing demographics of our country. Baby boomers are getting old. They're paying less in taxes than they used to, and they're beginning to draw Social Security. Who's going to pay for that? Taxes increased at the beginning of 2013, and you can safely bet that wasn't the last tax increase you'll see in your lifetime.

• As I write this, Washington has not dealt with the government's unsustainable debt and spending. (And if you're reading this ten years *after* I wrote this, I'm guessing not much has changed!) Politicians have kicked the can down the road again and again. But they can't kick it forever or the government will collapse. When they are *finally* forced to fix the problem, higher taxes are inevitable. I've asked thousands of people what they think will happen to tax rates in the future. Virtually all of them—including most experts—believe tax rates will go up.

• If tax rates *do* go up and you're successful in growing your nest egg, you'll only be paying *higher* taxes on a *bigger* number. If you were a rancher, would you prefer to pay a per-pound tax on that tiny calf or on the 1,500 pound animal that it will grow into when it's ready for market?

---

If tax rates go up and you're successful in growing your nest egg, you'll only be paying *higher* taxes on a *bigger* number.

---

• Typically as you age, you have fewer deductions or exemptions. For example, maybe you'll no longer have a home mortgage interest deduction or dependent children. Fewer deductions means paying more in taxes.

The government and Wall Street want you to believe you'll be in a *lower* tax bracket in retirement. Good, right? Paying a lower rate on your money? But the fact is that if you're in a low tax bracket in retirement, it means one thing: You're poor! (Or you've been smart enough to successfully shield your income from deferred taxation, perhaps using a Bank On Yourself–type strategy.)

---

**TIP**    **CONSIDER SPENDING DOWN YOUR QUALIFIED RETIREMENT PLAN FIRST**

---

Some Bank On Yourself revolutionaries say it makes sense for them to draw down their qualified plans within ten to fifteen years of retiring, while allowing their Bank On Yourself plans to continue growing exponentially. They cite several advantages:

• They're paying taxes at today's rates, which are presumably lower than future rates
• Because they're spending their qualified money over a shorter time period, they're able to draw more income per year, which helps them maintain their current lifestyle
• Meanwhile, their Bank On Yourself plans continue to grow, to provide more income later, with potentially no taxes due on it

A Bank On Yourself Authorized Advisor has the training and knowledge to help you develop a strategy to fit your personal situation.

---

The *Wall Street Journal* reported that the government has estimated that it lost $136 billion in revenue because of the taxes it did not collect on money going into tax-deferred retirement plans in 2012. The *Journal* pointed to a number of proposals on the table to increase tax revenue and noted that it's "a reminder that tax treatment of retirement accounts, once considered permanent, is anything but."[28]

## How to Minimize Your Lifetime Tax Bite

With a Bank On Yourself–type plan, it's possible to take retirement income *without* taxes due under current tax law. This is accomplished through a combination of dividend withdrawals and loans against your cash value, while making sure the policy doesn't terminate.

By building your nest egg through Bank On Yourself, you get to enjoy several advantages:

1. **You can take a retirement income with no taxes due.** There are two types of Bank On Yourself plans. In the most common one that we discuss through most of this book, the tax treatment is similar to Roth plans. (The other type is the Bank On Yourself for Seniors Plan, which we discuss in Chapter 10.) You put in dollars on which you have already paid income tax. On the gains you have each year (and you *will* have gains—guaranteed!), there are no taxes to slow the growth of your money.

Then, similar to Roth plans, you can access your principal and growth with no taxes due. Here's how: Dividends you leave in your policy to be reinvested are *not* taxable, and dividends you withdraw from your policy are *not* taxed unless you exceed your cost basis (the premium you paid in). If you get close to your cost basis, you can switch to *borrowing* against your cash value, with no taxes due on policy loans as long as the policy remains in force.

**2. You can reduce the taxes you may have to pay on your Social Security benefits.** Many people don't know that it's fairly common to pay taxes on your Social Security benefits. Currently, if a couple makes over $32,000 (from retirement account withdrawals and certain other sources), 50 percent of their Social Security income gets taxed. If they make more than $44,000, up to 85 percent of their Social Security benefits are taxed. That's bad.

However, the income you take in retirement from a Bank On Yourself policy is *not* included in the income totals the IRS uses to determine whether (or how much) your Social Security check is taxed. And that's good.

**3. If you're a business owner, you get extra tax breaks.** Professionals and other business owners are increasingly using Bank On Yourself to become their own source of financing for business vehicles, equipment, office buildings, and more. When you finance business expenses this way, you can qualify for tax deductions for interest and depreciation. Plus this strategy lets you recapture the interest you'd otherwise pay to banks and other financial institutions and never see again. See Chapter 9 for more on how business owners and professionals are using the Bank On Yourself method.

**4. The death benefit passes to your loved ones income tax-free.** It avoids passing through probate, too.

## Is Paying Deferred Taxes All That Bad?

Are the taxes you'll owe on your withdrawals from a tax-deferred plan really that big a deal? Let's figure it out together. Say you'd like to have $70,000 per year to spend in retirement. If you're investing in a tax-deferred plan and you're lucky enough to retire in only the 33 percent tax bracket (with perhaps an *average tax rate* of around 25 percent), your retirement plan would have to throw off $93,333—an extra $23,333 every year—to give you an after-tax income of $70,000 per year that you could get from a Bank On Yourself plan.

If your retirement plan *could* throw off $93,333 per year, wouldn't you rather spend that extra $23,333 enjoying life more rather than paying it out in taxes?

Here's an example comparing Bank On Yourself with a tax-deferred plan:

Retired brothers Bob and Bill are in the 35 percent tax bracket (and each has an average tax rate of 28 percent). Bob takes $100,000 per year in retirement income from his Bank On Yourself plan, with no taxes due.

Bill takes $100,000 per year in retirement income from his tax-deferred plan. However, because Bill has to pay income tax on his income, he ends up with only $72,000 per year to spend. The rest—$28,000—goes to the government. If Bill wants an *after-tax* income that equals Bob's, he will have to withdraw much more—about $139,000—and send 28 percent of it to the IRS. Only then will Bill have $100,000 to call his own.

Paying your taxes up front while you *know* what they are, and then having *no* taxes due on your gains, avoids unwelcome surprises. Both Roth plans and Bank On Yourself plans offer that strategy, but only Bank On Yourself has all the additional advantages and guarantees described here.

## Endorsed by Estate Planning Attorneys

Co-founder and chairman of the faculty of the College of Estate Planning Attorneys John Goodson says, "The idea of turning a life insurance policy into a more flexible Roth IRA substitute, when estates both large and small are involved, is a real winner. The Bank On Yourself strategy also enables setting up asset protection, stand-by emergency money, and tax and administrative savings. Bravo, bravissimo!"

# What if the Tax Laws Change?

Congress *could* change the tax laws regarding Bank On Yourself–type plans, just as they could change the laws for all retirement plans, including Roth plans. The tax benefits of a Bank On Yourself plan are simply an extra bonus. Even if those tax benefits were to disappear, the Bank On Yourself method *stands on its own merit* with unique advantages and guarantees.

This is why I've offered a $100,000 cash reward to the first person who can show that they use a different product or strategy that can match or beat Bank On Yourself. It remains unclaimed after nearly five years! Take the $100K Challenge, and see for yourself, at **www. BankOnYourself.com/challenge**.

## Bank On Yourself Protects Your Privacy

With a Bank On Yourself plan, you have privacy. Your plan and its growth are generally not reported to the IRS. When you access your money either by withdrawing money you previously placed in the plan by taking dividends up to your cost basis or by taking policy loans, it's not reported to the IRS. Only if there is a taxable withdrawal will there be any IRS reporting. A "taxable withdrawal" is one where you're withdrawing more money from your policy than the premiums you paid. You'll generally want to avoid that. Take a tax-free loan instead.

The other situation that can result in reporting to the IRS is if you allow the policy to lapse, in which case any gain there may be in the policy becomes taxable to the policy owner. You don't want to let your policy lapse. That's like killing the goose that lays the golden eggs.

## Fees That Compound Against You

We all know that when compound *interest* is working *for* you, it's a thing of beauty. But in traditional retirement plans, just like with deferred taxes, the compounding of *fees* works *against* you. It doesn't matter whether you win or lose in the stock market, one thing *is* guaranteed: Your stockbroker, or the advisor managing your money in the market, will *still* get paid. The impact of 401(k) fees is colossal. According to an exposé on *60 Minutes*, fees "can eat up half the income in some 401(k) plans over a thirty-year span."[29] Yikes!

Wall Street boasts about all the returns you'll earn in the stock market (Really? Starting when?), but it ignores all the compounded fees and commissions you pay. 401(k) plans layer on even *more* fees. Whether you buy a mutual fund that tracks the S&P 500 index outside of a qualified plan or you're investing inside a 401(k) or other government-sponsored retirement account, you'll pay fees. According to the U.S. Department of Labor, *fees of only 1 percent can slash the value of your savings by 28 percent* over the next thirty-five years. Think you're not paying 1 percent in fees in your retirement plan? Think again: On average, participants in small plans pay 1.9 percent in fees annually, and participants in large plans pay 1.08 percent per year.[30]

According to AARP, "What an investor pays in 401(k) fees could add up to significant costs over the life of a 401(k) plan. For example, for an employee who has been working for thirty-five years and contributes an estimated $5,000 per year to his/her 401(k) plan, with an annual return of 7 percent and no fees, he would earn about $469,000 over the thirty-five year period. However with an *annual fee of 1.5 percent* of the account balance, the employee would earn only $345,000 in a thirty-five-year period." [31] Poof! There goes more than 26 percent of your hard-earned dollars! *Somebody* made good money, and it *wasn't* the investor!

What about those target date funds that were supposed to "mitigate risk"—the ones that often significantly underperform the indexes? In *Common Sense on Mutual Funds*, John Bogle writes: "The largest target date funds include only the costs of their underlying funds in their expense ratio. The range of those costs runs from 0.18 to 0.86 percent. Shockingly, however, more than half of the target date funds carry their own hefty expense ratios—in addition to the expense ratios of the underlying funds, usually in the range of 0.70 to 1.30 percent. Together these costs can reach almost two percentage points, paid year after year." Hmmm ... I wonder who's stuck paying those extra points?

---

The fees projected in one popular target date fund
will eat up almost 25 percent of your savings just
in the first ten years.

---

As reported in the article "The Trouble with Target Funds" by William Baldwin in the June 24, 2013, issue of *Forbes* magazine, according to the prospectus of one popular target date fund, your projected fees and expenses for each $10,000 invested is $2,478 over a ten-year period (assuming it grows at 5 percent)—that's 25 percent of your savings! So if you had $300,000 in that fund for ten years, you'd get soaked for—are you sitting down?—$74,340! (And that's just over a ten-year period!)

---

### MYTHBUSTER

### IRA Fees Are Negligible

While all the attention has been focused on the confiscatory fees you pay in a 401(k) plan, IRA fees have gotten ignored. Many people assume they're very low. Hold on to your wallet, because a 2013 Government Accounting Office (GAO) report blew the roof off that myth![32]

Have you ever left a job and rolled your 401(k) into an IRA? Millions of people do every year. Financial firms often encourage workers who are leaving a job to roll over their 401(k) assets into an IRA also managed by the firm.

As recounted in the report, undercover investigators hired by the GAO called thirty of the largest 401(k) providers. Seven of them *incorrectly* stated there were no fees to open or maintain an IRA. And *half* of the ten largest firms *incorrectly* advertised free IRAs on their websites. The fee information was scattered in tiny print in hard-to-find documents on the site.

The study found that at one of the largest IRA providers, the annual advisory fee is 1.5 percent of assets for accounts with balances up to $500,000. As Representative George Miller noted when he released the report in Congress, "This comes as no surprise since IRAs often come with higher costs when compared to a 401(k)."

---

## But Didn't They Pass a Law Requiring Better Fee Disclosure?

In 2012, amidst considerable fanfare, the government announced new rules designed to force 401(k) plans to disclose the fees that we are paying. The new annual disclosure form often runs more than fifteen pages, but it doesn't provide a simple figure for the annual cost you're paying.[33] What we need is an easy-to-read summary that says, "You're paying this much for your 401(k), and here's how that compares to other plans," right?

It's important to know how much your plan is charging you because the growth you were *hoping* for is reduced each year by the fees you pay. Even with new laws requiring better fee disclosures, surveys show most participants still have *no* clue how much they're actually paying. The Employee Benefit Research Institute's *2013 Retirement Confidence Survey* revealed only *half* of plan participants even noticed the fee disclosure information, and only 7 percent have made changes to their investments as a result of receiving information about the fees they're paying.

## What About the Fees in a Bank On Yourself Plan?

Bank On Yourself is based on a whole life policy, and whole life policies have been given a bum rap by stockbrokers and others tied to Wall Street. "Look at those hefty initial fees! They don't even tell you how much your advisor is making off it!" It's true. You won't see the detail of this fee and that expense.

But it's kind of like buying a vacuum cleaner at Sears. You just want to know the bottom-line price you're paying, right? Do you really care about the details of how much commission that guy at Sears is making, how much the truck charged to deliver it to the store, or how much it cost the factory to build it? No. You care about what comes out of your pocket and what you end up with, don't you?

The projections *and* guaranteed values of Bank On Yourself–type plans have already had *all* costs—*including insurance costs and commissions*—deducted, so you *know* your bottom line, and there are *no* surprises in the future. No unknowns. No smoke and mirrors, just clear information so you can know in advance the *true* value of your plan at any point in time.

---

Bank On Yourself lets you benefit from the magic of
compounding *returns*, rather than having your nest egg
severely eroded by the tyranny of compounding *costs*.

---

## Do You Have a Crystal Ball?

Let's face it: If you have a conventional retirement plan, you don't have a clue what your retirement account will be worth on the day you'll finally tap into it. Considering the unknown of how much you'll be paying in fees, the volatility of the markets your money is thrown into, what tax rates will be when you retire, changing government regulations, and that the people administering your fund may have limited skill and knowledge, no matter *what* conservative number you plug into that spreadsheet, you simply don't know what the heck you'll end up with.

So how can you make plans for the future? How can you set a date for retirement or figure out the lifestyle you'll be living? When you don't know what you'll have, can't plan for the future, don't know when or *if* you'll be able to retire, and can't even predict your lifestyle with any certainty, isn't that the *ultimate loss of control*?

Contrast that with the certainty you have with a Bank On Yourself plan. Before you even sign on the dotted line of your policy, you know exactly how much money you'll have—*guaranteed*—at any point in time. That means you can know how much you will have in your plan ten years from now and forty-five years from now. Rather than dreading opening your latest retirement account statement to tell you whether you even *can* retire, you'll be confident making decisions about when you want to retire, how you want to live, and where you want to live. The only thing that's *unpredictable* is how much *better* you might do than the guaranteed returns, based on potential dividends!

## Retirement Planning Made Easy

The majority of this chapter talked about the pitfalls of conventional retirement plans—those very plans that you, like most Americans, probably based your future on. (Bummer!) But I've also shown you a solid alternative in Bank On Yourself. (Yay!) So let's sum it all up in a simple comparison chart that doesn't require a Stanford MBA to understand:

| Does the Retirement Plan You Currently Have or Are Considering ... | 401(k)s and 403(b)s | IRAs | Roth Plans | Bank On Yourself Plans |
|---|---|---|---|---|
| Give you guaranteed, predictable growth? | X | X | X | ✓ |
| Lock in your principal and growth, even when the market crashes? | X | X | X | ✓ |
| Give you control of your money without government restrictions and penalties? | X | X | X | ✓ |
| Give you tax-free retirement income? | X | X | ✓ | ✓ |
| Let you use your money in the plan without penalties, however and whenever you want? | X | X | X | ✓ |
| Let you use your money in the plan yet still have it grow as though you didn't touch it? | X | X | X | ✓ |
| Let you access your money without liquidating your investments? | X | X | X | ✓ |
| Allow you to fund it every year, without limits imposed by the government? | X | X | X | ✓ |
| Finish funding itself if you die prematurely? | X | X | X | ✓ |
| Tell you the minimum guaranteed value of the plan on the day you expect to tap into it, and at any point along the way? | X | X | X | ✓ |

Bank On Yourself plans also make sense for people who have seen the promised security of pensions and defined contribution plans evaporate. A Bank On Yourself plan can provide a much-needed supplement to whatever your pension plan manages to deliver.

With traditional retirement plans, you have surrendered control to the government and Wall Street. You cannot easily calculate all the fees and expenses you're paying, and over time, these fees and expenses will dramatically reduce the size of your retirement nest egg. Bank On

Yourself plans, on the other hand, remove all the mystery by clearly stating your guaranteed bottom-line results *after* taking *all* fees and expenses into account.

But by joining the Bank On Yourself Revolution and using a strategy that has been successfully building wealth and retirement security for well over 160 years, you can conquer the problems of predictability, control, liquidity, tax consequences, and fees and expenses.

## KEY TAKE-AWAYS

There are (at least) eight reasons Bank On Yourself makes an excellent alternative to conventional retirement plans:

**1. Guaranteed, predictable growth and retirement income—** with no luck, skill, or guesswork required.

**2. No volatility.** Your plan doesn't go backward when the markets tumble. Your principal and growth are locked in. It's not subject to market risks.

**3. You're in control.** You have control of your money without government penalties or restrictions on how much income you can take or when you can take it.

**4. Tax advantages.** You can access your principal and growth with no taxes due, under current tax law.

**5. Liquidity.** Your cash value can easily and immediately be tapped for any purpose at all, and your plan continues growing as though you never touched a dime of it.

**6. Fees don't compound against you.** Studies show that the fees in traditional retirement plans can consume as much as one-third to one-half of your savings over time. With a Bank On Yourself plan, *all* fees have *already* been deducted from the bottom-line numbers and results you'll get.

**7. Income tax-free legacy.** The death benefit is likely to be many times larger than the total amount you've paid into your policy. This passes to your loved ones and/or favorite charities income tax-free and without going through probate. If you die prematurely, the death benefit allows your plan to finish funding itself. That won't happen with traditional retirement plans.

**8. Peace of mind**. Perhaps the best reason of all: You'll know the minimum guaranteed value of your plan on the day you plan to tap into it—and at every point along the way!

# CHAPTER 6

# The Secret to a Financially Stress-Free Life

*By failing to prepare, you are preparing to fail.*
—BENJAMIN FRANKLIN

IN THE LAST CHAPTER, we talk about finding financial peace of mind. But is that even possible? Has *financial stress* become the new normal for most of us? Let's start with the bad news:

A recent Wells Fargo study revealed that:

- In 2012, 19 percent of participants had an outstanding loan against their 401(k) plans, and many were using those funds to pay their mortgages, credit card debt, or other bills.
- More than 34 percent of people in their fifties took money from their plans in the last quarter of 2012 alone. Twenty-seven percent of those in their forties also tapped their retirement accounts.

---

**INSIDE THIS CHAPTER . . .**

- Is There a Difference Between Saving and Investing?
- Is Your Financial Pyramid Upside Down?
- How Having Money You Can Get Your Hands On Helps You Sleep at Night
- How to Find the Seed Money You Need to Fund Your Plan
- Navy Commander Puts Financial Planning on Autopilot

---

Based on these statistics, it seems obvious folks are cash-strapped and definitely have a good reason to be stressed!

The National Institute of Personal Finance says that up to 50 percent of employees admit to spending an average of twenty-one hours per month dealing with personal money matters while on the job. Another report from the Personal Finance Employee Education Foundation found that 30 percent of U.S. employees are *seriously* financially distressed.

But we don't really need these stats, do we? These days, we all know friends who have lost their homes, neighbors who have lost their jobs, young families who have moved back with Mom and Dad because they couldn't afford housing on their own. We look around and see more and more people who are struggling to make ends meet today—much less building security for their future. It's become epidemic!

So if you're feeling financial stress and worry, you're not alone. But even if the statistics seem to tell us that this stress is inevitable, I'm here to tell you, it isn't! You don't have to panic about your financial present or agonize about all the what-ifs in the future.

*You actually can be financially stress-free.*

In this chapter, I'll share a few time-tested keys to achieving this financial peace of mind. Much of this is basic money sense that your great-grandmother lived by, and it includes a set-it-and-forget-it wealth-building vehicle many of our grandmas and great-grandmas used. It's simple—but powerful—wisdom that we somehow lost over the past couple of generations. Grandma may not have been perfect (well, mine was, but I don't know about yours), but she was a pretty sharp cookie when it came to handling money.

## Saving Versus Investing

Is there a difference between *saving* money and *investing* money? You can bet your bottom dollar there is!

*To save* means to place money you *can't afford to lose* in a vehicle that is *safe* and has *guaranteed* growth. You are *certain* your money will be there when you need it. In contrast, *to invest* means to place money in a financial vehicle or an asset that has a certain amount of risk. You *hope* to make a gain, but it's not guaranteed. In fact, you might even lose your original investment money. The only money you should *invest* is money you can afford to lose—or money that you're able to let languish in the market for *at least* twenty years, if necessary, until it recovers.

Unfortunately, over the past thirty years or so, we've been seduced by Wall Street into believing we must risk our money in order to achieve growth of any significance. That boring savings stuff? *Not* sexy. We're too sophisticated for that. We invest. We go for the gold. We take risks. And we do this with our emergency fund, our children's college fund, our retirement nest egg—the very money we *absolutely cannot afford to lose*. And we do this because we've been led to believe there are no better alternatives.

Great-grandma says, "Say *what*?"

## Everybody Has a Pyramid of One Shape or Another

Think of your money as a pyramid. If you're like the vast majority of people, your current financial picture may look something like this:

**FINANCIAL *INSTABILITY* PYRAMID**

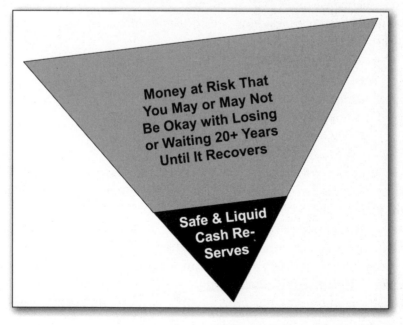

Many people *invest* before they *save*. The result? Only half of workers *and* retirees say they could definitely come up with $2,000 within thirty days to cover an unexpected expense. Of those who could, many say they'd have to rely on *extreme measures* (hopefully, that doesn't involve a guy who collects debts with a baseball bat!) to come up with the money.[34] Two thousand bucks. What is that? The transmission goes out in your car? Your teenager needs braces? Your mom who lives halfway across the country is in her last days, and you want to say your good-byes? Yep, that's two thousand dollars.

And *two-thirds* of employees say they would have trouble meeting their current financial obligations if their paycheck were delayed for *just one week!*[35] They couldn't go to the grocery store. Make the car payment. Pay the mortgage.

Ever been there? Or close?

You may *think* you're investing money you won't need for twenty years or more. But if you haven't yet built a solid financial foundation to help you weather whatever life throws at you, you're taking an enormous gamble putting your money at risk in stocks, real estate, and other volatile investments. (If you need a refresher on how risky this is, head back to Chapter 2.)

Life happens, and we should all expect the unexpected. Without safe and liquid cash reserves, how will you cope with:

- A medical emergency?
- Disability?
- A broken major appliance or leaky roof?
- Loss of a job?
- A family member needing assistance?

Without a *sizeable liquid rainy-day fund*, you may be forced into selling or liquidating your nest egg assets prematurely—the investments you planned on keeping over the long haul. When this happens, the timing is often terrible. You're at the mercy of current market conditions and forced to sell at the worst possible time.

Honestly? That's how the majority of people live. Their fortunes depend on Wall Street, the Dow Jones, the next paycheck coming in. (Great-grandma at least had that old jelly jar filled with cash!)

But what if your financial pyramid looked like this instead?

**FINANCIAL STABILITY PYRAMID**

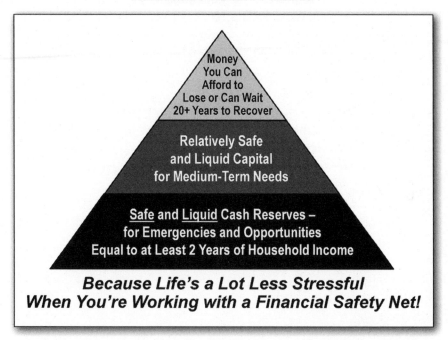

Money You Can Afford to Lose or Can Wait 20+ Years to Recover

Relatively Safe and Liquid Capital for Medium-Term Needs

Safe and Liquid Cash Reserves – for Emergencies and Opportunities Equal to at Least 2 Years of Household Income

*Because Life's a Lot Less Stressful When You're Working with a Financial Safety Net!*

Can you sense how much better that would feel? When safe and liquid cash reserves are the *foundation* of your pyramid, life is a lot less stressful. Rather than walking a tightrope in a strong wind with nothing to catch you, you're working with a financial safety net. A core built on savings gives you stability, accessible resources, and restful nights. A core built on the inherent gamble of investments? Pull out the Dramamine and Ambien!

**TIP  HOW GRANDMA BUILT SAVINGS**

One of the most powerful pieces of financial wisdom I've ever heard is what I call the **10/10/10 Savings Formula**. My husband and I have used it in our own lives for decades, and we've taught it to all our children and grandchildren.

My colleague, Tim Austin, who you'll meet in Chapter 11, says that people in the 1940s and 1950s commonly used this formula. They would set aside 10 percent of their gross income for short-term needs (vacations, gift giving), 10 percent for anticipated mid-term needs and potential emergencies (a new car, replacement of major appliances, a new roof, and college tuition), and 10 percent for long-term retirement planning.

The 10/10/10 Savings Formula can allow you to avoid all conventional bank and credit card debt. You can pay cash for even large purchases, such as appliances or a car, and save tons in interest and fees. How's that for a winning formula! What worked back then still works today.

For more helpful money and financial literacy tips, head over to **www.BankOnYourselfNation.com**.

---

## Liquidity Is the Key

How much cash should you stash? The conventional advice is to have a fund equal to three to six months of your household income. But during the recession that started in 2008, many people discovered too late that three to six months' income wasn't even close to being enough. Millions of people who lost their jobs remained unemployed for well over a year, or even two. At the same time, we lost the ability to use our homes like ATM cash dispensers as real estate took a hit and lenders clammed up.

To have the security of a *real* safety net, why not build a fund equal to at least two years of your income? Put that money in a place that is safe and liquid, so you can easily get your hands on it when the proverbial you-know-what hits the fan.

Does it seem impossible? You probably won't build this fund overnight. You may not be able to follow the 10/10/10 Savings Formula immediately. But if you increase your savings by even just 1 percent or 2 percent each year, you won't feel the pinch, and you'll be surprised by how quickly your rainy-day fund will grow.

I know, I know! Who wants to put that much money in a savings, money market account, or CD, where it earns so little interest these days that you need a magnifying glass to see it? Keep reading because there's a better place to keep money you need to keep safe and liquid.

 **FIND OUT WHERE YOUR MONEY IS GOING**

Call me brash, but I'd bet a pretty penny that Grandma had a much better handle on where the family's money went each month than most folks do today. Of course, she didn't have credit cards stuffed in her wallet, automatic withdrawals, ATMs, teenagers wielding Starbucks cards, and multiple checking accounts.

Do you really know where your money goes every month? Honestly, most of us don't to any degree of detail. But it can be an incredible eye-opener! To get a grip on this, it can be as simple as starting with a piece of paper and listing your ongoing expenses for the month. Then track your daily purchases: that newspaper you buy, the latte, the four boxes of Girl Scout cookies. Get your spouse and children to write everything down for at least a week. Add that to your monthly list.

What do you see? How much value are you getting from each of your expenditures? Are there places where you'd feel better if you put that money into the base of your pyramid rather than tossing it away?

## A Liquid Fund That Builds Real Growth

We tend to vastly underestimate the value of a substantial emergency fund. And it's not just lower-income workers. We've found affluent families are just as squeezed when unexpected expenses arise. Maybe they can handle $2,000, but what about the bigger hits? Your twin daughters both decide to get married in the same summer with guest lists of over 200 each. Your billable hours drop significantly and you need $20,000 pronto to cover your staff. That land dispute from decades ago settles—but not in your favor. Where are you going to get the boatload of cash you need?

It may not seem like much fun to have a lot of cash sitting around idling when there are so many things we need and want. And whatever extra we've got, we'd prefer to invest those dollars and (hopefully) earn a lot more than the interest the bank will pay us.

There are lots of compelling reasons to have a substantial rainy-day fund, but you don't have to keep your money sitting under your mattress or languishing in a bank vault. You can have a *safe and liquid fund that gives you healthy growth* at the same time.

But first let's nail down the **definition of liquidity**. It's money you can get your hands on:

- When you need it
- For whatever you need
- Without begging for it or applying for it
- With no penalties for accessing it and no restrictions
- Without sustaining a loss

That short list of requirements rules out many financial vehicles. But by joining the Bank On Yourself Revolution, you get *all those advantages*, plus:

- Growth that historically has beaten savings and money market accounts and CDs
- You aren't required to liquidate or sell income-producing assets to get cash
- You can use your money and have it continue growing as though you hadn't touched it (if your policy is from one of the handful of companies that offer this feature)

**WHERE GRANDMA PUT THE FAMILY'S SAVINGS**

Grandma had more than her jelly jar going for her, as Tim Austin learned from some of his elderly clients. "In the 1940s and 1950s, it was very common for the whole life insurance agent to come around on Friday mornings to collect the $1 or the $5 premiums. They called him a debit agent, and he literally showed up every week just like the milkman and collected the $1, $2, or $5 premiums."

Tim's clients set up those policies not only for the death benefits. These folks knew they could borrow cash from them whenever they needed to. "A whole life policy was very routinely used for emergency funds, car loans, business loans, and such, and it was common for whole life insurance to be a foundation of a family's financial plan in those years."

In Chapter 3, I mentioned that one-third of American families owned whole life policies back in 1950. Maybe they knew something we've forgotten.

## Seven Benefits of Liquidity

Life does have a tendency to throw us curveballs, and they have a perverse way of coming at the most inconvenient times. Here's a partial list of the many ways having a sizeable liquid emergency fund can come in handy and substantially reduce the stress in your life:

### 1. No high-interest finance charges
Cars break down, roofs leak, and teeth need crowns. Having a pool of money in a Bank On Yourself plan lets you avoid putting charges on a credit card, or worse, getting gouged by a payday loan.

Right after Larry and I bought a home in 2009, we discovered the roof needed a lot more than patching after a season of unusually heavy snow. Even though we got quotes from four different roofers, the price tag made us gasp—$55,000! That's assuming we wanted to replace the roof with one that would last more than a couple seasons. We live in New Mexico, where flat roofs are common—and shockingly costly! We'd just moved in and already bitten the bullet paying for moving costs, remodeling, and all the zillions of extra expenses of owning a new home.

Bank On Yourself to the rescue! We filled out a simple form indicating how much money we wanted and where we wanted it sent, faxed it in, and had the money in our checking account within a week. We then set our *own* repayment schedule to pay it back to our plan so the funds would be there the next time an unexpected expense came up. (And our policy kept growing as though all $55,000 were still in it! Woo-hoo!)

And while you do pay interest on policy loans, typically at a competitive below-market rate, that interest ultimately benefits you, as I explain in the next chapter.

Based on your current financial pyramid, how would you have handled a $55,000 roof replacement? Scary thought, isn't it?

### 2. A cushion if you lose your job

Do you know someone who lost their job and couldn't find another for a year or more during the Great Recession? It happened to millions of people. But I heard from many who had the foresight to start a Bank On Yourself plan who credit their plans for bridging the financial gap until they could get income flowing again.

### 3. Lower insurance premiums

When you have a cash cushion to fall back on, you can opt for higher deductibles (the amount you pay before the insurance kicks in) on your auto, homeowners, and other insurance policies. If you think of your insurance policies as safeguards against *major* catastrophes rather than something that covers smaller expenses, the savings can be huge.

For example, an ABC reporter recently ran an analysis on health insurance for a healthy forty-one-year-old woman friend.[36] He compared five plans, all with the same company, and every aspect of the coverage was the same except for the deductibles. Here's what he found:

| Deductible | Premium |
|------------|---------------|
| $500 | $4,236/year |
| $1,500 | $2,808/year |
| $2,500 | $2,352/year |
| $5,000 | $1,536/year |
| $10,000 | $1,164/year |

Bumping up her deductible by just $1,000 saved her $1,428 per year in premiums. A higher deductible will mean lower premiums in *all* kinds of insurance—but you definitely wouldn't want a deductible that is higher than your liquid cash fund.

### 4. Sense of control

Having a pile of cash provides peace of mind and a feeling of being in control. Even if your worst fears never materialize, that feeling of being in control is priceless. It's like walking down a dark alley at midnight with the confidence that comes from knowing you're a master at self-defense. Even if you never see a bad guy, nothing beats knowing that you've got what it takes to protect yourself and those you love.

### 5. Steady year-round income

If your income varies, you'll need a cash cushion to even out the highs and lows. We cover this dynamic with business owners in Chapter 9. But fluctuating income is also a fact of life for those who work on commission or who rely on tips or bonuses beyond their basic salary. In these cases, income may ebb and flow, but expenses typically remain constant.

### 6. Give yourself options

If you don't have money stashed away, your choices might be made by your cash situation rather than by what's really important to you. For example, you might decide you can't afford to pay for an airline ticket to visit a sick relative, or you may have to forgo an operation that would save your pet's life. With a cash stash, you won't have to make choices you'll regret.

The Gammon family, who I profiled in my first book, had an unusual emergency come up. Out of the blue, Greg got a call from his stepbrother letting him know they wouldn't be able to keep the baby girl they were expecting in four days because of a difficult personal situation. They didn't want just anyone to adopt her. Would Greg and his wife consider becoming her new parents?

Greg and Christy didn't have to think twice before saying yes. As they prepared to fly across the country to the hospital where the child would be born, they realized that there were fees involved in the adoption. Greg's alternatives weren't very good: He might be able to put the fees on a credit card, but he'd need to get an increase in his limit. Taking out a home equity line of credit was going to be tough because the real estate market was in the toilet.

Instead they called their Bank On Yourself Advisor, who handled the simple paperwork. The needed funds were in the Gammons' checking account within days, and they flew home with their beautiful new baby girl.

You can watch a video of Greg telling the family's moving story at **www.BankOnYourself.com/adoption-story**.

### 7. Ability to take advantage of opportunities

Just as emergency expenses come up when we least expect them, so do opportunities! Imagine the opportunities you might be able to take advantage of if you had safe and liquid cash reserves equal to one or even two years of your household income.

---

  **CONVENE A FAMILY COUNCIL**

---

Can we agree that families in past generations had a little more time around the family dinner table to discuss what was going on in their individual and collective lives? No television blaring, fingers texting, or iPods jammed in children's ears. Mom and dad weren't usually racing in from ten to twelve hours on the job, and life wasn't rushing by so quickly that you hardly had time to think.

But that was then and this is now. In order to have good discussions with one another, we have to schedule them.

One thing I recommend is to hold a monthly Family Financial Discussion Night during which you focus together on the things like a family budget. Much like diets, budgets are no fun. But a **strategic spending plan** can be, and even children as young as four or five can get involved. Create your family's "Personal Spending Rules" together to work toward family goals and help you make spending decisions today that build happiness for you now *and* in the future. Your children will not only learn good financial skills through this process, but they'll take pride in being part of it.

It's also important for couples to regularly get together and discuss the more sophisticated parts of the family financial picture. Sit down at least once per year and look at everything: Do you need to update your wills or update trusts? How are your accounts doing? Are you on track to meet financial needs in the short term and long term? One of you may keep the checkbook and pay basic expenses while the other handles big-picture wealth-building strategies. But when *both* partners stay abreast of the overall picture, you both feel more confident and in control.

---

## When Should You Start With Bank On Yourself?

The key, of course, is to start building your emergency fund right now—TODAY! Remember, it was *not* raining when Noah built the ark. He got the message then got to work. He didn't say, "Yeah, that makes sense. But the sky looks pretty clear for now. I'll start on it later. Maybe tomorrow." Tomorrow never comes, does it?

The cash you save in your Bank On Yourself plan can be that ark, ready to set sail at the least sign of trouble. But it doesn't work as well if you start building it in the middle of a financial storm!

The unexpected doesn't wait around for us to get our act together. The unexpected just shows up when it does. Please note that I said *when* it does, not if it does. As smart as we are, we can't anticipate everything that will happen in our lives. We can only be like Noah: Get the message, then get to work.

The bottom line is that the more cash you have in a place that's safe and liquid, the more options you'll have, the *more peace of mind* you'll have, and the *less financial stress* you'll have.

---

### MYTHBUSTER

### Whole Life Insurance Is Nothing More Than a Forced Savings Vehicle

Like that's such a bad thing? Isn't the 401(k) plan that you have some of your paycheck deposited into before you can spend it a way of forcing yourself to save? (Except with Bank On Yourself, you don't have to worry that your savings will vanish in a market crash.) Some of us are very disciplined, but most of us will save more when we make a *commitment* to save.

As mentioned throughout this book, Bank On Yourself gives you lots of flexibility if you hit a rough patch. And you may be surprised to find out how much fun and motivating saving becomes when your money only goes in *one* direction (Up!), and you can use your money and still have it grow!

## Where Will You Find the Money?

Okay, I know how you're feeling. If you're like many people, you probably don't have a pile of cash lying around at the end of each month. Many of us are living a thirty-day month on a twenty-eight-day paycheck.

So how and where do you find the money to get started with Bank On Yourself to build your extremely valuable liquid cash fund?

Your plan will be custom-tailored to *your* unique situation, goals, and dreams, and there's no set amount you need to put in to start a policy. As a general guideline, plans funded with a minimum of $250–$300 a month grow more efficiently, and you can put in as much money as you wish. The upper limit is determined by your income, assets, and need for insurance.

Not sure you can set aside at least $250 a month to grow your wealth safely and predictably while building a solid financial foundation that can help you weather just about any curveball life throws you?

Tim Austin, who has loads of experience with thousands of clients, says, "I have been specializing in this area for twenty years, and I haven't met a family, *no matter what income level they are at*—from $40,000 a year to $400,000 to $1,000,000—that I *haven't* been able to help find some things within their monthly expenses that they can trim by using some very simple tweaks."

So don't rule yourself out! Bank On Yourself Authorized Advisors are black belts when it comes to helping people restructure their finances to free up seed money to fund a plan to help you reach your goals and dreams. Sometimes this can even be done without reducing your cash flow or lifestyle at all. (You can get a free Analysis and a referral to one of the Authorized Advisors by going to **www.BankOnYourselfFreeAnalysis.com** or by completing and submitting the Analysis Request Form on page 265.)

## Eight Ways to Free Up Money for a Plan

### 1. Restructure debt

In some situations, strategically reducing debt can free up a significant amount of monthly cash flow to help fund a policy that could help you achieve your goals more quickly.

**2. Reduce funding of your 401(k) or other retirement plans**

Many people find money to finance their Bank On Yourself policy by reducing the funding of their 401(k) or other retirement accounts. They pay only the amount that their employer matches. This brings them the guarantees, tax advantages, and flexibility of Bank On Yourself that traditional, government-endorsed 401(k)s IRAs and pensions plan do not.

**3. Tap your IRA or 401(k)**

You can use a federal rule (called 72(t) after the tax code section that describes it) to **pull money out of your traditional retirement plan** to fund your policy. The 72(t) rule enables you to avoid the 10 percent penalty anyone younger than 59½ would typically be required to pay. You should consult with a qualified advisor and tax professional before considering this option.

**4. Make your savings work harder**

A policy designed to maximize the power of the Bank On Yourself concept also serves as your emergency fund. So you may want to consider moving some of your savings into a Bank On Yourself policy. The return on a Bank On Yourself policy typically beats the interest rates of savings and money market accounts and CDs—*without* increasing your risk.

**5. Rethink that tax refund**

People love getting a big tax refund check in the mail every year. But that's *your own money* you're getting back. In essence, you're giving the government an interest-free loan while you're getting a zero rate of return on your money. It's fast and easy to adjust your withholding on a W-4 form at work. You can change your withholding amount as many times as you want until you are comfortable with the adjusted amount. By doing this, you may be able to immediately increase your monthly cash flow, perhaps by hundreds of dollars every month, and you can then use those dollars to fund your policy.

**DO YOU *NEED* IT OR JUST *WANT* IT?**

Grandma, especially if she grew up during the Depression, was a lot clearer about the difference between *want* and *need*. But then again, Grandma only had to deal with the occasional salesman at the door. Today Madison Avenue has got us surrounded! And Madison Avenue is fully aware that spending is triggered by emotion. They've hypnotized many of us to react to our emotions and go on automatic pilot when it comes to spending.

But we're smart. We know that keeping up with the Joneses is *not* the road to happiness those Mad Men try to tell us it is. And when we take a moment to stop and reflect, we do really know what we *need* versus what is just a momentary flash-in-the-pan, won't-outlast-a-bowl-of-popcorn kind of desire.

Before each purchase, get yourself off emotional autopilot. Take a deep breath (and a couple of days) to consider whether you really *need* whatever it is. An odd trick to shift your mind-set—that really works!—is to clench your fist or biceps when you're considering making a purchase.

And teach your children about the difference between *need* and *want*—not by your lectures, but by your good example.

Grandma would be proud!

## 6. Make lifestyle changes

An option that could enable you to start a plan sooner is taking small practical steps to reduce spending. One of the easiest ways is holding on to your car a few years longer than you normally would before buying a new one. It's also easy to cut monthly costs through simple changes like eating out less; bundling your Internet, cable TV, and phone services; or calling your mobile phone carrier to see how to sensibly reduce your monthly plan. While each individual change in lifestyle habits may be small, the total savings can be significant.

### 7. Convert existing life insurance policies

Transferring the cash value from an existing policy may be an option, especially in the case of an underperforming variable or universal life policy. In some cases, taking a withdrawal from the old policy and using that to fund a policy that meets the requirements for Bank On Yourself is a good option. A word of caution: Giving up an old insurance policy is not *always* in your best interests. A Bank On Yourself Advisor can explain the pros and cons and show you the impact of doing this.

### 8. Manage your home equity wisely

You may find that you can restructure your mortgage or stop making extra payments of principal and free up more seed money to help fund a policy, so you can move closer to a secure financial future. (The next chapter talks about the hidden dangers in having too much equity in your home.)

---

Take our "Love and Money Self-Assessment"
and discover how to increase financial
intimacy with your partner at
**www.BankOnYourself.com/financial-intimacy**

---

Here's a modern-day example of how Grandma's wisdom works:

## Navy Commander Puts Financial Planning on Autopilot

Bob Chambers is a Navy commander who retired before he turned fifty. Early on, Commander Chambers knew he wanted to attain financial independence, enjoy a comfortable lifestyle in retirement, and leave a legacy for future generations.

Commander Bob wrote a booklet titled *Financial Independence Made Easy*, consolidating all the financial planning information and wisdom he had collected over the years so he could share it with his friends and twin teenage boys. He had conducted extensive research because he knew he would be retiring early. And through his research, he came to some major insights into why the conventional wisdom about saving and investing has failed so many.

But Bob discovered a positive alternative, and his booklet spells out more than *thirty unique benefits* of the Bank On Yourself method. (He just told me he's now listed over *sixty* benefits!)

In 1985, when Commander Bob first joined the Navy, he put together a "financial autopilot system," a set of three-by-five-inch cards outlining the accepted best practices of money management and investing. As he explained, "They included such ideas as: Put your household inventory together. Calculate the amount of insurance you'll need for both you and your wife. Create a will. Obtain a line of credit with credit cards. Watch your credit rating. Learn about taxes. Learn about investments. Write down realistic financial goals. Create a portfolio." The idea was that once he established a portfolio of investments, he'd be on financial autopilot.

Commander Bob started off by investing in no-load mutual funds, assuming he could just let them grow for twenty to thirty years and his retirement would be set. He followed that strategy for quite a while until he realized it just wasn't working. The concept of financial autopilot was sound, but the vehicles he was using were not.

## Navy Commander Bob Discovers the Big Leaks in His Financial Ship

One of the biggest leaks in his ship was his dependence on his conventional savings and investing vehicles, mutual funds, his wife's 401(k) plan, home equity, Social Security, etc. for his eventual retirement. He came to realize those sources might not exist or be viable in the future. He also lacked control over his retirement programs and couldn't predict where his various investments would end up.

He couldn't say with any level of certainty, "This is the income I'll have from these investments in ten, twenty, or thirty years."

His defining moment came while he was stationed in Washington D.C. He was a short distance away from the Pentagon when the plane crashed into it on 9/11. A tragic day for America and the whole world. In the days afterward, Commander Bob, like many others, lost half of his net worth as the stock market crashed. And he knew he *had* to find a better way to secure the future of his family.

Commander Bob got serious about finding alternatives. When he checked out Bank On Yourself, he discovered that it embraced all the principles of sound financial planning that were vitally important to him. "To me, a Bank On Yourself policy is like having a Swiss Army knife."

He described the three most important advantages to him of Bank On Yourself as:

1. **Simplicity.** "You fill out an application, have a medical screening, and you fund the policy. But that's about it. It's on autopilot after that. I can use the time I once used to track my investments for more important things."

2. **Giving back to others.** "Bank On Yourself allows me to experience the goodness of planned giving. I can guarantee that I can give back to others. And if I want to give back before I pass away, I can do that, too."

3. **Dreams can live on.** "If I die, my dreams and goals don't die with me. They continue with a financial and educational legacy through my family. That was most important for me."

Commander Chambers is also using his Bank On Yourself plan for its liquidity, to become his own source of financing. Through one Bank On Yourself policy, he financed a trip to Italy with a Navy friend who has been a personal mentor, and then another trip with his sons and several other Boy Scouts to the Philmont Scout Ranch in New Mexico.

As he did this, he paid close attention to how easy it was to take out a policy loan. "It was easier than getting a loan from the bank I've been with for twenty-five years."

When talking to people who are trying to figure out which way to turn financially, Commander Bob tells them to keep an open mind. "Don't say 'no' until you've done your research."

"My driving force was twofold: to retire to spend time with my family, and to leave a legacy that was both monetary and educational. That's not out of reach for anyone. You just have to have faith in yourself and your Bank On Yourself Advisor.

"Now I'm relaxed when it comes to financial planning because of the Bank On Yourself concept. It makes it super easy. I'm finally on financial autopilot, and I've found financial independence all in one product."

To read or listen to my interview with Commander Bob Chambers, and to download a copy of his booklet, *Financial Independence Made Easy*, go to **www.BankOnYourself.com/navy-commander**

## KEY TAKE-AWAYS

1. **Investing and saving are two totally different animals!** Saving is what you do with the money you *cannot* afford to lose like your retirement, kids' college funds, and emergency stash. Investing is what you do with money you *can* afford to lose—because you very well might lose it!

2. **In life, you can always expect the unexpected!** Whether it's a positive opportunity that comes your way or a critical emergency that hits, you want to be ready for anything life has in store.

3. **Financial peace of mind comes from building a pyramid with a strong pool of savings and liquidity at its base.** Liquidity

ensures that you'll never have to beg for, pay exorbitant interest on, or simply go without the money you need when you need it.

**4. Grandma was a pretty smart cookie.** Financial wisdom of yesteryear still applies: the 10/10/10 Savings Formula, knowing where your money is going, separating *want* from *need*, and stashing funds in a properly designed whole life policy!

**5. Bank On Yourself lets you sleep at night.** Not only can you feel confident that your money is growing safely so you have funds for retirement and can leave a legacy, you also have easy access to funds when the inevitable unexpected occurs.

**6. Where there's a will, there's a way.** Your Authorized Advisor can help you find the money you need for your Bank On Yourself policy so you can move forward financially stress-free!

# CHAPTER 7

# Fire Your Banker

*Banks take money from the public or each other on call, skim it for their own reward, then lock it up in volatile, insecure illiquid loans that at times they cannot redeem without public aid.*

—JAMES BUCHAN, SCOTTISH JOURNALIST

I'M PRETTY SURE the last banker who was portrayed as a good guy was George Bailey in *It's a Wonderful Life.* Typically, bankers are cast as the greedy villain, preying off good, honest working folk—an image they certainly lived up to in recent decades.

And even after forcing the world's economy into ruin, they aren't finished yet! JP Morgan Chase hid losses on bad bets that cost the bank *at least $6.2 billion* tied to "synthetic credit derivatives," one of the latest smoke-and-mirrors plays Wall Street has come up with to fatten their wallets at the expense of yours. The Justice Department and FBI investigated them. But nothing has changed, and it's likely nothing ever will. Wall Street investment bankers will just invent a new, obscure investment that nobody can figure out until it's too late.

In an article on MSN Money, Anthony Mirhaydari noted, "The bankers know the bigger they get during the bull market, the safer they'll be in the next downturn since taxpayers will have no choice but to support them. And

> **INSIDE THIS CHAPTER . . .**
> - How to Make Money You Spend Continue to Grow for You
> - How to Beat the Banks at Their Own Game
> - FAQ's of Self-Financing through Bank On Yourself
> - Savings Account Versus Bank On Yourself

according to comments from Attorney General Eric Holder back in March of 2013—comments he's since tried to tone back—the CEOs leading these monstrosities have become too big to jail for fear of damaging sentiment and shaking markets."[37]

The banks may be too big to fail, but you and I are apparently too small to save. There's no bailout coming for us, no knight in shining armor, no Mighty Mouse to save the day. We don't have lobbyists in Washington or tentacles throughout the world economy. The guys who crashed global markets get a slap on the wrist, a bailout, and the right to keep on doing much of what they've been doing. We get *bupkus*.

But wait! What about your friendly *local* banker? The one who almost sometimes kinda remembers your name when you visit to make a deposit? *He's* not responsible for the debacle of the last several years. He's the good guy who extends us credit for our major purchases, safeguards our savings, and lets us take out loans for the tough times, right? Do we really want to fire him? Or even if we did, is it even possible?

Yes and yes.

Mark Twain described your friendly local banker eloquently many years ago:

*"A banker is a fellow who lends you his umbrella when the sun is shining, but wants it back the minute it begins to rain."*

There are three main ways you use your bank: 1) for consumer credit, 2) for loans for a variety of expenses, and 3) as a place to keep cash in checking accounts for convenience and savings accounts that receive interest.

Even if your banker is a charming guy, what if I told you that you can bypass banks, finance companies, and credit companies altogether? That you can use your bank but not let it use you? Use your bank for the convenience of a checking account, debit card, and a credit card (that you pay off every month while earning perks). But rather than letting your bank feed off you when you need money, you can join the Bank On Yourself Revolution and beat the banks at their own game.

You can become your *own* source of financing and get access to money *when* you want it, for *whatever* you want, by answering just one question: How *much* do you want? And even while you use your money for purchases or to take advantage of opportunities, it keeps growing just the same.

Sound good? Keep reading.

## Are You Stuck in a Credit Crunch?

Let's start with business as usual. Conventional wisdom says there are the three ways we buy big-ticket items like a car.

1. We finance it
2. We lease it
3. Or we pay cash for it

When you **finance** a car, you take out a loan, pay interest according to your credit rating and the economic climate, and pay it back according to a pre-set schedule, right? But after your loan is paid off, what do you have show for your money? Only an old car, worth whatever its trade-in value happens to be (which is *never* equivalent to the total of the payments you made).

Or you might **lease** your new car. After all, monthly payments may be lower than if you financed it. However, when you lease a car, what do you have to show for it when the lease is up? Even less. You'll turn the car in and have *nothing* to show for the money you spent. Leasing is actually the *least* efficient way to finance something.

Other people figure they can beat the financing and leasing rackets by **paying cash** for the car. But here's the rub: If you save up for your car in a savings or money market account and then pull your money out to pay cash, how much interest are you now earning on that money?

Nothing, of course, because the bank's going to stop paying you interest. And you'll only start earning interest again very slowly as you put money back in your savings account.

The reality is, you finance *everything* you buy because either you *pay* interest when you finance or lease, or you *lose* interest and investment income you *could* have had if you'd kept the money invested instead.

---

You finance *everything* you buy because either you *pay* interest when you finance or lease, or you *lose* interest and investment income you *could* have had if you'd kept the money invested instead.

---

The conventional wisdom says there's no way to get around that. I beg to differ!

## Make Money You Spend Continue to Grow for You

There's a fourth way to finance what you want—and banks and credit card companies are desperately hoping you never hear about it. This little-known method lets you *bank on yourself* and bypass lending institutions *altogether*.

When you save up your money in a Bank On Yourself plan, you can then borrow it to pay cash for a car or anything else you might want, and *the money in your plan will continue growing as though you never touched a dime of it.* I'll show you how that works in a moment.

Becoming your own source of financing will take a shift in your thinking.

If you make your major purchases the traditional way (financing, leasing, or directly paying cash), your money is *gone forever*, other than the potential asset value of something like your home or car. However, when you save up in a Bank On Yourself policy, your money is safe, liquid, tax-advantaged, and growing by a guaranteed and predictable amount every year. And it can continue growing, even while you're using it to make purchases.

Let me repeat that: A dollar you spend is gone forever. But a dollar you save in your Bank On Yourself policy first, *then* use for major purchases, continues compounding and growing exponentially for as long as you have your policy. And that happens whether you use your dollars one time or a hundred times. It solves the problem of having to constantly interrupt the growth of your money when you spend it or invest it elsewhere.

---

The Bank On Yourself strategy solves the problem of having to constantly interrupt the growth of your money when you spend it or invest it.

---

## Exactly How Friendly *Is* Your Banker?

To get a loan from your friendly banker—any kind of loan, from personal emergency to a loan secured by an asset—you start by filling out a credit application. They run a credit check, and if you don't qualify, you don't get the loan. Or if your credit isn't perfect, they'll charge you a higher rate. Even if you qualify, your friendly banker might set a limit for what you can borrow that is *lower* than what you've asked for, or they may require you to put up cash or assets as collateral.

During the credit crisis that started in 2008 and put banks on lockdown, many of us discovered we couldn't get access to credit at *any* price. Credit card accounts were closed and/or limits reduced. Interest rates were jacked up with little or no warning. Homeowners were also caught off guard when banks yanked their home equity lines of credit because their home values declined—even if they had a perfect payment record!

Why did banks do this? Because they can. Even today, years after the peak of the credit crisis, gaining access to capital is no easy feat.

If you borrow from a bank using your savings account as collateral, you still have to go through an approval process, and you must pay your loan back on a pre-arranged schedule. You'll be charged a penalty if you're late making a payment. Many banks will only allow you to borrow up to 50 percent of your account value, and they can seize your money to cover your loan in full if you miss a payment—even though it's *your* money!

When you borrow from a bank, who sets your repayment terms? Your friendly banker. What happens if you miss a payment on a bank loan? Your friendly banker charges you late fees and dings your credit score. He might resort to collection calls or repossession or foreclosure. Even if you miss a payment in the last months of a loan, your banker has the right to repossess your stuff. Finally, when you pass away, your friendly banker goes after your estate to settle all your bank loans.

Your friendly banker will pay you 1 percent or less on your savings account today, but if you need money to buy something like a car, they'll charge you 4–7 percent interest, depending on your credit score. And if you get a credit card from them, they'll apply a 10 percent to 20 percent interest charge whenever you run a balance!

What's wrong with this picture?

The guy may have given you a new toaster to open your account, but he's seeming a little less friendly, isn't he?

## You, a Better Banker

When you hold a Bank On Yourself policy and want a loan, there's no qualifying. You *cannot* be turned down, and you can borrow up to 85 percent to 90 percent of your cash value. Pure and simple.

When you Bank On Yourself, you get competitive interest rates (generally below-market) *regardless* of your credit rating. If you don't pay the loan interest, which is due the end of each policy year, the company will simply add the interest to your loan balance. It's a good idea to at least pay the annual interest due on your policy loan out of your pocket each year to keep your loan balance from increasing (unless you are taking retirement income), as covered in greater detail in FAQ #6, later in this chapter.

With Bank On Yourself, it's *your* money, and *you* set your own repayment terms. And if you hit a rough spot financially? With a Bank On Yourself loan, you can reduce or even skip some payments with absolutely *no* impact to your credit rating.

And after you pass away, unpaid loans with Bank On Yourself are merely deducted from your death benefit (along with any interest due) before the company pays out the claim. By that time, though, because the death benefit increases as your policy matures, the death benefit may have grown by a significant amount.

## M Y T H B U S T E R

### It's Stupid to Pay Interest to Use
### Your Own Money

That's a nugget of advice often repeated by Dave Ramsey and others, to explain why permanent life insurance is a bad deal. "It's stupid to pay interest to use your own money when you take a policy loan," they say.

There's a principle of economics called **opportunity cost**, which is defined as "the loss of potential gain from other alternatives, when one alternative is chosen."

This means there's an interest cost, no matter *where* you get the money from when you buy something. You pay interest to a third party (credit card company, banker, or Uncle Fred). And if you use cash from a savings account, you *just lost out* on the opportunity to earn interest on that money.

By borrowing on your own policy, you not only continue to receive the same growth, but the interest you pay on your loans will benefit *you*, as you'll see later in this chapter.

## How the Savvy Consumer Does It

There's a reason it's called *life* insurance, not death insurance: You don't have to die to reap the benefits!

Stop and think about it: zero balances on whatever credit cards you choose to keep. No auto dealership interest charges, student loans, or maybe even home loans. This isn't smoke and mirrors with a hidden trapdoor under the stage. This isn't some weird, fringe strategy. In fact, the latest statistics from the life insurance industry report that consumers had $129 *billion* in outstanding policy loans.

I've done it. Millions of people have done it over the last century. And you can do it, too.

It won't happen overnight. But if you're patient, determined, and disciplined, you'll feel like the savvy consumer you always wanted to be. You'll use money from a Bank On Yourself whole life plan that you build. And even when you tap this unique source of funds, if your policy is from one of a handful of companies that offer this feature, you'll continue to earn uninterrupted growth and any dividends, as if the loan money were still sitting in the plan.

---

*"I still get plenty of promotional ads in the mail for credit cards and equity loans. It gives me great pleasure to tear them up. I no longer need anyone else's money, since I'm using my own. That is a powerful and emancipating feeling."*
—Joe Goldsmith

---

And there's an added benefit that all savvy consumers know: Cash is king. Say you take out a $30,000 policy loan to purchase a new car. When you pay cash for major purchases, you're literally in the driver's seat when it comes to making your best deal.

So not only are you able to negotiate a great deal and drive off the dealer's lot in a spanking-new vehicle, but your life insurance company continues to pay you your guaranteed, pre-set annual cash value increase, plus any dividends on your policy—just as if the $30,000 you paid the auto dealer never left your account.

It's like having your cake and eating it, too—but not getting stuck with all those calories!

The insurance company *does* charge interest on your policy loan. But rates charged are often less than you'll get from conventional lenders. And rather than air-expressing your payments off to benefit some mega-credit card or finance company, your interest payments ultimately benefit *you*, the policy owner.

Wait! How is that possible? Here's the deal: As an owner of a policy from one of these select insurance companies, you're like a shareholder (we talked about *participating companies* in Chapter 4). At the end of each year, if your insurance company earns a profit, it distributes those funds to policyholders in the form of dividends. And the companies recommended by Bank On Yourself Authorized Advisors have never failed to pay a dividend, year after year, for over 100 years. It's as if VISA or MasterCard were to announce, "Hey, we made a lot of money this year! Let's share our profits with card holders!" Uh-huh. Like *that* will ever happen.

**Tale of a Savvy Consumer**

Former teacher Ed Ingle and his wife decided to take a policy loan to do some home improvements soon after starting a Bank On Yourself policy, "Just to see how this whole loan thing worked. It was so easy that now we laugh at the idea of trying to understand the process. There *is* no process. It's our money!"

In two years, Ed and his wife have put the policy to work in several ways. They are putting their son through a private college through the plan. "No money goes to the bank," Ed notes.

He purchased a car using the policy…and "no money goes to the bank!"

He also financed his wife's graduate school through the plan. ("And no money goes to the bank!")

Ed says he no longer worries when the stock market rises and falls. He no longer worries about the interest rates banks are charging. He's in charge of his own finances from here on out. (And no money goes to the bank!)

# FAQs About Bank On Yourself Policy Loans

As good as this strategy is, it's also misunderstood by many people, including many financial advisors. So here are the answers to the six most frequently asked questions about Bank On Yourself whole life insurance policy loans.

### 1. How much and when can you borrow from your policy?

You can borrow against up to 85–90 percent of your cash value through one or more policy loans at any time for any reason. The only question you'll be asked is "How much do you want?"

You are contractually guaranteed to be first in line to get access to your cash value, and you *can't* be turned down for a loan. You don't need to fill out any nosey credit applications or pledge your firstborn. Most financial experts talk about whole life policies that generally have no cash value in the first year or two. But a properly designed Bank On Yourself–type policy will have cash value by the end of the first *month*. (My general recommendation is not to plan on taking a policy loan in the first year, although that option is available to you.)

The ways you can use a policy loan are limited only by your imagination. Many of us use them to finance big-ticket items such as cars, vacations, home repairs and improvements, college educations, and business expenses. But folks have also used them in very creative ways, such as:

- To pay the expenses of adopting a baby on very short notice (see the Gammons' story in Chapter 6)
- To buy a prize-winning racehorse
- To help raise $100,000 for their church's very creative capital campaign—watch the video to see how they did it, at **www.BankOnYourself.com/fundraiser**
- Grammy-nominated singer Karyn White took a policy loan to produce her new album and pocketed the profits the record producers used to make off her (her story is in Chapter 9)
- A photographer used a loan to buy an expensive machine for her business that prints photos on chocolate

At the risk of sounding like your mother, I'll remind you that having money available to you in your policy does not give you a license to spend more than you make or more than you can afford!

## Planning Ahead

"I like being able to leverage the equity in my policies for major purchases," says Glyn Milburn. Glyn is a Stanford graduate, retired NFL football player, real estate investment fund manager, and entrepreneur. Milburn and his wife Toya have two children, a six-year-old daughter and a four-year-old son. "My family is secure in the knowledge that our funds are backed by a proven 160-year-old strategy. Bank On Yourself helped us purchase two new family vehicles. We're paying ourselves back and continue to see our policies grow every year. We're also planning to use our policy to help pay for college expenses for our two children."

**2. Do you have to pay your policy loans back? And what are the repayment terms?**

You are *not* required to pay back your policy loans. But think of it this way: If you borrow money from a bank and don't pay it back, it's like stealing from the bank. If you borrow against your life insurance policy and you don't pay it back, you're stealing from *yourself.*

One comment we often hear from Bank On Yourself policy owners is how much they *enjoy* paying back their loans. Rather than lining the pockets of banks and finance companies, they can see how their payments build their plan value back up,

But the reality is that sometimes stuff happens. And when it does, you can reduce or skip some payments and not have to worry about collection calls or black marks on your credit report. Knowing that you have that flexibility brings great peace of mind.

I recommend that you set up a loan repayment plan at the same time you take a policy loan with the payments that will automatically come out of your checking account each month. Your Bank On Yourself Authorized Advisor can help you create a repayment schedule that meets your needs and set up the automatic loan repayments.

## Why Would Someone Own Multiple Policies?

A number of Bank On Yourself revolutionaries profiled in this book mention they own a number of policies. You may be wondering why they do that, rather than taking out one bigger policy. There are three main reasons people often start more than one Bank On Yourself policy:

1. Each policy can have a different owner, insured, and beneficiary, so a family might start one policy for each spouse and one for each child (and/or grandchild). If the family has a business, they may start one or more policies just for business financing needs.

2. There are limits to how much premium you can put into a policy, which varies according to the policy design. As a family's income

*continued*

*continued from previous page*

increases and/or they decide to cut back on funding their traditional government-controlled retirement plans that have disappointed them time and again, they open new plans so they can achieve even *more* of their goals (without the risk and volatility of traditional investments).

3. Once people experience the power of the Bank On Yourself concept and realize their plans have met or exceeded their expectations, they have the confidence to start new policies. And seeing their plans go in only one direction (Up!) gives them the motivation to save more.

### 3. How can your policy continue growing even on the money you've borrowed?

I realize this benefit of the Bank On Yourself method may sound too good to be true, especially because there is no other financial product I'm aware of that works this way. Here's how it works:

When you take a policy loan, the money doesn't actually come from *your* policy. It comes out of the company's general fund because all the cash value of all the policies is pooled together. Your policy's cash value and death benefit are used as collateral for the loan.

As you pay back a loan, it works the same way in the opposite direction. The payments you make don't go back into your policy. They go back into the company's general fund.

The company applies your payments of principal to reduce your loan balance. Then at the end of each year, the company calculates their income from all sources, including the loan interest you and others paid, and they calculate the company's expenses and the death claims they paid out.

If that yields better results than the worst-case scenario they projected, they pay a dividend to all the policy owners. So you end up getting the benefit of the interest you pay through a combination of guaranteed annual increases plus any dividends the company pays. That means both the principal and interest you pay can ultimately end up in your Bank On Yourself policy for you to use again—for a car, vacation, business equipment, a college education, retirement, or whatever you want.

If you *don't* pay your loans back, the company will just add the loan interest to your outstanding loan balance at the end of the policy year.

How is the interest rate on policy loans determined? The companies preferred by the Bank On Yourself Authorized Advisors generally charge a variable loan interest rate that's based on Moody's Corporate Bond Yield Average, which can be similar to the prime rate a bank charges its best customers. The rate can be adjusted once each year, on your policy's anniversary.

**Here is an important point:** If your policy is from one of the companies that offer this feature, when you pay your loans back at the exact same interest rate the company charges, you'll end up with exactly the same cash value as you would have if you didn't use your plan to finance purchases. For example, suppose your policy is projected to have $400,000 of cash value in Year 25. And let's say you decided to borrow $30,000 in the fifth year to buy a car then you pay it back at the interest rate the company charges over the next five years. Then you repeat that cycle three more times. At the end of twenty-five years, your cash value would still be $400,000—the same as if you hadn't used it to finance anything.

## Enjoying the Sun

Joni Schultz figured it would be a smart move to convert their home's electric system to solar power. It would save thousands of dollars every year on their electric bills, which would come in handy since she hoped to retire in five years and her husband Dave had already retired. Plus, they wanted to make a contribution to a greener planet.

But converting to solar can be expensive. Fortunately, Joni discovered that their electric company was offering a 50 percent credit to anyone putting in a qualifying solar system—but only for a limited time. So she borrowed $23,500 from her Bank On Yourself policy and paid for her solar system in cash.

The Shultz's electric bill fell from hundreds of dollars a month to under $15 a month, saving them thousands of dollars every single year! Joni

*continued*

*continued from previous page*

and Dave also qualified for generous federal and state tax credits for the solar system when they filed their tax returns, bringing their out-of-pocket cost to close to zero.

Joni borrowed the money from her policy without an application or the approval of a loan committee, and she could not have been turned down for a loan. She set her own loan payback schedule, and when she finishes paying it off, she'll have the solar system *and* all the money she paid for it will be available to her again, to help fund her retirement.

**4. Will your policy's cash value grow faster if you *don't* take a loan?**

All dividend-paying whole life companies pay you your same guaranteed annual cash value increase when you borrow against your policy. However, a handful of companies offer what are known as *non-direct recognition* loans. With one of these loans, the insurance company doesn't *recognize* that you took a policy loan when they dole out the dividends. If you *don't* have a non-direct recognition loan, they'll pay you a different dividend on that portion of your cash value that you borrowed against.

Pay attention! This is important: Your policy must be from one of the handful of companies that offer *non-direct recognition loans* to get full benefit. Only these companies pay you the exact same dividend regardless of whether or not you have any policy loans—another reason to work with a Bank On Yourself Authorized Advisor who will really know the ropes. You can get a referral to one, and a free Analysis that will show you how much more lifetime wealth you could have when you become your own source of financing, at **www.BankOnYourselfFreeAnalysis.com** or by completing and submitting the form on page 265.

**5. If you can get a *lower* interest rate from a finance company than the insurance company charges, should you go that route instead?**

Excellent question. If you can *truly* get a lower rate than the insurance company charges, then you may want to consider taking advantage of that lower rate and putting the interest you save into your Bank On Yourself policy. But I say this with two critical caveats:

**Caveat 1**: You should *only* do this if you have enough cash value in your policy to transfer the loan to the policy if you happen to hit a rough patch financially down the road. Then *you* would be in control of the repayment schedule, and you won't have to worry about collection calls, repossession, or having your credit score slashed.

**Caveat 2**: In most cases, those low-interest rate offers are not all they're cracked up to be. There's no such thing as a free lunch. A low rate is usually offered *instead* of giving you a discount or rebate on whatever you're purchasing. So always bargain hard to get an amount equal to the interest savings knocked off the price of the item.

For example, if the lower loan rate offered would save you $2,500 of the ultimate total price of a car (including the cost of financing it), bargain for a $2,500 discount off the price of the car instead of the lower rate. Then use a Bank On Yourself policy loan to pay cash for the car.

And think about this for a moment. Do you truly love banks? They pay you a pittance in interest, then turn around and loan out *your* money at exorbitant rates! Have they been doing you a lot of favors? If not, why continue to play the game by their rules just to shave a couple points off your interest rate?

---

## M Y T H B U S T E R

### Loan Payment *Plus* a Premium Payment?

A concern some people have is "But if I take a policy loan to buy a car, now I've got to not only make the loan repayments, I've also got to pay the premium every month."

Remember that a Bank On Yourself plan is doubling as *both* a safe way to save for your retirement *and* a source of financing. Would you stop funding your 401(k) or IRA because you bought a car and had loan payments? Of course not. And if you *would* have to stop funding your retirement plan to buy a car, you can't afford to buy that car!

**6. If you're taking out policy loans for retirement income, do you have to pay them back? If not, how does the interest due on those loans affect your policy?**

There is no requirement for you to pay back the principal of your policy loans. Interest will continue to accumulate and can be added to your loan balance, if you choose.

Generally, loans you take to make major purchases should be paid back on the schedule you set. If you borrow and never pay back your loans or at least the loan interest, the policy could potentially lapse if you have no cash value left to cover the loan interest. That could result in an income tax liability on any gains. That said, loans used to provide income in retirement aren't typically repaid. They are deducted from the death benefit on the death of the insured.

Recall from Chapter 5 that you'll typically withdraw your dividends up to your cost basis first, which you can do with no taxes due. After that, you can switch to taking policy loans, which also are not taxable. If the loan balance ever does exceed the available cash value, paying some or all of the loan interest out of pocket solves the problem. Your Bank On Yourself Authorized Advisor can help you monitor your policy to make sure it stays in force while you take out money for retirement.

## Should You Pay Off Your Mortgage?

So by now you've had it with your banker and are ready to pay off all your consumer debt and maybe even pay off your mortgage. Fire that banker!

But hold on a minute. Let's step back and think about that.

Many of us think we'd feel more secure if we had more equity in our homes or owned them free and clear. Some of us even tightened our belts to make extra mortgage payments or refinanced to a fifteen-year mortgage. But is creating lots of home equity really the holy grail that financial pundits claim it to be? Think about this:

- Payments of principal you make into your home do *not* earn interest or make you any money
- The equity in your home is *not* liquid

- The equity in your home is *not* guaranteed—a fact that came as a shock to many when the real estate market crashed
- There is absolutely *no* tax benefit to having equity in your home

Not feeling so warm and fuzzy, is it? Unfortunately, many people don't think about these downsides until it's too late!

Case in point: Larry and I were connecting to a plane in the Atlanta airport and grabbed lunch at a restaurant. We struck up a conversation with a couple at the next table, which got around to whether it's a good idea to pay off your mortgage. He told us how he had begged his ex-wife not to use her divorce settlement to pay off the mortgage on the home they used to share. But her overriding concern was the feeling of security that comes with not having any mortgage payments.

Shortly after she paid off the mortgage (who listens to their ex's advice, anyway?), the real estate market plunged and she lost her job and became disabled. She desperately needed money, but now all her money was locked up in her home with no way to get at it. It was a heartbreaking story of the dangers of following the conventional wisdom.

For all the reasons I've just mentioned, having a mortgage is one situation in which using bank financing *can* make sense. (Remember, you can use banks for *your* convenience, not for theirs!)

---

### Remember, you can use banks for *your* convenience, not for *theirs!*

---

Rather than trying to pay down your mortgage with every spare buck you can find, if you put those dollars into a Bank On Yourself policy, you'll have all the benefits that are missing from building home equity: That money will grow by a guaranteed amount each year. It's liquid, and you can borrow against your equity in the plan to make major purchases. So if you *really* want to feel more secure, where should you be building up equity?

Larry and I decided to refinance our home with a thirty-year fixed-rate mortgage, taking advantage of historically low rates, and we still get a tax deduction for the interest we pay. That made more sense to us than trying to pay down our mortgage faster. The dollars we save are going into our Bank On Yourself plans.

That strategy has given us the option to write a check today to pay off our mortgage *in full* if we choose to. But having all that money in our policies gives us *far* more peace of mind and security than paying off our mortgage and leaving all that money locked up in our home where we might not be able to get to it when we want or need it.

## Paying Off Debt Versus Saving

Okay, but what about credit card debt? Isn't it just common sense to get rid of as much consumer credit card debt as fast as you can? While I'd agree that carrying credit card debt for extended periods of time is *never* a good idea, if you're already in that situation, there are some things you should consider.

If, because you're trying to pay off your debts more quickly, you are not able to put aside any savings, you're setting yourself up for a vicious cycle. When something hits the fan (your car breaks down, you're laid off, you have an unexpected medical bill, etc.), if you have no savings to cover it, you end up incurring *more* debt, right? You're back to where you started, or worse!

Each situation is unique, but consider the option chosen by this Bank On Yourself policy owner:

### Pay Down Debt Before You Save?

One family from the Midwest had credit card balances of over $70,000, at an interest rate of over 20 percent. Like so many other people, they got addicted to using their credit cards and before they knew it—wham! Their debt had snowballed beyond belief. No one plans to rack up debt, but even people with high incomes fall into this trap. This couple was doing their best. They wrote checks for more than $3,000 each month to pay down their credit cards. This was *twice* their required minimum

*continued*

monthly payment. They were tired of being in this mess, and they were open to change.

Their Bank On Yourself Authorized Advisor helped them start a Bank On Yourself policy for $1,500 per month, which was about half of what they had been sending to the credit card company every month. Meanwhile, they kept making their $1,500 minimum monthly credit card payments. There was *no increase* in their monthly out-of-pocket payments.

As cash has built up in their policy, they have been able to borrow from it systematically and pay off large chunks of the credit card debt. Their Bank On Yourself policy has allowed them to pay off over $50,000 of credit card debt in just four years. But it's going to get even better.

Once they've paid off their credit card balances and paid back the loans to their Bank On Yourself policy (by redirecting the $1,500 per month they had been paying to the credit card company), they can start a second Bank On Yourself policy for the family, using that same $1,500 per month. So their total monthly outlay need never be more than the $3,000 they were paying when they first met their Authorized Advisor.

Then, at age sixty-five, their two policies could have a total cash value of over $883,000 and death benefits of over $2,283,000 that can pass income tax-free to their heirs or charities of their choice! And if they suffer a serious illness, they could have over $300,000 to use for long-term care expenses.

## What About Using a Savings Account?

"Okay, I get your point about credit and loans. And the Bank On Yourself loan thing sounds pretty good. But why not just save up my money in a savings account, earn a little interest, then pay cash as I go?"

Good question (thank you for asking it). People often ask how financing purchases through policy loans compares with putting money aside in a savings or money market account and directly paying cash. So let's break it down. A properly designed dividend-paying whole life policy gives you many advantages over a savings or money market account or CD. Some key differences:

1. The growth you receive in a Bank On Yourself policy is typically greater than you can get in a savings or money market account or CD.

2. True, you can immediately withdraw 100 percent of the money you put into a savings account while you can only borrow 85–90 percent of your equity in a dividend-paying whole life insurance plan. But the money you withdraw from your savings will cease to earn interest. The money you borrow from your plan (from one of the right companies) will continue to earn for you.

3. The interest you earn from a savings account is taxable at the federal level and usually at the state level, too. However, with a Bank On Yourself–type policy, you can access your principal and growth with no taxes due under current tax law, through the proper combination of dividend withdrawals and loans against your cash value.

4. Life insurance companies are even more highly regulated than banks. They are legally required to maintain sufficient reserves to pay future claims. But by law, your bank can lend out or invest each dollar it has in reserves *ten times*. (The technical name for this disaster in the making is *fractional reserve banking*.) Prior to the financial crash in 2008, banks had figured out complex products that allowed them to leverage each dollar as many as *thirty* times. The difference with a life insurance company is that they can only invest what they have.

5. The money in your life insurance policy may be protected from creditors and lawsuits. For example, one Bank On Yourself policy owner in Texas said that the equity in her policy was the only significant money she was allowed to keep when she declared bankruptcy. (Be aware that rules vary from state to state. Check with a professional for the rules in your state.)

## An Interest Rate of More Than 1,600% Per Year?

My husband and I haven't run a balance on a credit card in years. We have a handful of cards we use for convenience and to get points and airline miles. We get our statements e-mailed to us, then pay them off in full online each month.

Last month, Larry realized we didn't get the statement for the card we use for personal expenses. When he checked the account, he realized it was one day past the due date, so he immediately paid it. We discovered there would be a late fee and some interest due. The balance was around $3,500, so we figured the interest would be maybe a few bucks, right? Wrong!

A week later we got an e-mail that floored us. It notified us of a $15 late fee, PLUS a $162.30 interest charge for being *one day late* with our payment! That's 4.64 percent interest *per day*—1,693 percent interest *per year*!

A whole page of fine print on the statement tried to explain all the "gotchas." But it's a fact that banks and finance companies are gonna get you one way or another. Why? Because they can.

Bank On Yourself offers two critical benefits in one financial tool: It lets you beat the banks at their own game, and it provides you with a safe, predictable way to grow a nest egg. When you use the Bank On Yourself method, you can know the guaranteed value of your plan at any given point in time.

Yep. Time to give your friendly banker his toaster back.

---

*"If you want to continue to be slaves of the bankers and pay for the cost of your own slavery, allow them to continue to create money and control credit."*
—Josiah Stamp, Former Director of the Bank of England

---

**An Easy Move**

Bank On Yourself revolutionary John Chiappetta writes:

"I was out of work and had to move across the country to take a new job. My new employer was not going to cover this move, but fortunately, I was able to borrow $5,000. I used my American Express card to pay for the move, in order to get the points for all the costs. Then I immediately paid off the credit card balance using a Bank On Yourself policy loan. I then paid my policy loan back—with interest—from the earnings from my new job. To top it all off, I'll be able to write off all the interest charges on my tax return because it was a job-related move. Seriously, does it get any better? Plus, I'm still earning the same on my policy, while I'm paying back my loan.

"I think of Bank On Yourself like recycling: good for your financial environment, and the right thing to do. Saving and spending is like putting water in a bucket with a giant hole at the bottom. *Borrowing* and spending is like standing in water with your finger in an electric socket. *Bank On Yourself plugs the hole in your bucket.*"

## KEY TAKE-AWAYS

1. **You finance *everything* you buy.** Either you *pay* interest when you finance or lease, or you *lose* interest and investment income you *could* have had if you'd kept your money invested. Saving money in a Bank On Yourself policy first—and *then* using it to make major purchases—allows your money to compound continuously even when you spend or invest it elsewhere. It solves the problem of having to continuously interrupt the growth of your money when you spend or invest it.

2. **Taking a loan out from a bank is a cumbersome process.** Your friendly banker will do a credit check and possibly deny you a loan. He'll charge you more interest if your credit rating isn't perfect. He'll impose a payment schedule that works for the

bank—but not necessarily for you—that could lead to collection agency calls, threatening notices, and possibly repossession of assets. Becoming your own source of financing through Bank On Yourself policy loans avoid all of this hassle. It's *your* money.

3. **Policy loans are easy with many advantages.** The process basically goes like this: Ask for what you need, and get it within days. You can borrow up to 85–90 percent of your cash value in the policy. Your policy continues to grow as though you never touched it, if you use the right companies. You can pay the loan back at your own pace. The interest you pay ultimately benefits you. You call the shots.

4. **If you borrow against your policy (which is like borrowing from yourself), and don't pay it back, you're stealing from yourself.** Paying your loans back (unless you're taking retirement income) enables both the principal and interest you pay to ultimately end up in your policy, for you to use again for a purchase, retirement, or whatever you want.

# CHAPTER 8

# The Smart Way to Pay for College

*It is virtually impossible to compete in today's global economy without a college degree.*

— BOBBY SCOTT, CONGRESSMAN

Is THE EXORBITANT COST of a college education really worth it? I think the answer to that question depends on the individual child. But as a parent, here are a couple of stats you might want to consider:

A U.S. Census Bureau report reveals that the average high school graduate can expect to earn $1.2 million compared to the average $2.1 million that those with a bachelor's degree will earn.[38] For 2012, the Bureau of Labor Statistics reported a 4.5 percent unemployment rate for workers with *bachelor's degrees* while *8.3 percent* of workers with *high school degrees* were unemployed. And unemployment for those with *no* high school diploma is at 12.4 percent!

So a child who pursues a college education will have definite advantages. But the skyrocketing cost of this valuable education is making financing it more and more difficult. *MarketWatch* reported that over the past two

---

**INSIDE THIS CHAPTER . . .**

- The Pitfalls of 529 Plans
- Drawbacks of UGMAs and UTMAs
- College Loans That Can Haunt You for Decades
- How to Pay for College *and* Grow Your Nest Egg at the Same Time
- College Financing Options Comparison Chart

decades, college tuition has risen twenty times as fast as the average college grad's wages.[39]

Private institutions can cost more than $50,000 per year. Based on 2013–2014 tuition numbers, four years of undergrad education will cost $234,000 at Boston University, $218, 000 at Harvard, and $201,000 at Emerson. Public universities have become more expensive as well. In 2010–2011, the average cost of tuition, room, and board at public institutions was $15,605.[40]

And costs keep rising as state legislatures, desperate to balance state budgets, are cutting funding and increasing tuition. In 2012, California cut funding to the state's higher education by 14.3 percent. Other states averaged cuts of more than 8 percent.[41] According to the State Higher Education Executive Officers Association, state and local funding for higher education has dropped to a twenty-five-year low after adjusting for inflation. The result? Universities pass the burden of paying for this shortfall on to students. Ouch!

Meanwhile, the average family's income on an inflation-adjusted basis is *down* over the last decade. The real estate crash and credit crisis have made it almost impossible for parents to refinance or get home equity loans to help cover tuition costs. Even with the aid of scholarships and grants, the cost of college is rising beyond the means of many middle-class families.

Is this trend going to change? Unlikely. College tuition and fees continue to rise steeply. Costs for public schools, where the majority of students go, have doubled in the last decade. Whether your college-bound child is six months or sixteen years old, the cost of their higher education will be daunting.


## How Are We Paying for College Now?

As parents, we want to give our children every chance to succeed in life. So we face a tough decision: We can either help our children pay for college by sacrificing our own retirement savings or diving into debt, *or* we can saddle our kids with debt that may last a lifetime.

According to Sallie Mae (aka the Student Loan Marketing Association), 28 percent of college costs in 2011–2012 were paid out of parents' income and savings. But when Mom and Dad rob Peter to pay Paul, they put themselves in an awful bind. Half of parents surveyed in a MassMutual study in 2011 said that *after they pay for their kids' college education, there won't be enough money left for their own retirement.* They've put their own financial futures at risk by raiding retirement savings to pay for college costs.

---

### Half of parents surveyed say they won't have enough money for their own retirement after paying for their kids' college educations.

---

And it's worse for students taking out loans for themselves. Today's crop of young adults is called the Boomerang Generation for good reason. All too often they go off to college, graduate, then return home. Why? Their earnings straight out of college simply can't cover both their loan payments and their living expenses. According to David Shapiro, senior vice president for Western Union, *more than a quarter* of graduating college students with student loan debt say they plan to move back in with their parents.[42] The burden of borrowing for higher education is a dark cloud that will hang over this generation for decades. And student loan debt is extremely difficult to wriggle out of by declaring personal bankruptcy.

Even retirees are impacted by student debt. In 2012, the federal government started garnishing Social Security benefits of retirees who were delinquent on federal student loans, withholding up to 15 percent of their benefits. Many of these retirees were in trouble because of student loans they'd taken out for their children.[43]

Other seniors are still making payments on their *own* student loans, and more than 10 percent of those loans are delinquent. As shown in research by the Federal Reserve Bank of New York, it's not uncommon for debt collectors to harass borrowers in their eighties over student loans that are decades old.[44]

Not a pretty picture. How can you pay for college without spending your life savings, seeing your children in horrendous debt, or being there yourself?

The traditional ways of saving for college—529 college savings plans, Uniform Gifts to Minors (UGMAs), Uniform Transfers to Minors (UTMAs), and student and parent loans—were all meant to help, but they all have serious drawbacks. To help you to make the best choices, let's review each of these programs, *and* I'll show you a smarter way to finance your child's education. This is vitally important. Making the wrong decisions with such large sums can make your financial picture bleak and stressful for decades.

## 529 Plans

529 Plans are a popular way to save for college. You can set up a 529 Plan regardless of how much money you have. Contributions cannot exceed the amount necessary to provide for the qualified education expenses of the beneficiary, and there may be gift tax consequences if your contributions, plus any other gifts, to a particular beneficiary exceed $13,000 during the year. The primary attraction of a 529 Plan is its tax benefit. Once money is deposited in a 529 account, it grows tax-free. When the money is withdrawn for college, it's not taxed at the federal level, and most states don't tax withdrawals either. Yahoo!

However, these plans have several severe restrictions.

The most significant constraint is that the money must be used for *qualified educational expenses.* If money is withdrawn for *any* other reason before you're 59½, you not only have to pay income tax on any gains, but you're also going to be hit with a *10 percent federal tax penalty* on earnings. So what if your child decides not to go to college, or gets a scholarship and doesn't need the money for tuition? Your money may be locked up for years, unless you decide to change the account beneficiary to another one of your children—or go back to college yourself.

529 Plan account holders can choose among several investment options, including stock and bond mutual funds and money market funds. Most people invest in mutual funds, thinking their money will grow faster. But if you do this, you're pinning your kids' college education on a hope and a prayer that the volatile stock market will not sabotage your plans.

And that brings us to another restriction that can wreak havoc on your 529 Plan. Unlike 401(k)s, IRAs, and other types of tax-deferred plans, IRS rules for 529 Plans only allow you to make *one exchange* or reallocation of assets *per year*, at the beginning of the plan year. So if you decide your plan is losing too much money—or making too little—tough luck. If you just tweaked your asset allocations in January and your fund tanks in February, you have to wait eleven long months before you can do much about it. If you make changes more than once each year, you'll incur severe tax consequences.

## The Market Crashes but You Can't Bail

As Bank On Yourself revolutionary Bill Liebler discovered when his daughter Shelby's 529 Plan tanked with the market crash in 2008, "I couldn't easily pick up the phone and call a broker and tell him to get out of those mutual funds and put my money in cash and bonds. I could only move it between funds."

Of all the 529 Plans tracked by Morningstar, *93 percent* fell in value in the market crash in 2008, and almost *one-third lost at least 40 percent*—about the same amount the overall market plunged. [45] That's *despite* the popular *age-based option* for 529s, which is supposed to protect investors. A plan with an age-based option gradually moves your money into supposedly less-risky investments as the child gets closer to college age. Just ask any parent who saw their child's 529 Plan evaporate in 2008, *despite* having this age-based option, how well *that* turned out.

Another problem with these plans is that students have a pretty short window—typically just four or five years—within which to spend their 529 savings. So if these funds for college savings are in the stock market, you won't have the luxury of waiting for stocks to recover from a market downturn before drawing the funds out.

An article on MSN.com titled "The Great College Savings Fiasco" noted, "Many parents who have invested in 529s, counting on the market to cover the soaring costs of college, would've been better off putting the money under their mattresses…. Simply put, 529 Plans don't live up to the hype."

### John's 529 Plan Got 5% While the Dow Went Up 41%

Even if the stock market does well, that doesn't mean your 529 Plan will follow suit. John Phillips is a Bank On Yourself policy owner who funded his newborn daughter's 529 Plan in November 2008 (before he realized he had a smarter option). John put $1,000 in a 529 Plan run by a major mutual fund company, and instructed them to place the money in a fund invested in large growth companies. He wrote down the closing prices of the major stock indexes on the day he opened the account.

John figured he'd "set it and forget it." But when he decided to check on it three years later, in early November 2011, he realized his daughter's college fund had grown by only $50—just 5 percent—during a period when the market was up by more than 40 percent!

To add insult to injury, shortly after John checked the account balance, the mutual fund company liquidated the account and swept the funds into a money market account—without asking for permission or even informing him. John didn't discover this until early 2013, and when he did, he found the account had shrunk to $1,038. "At this rate, my daughter may be able to afford tuition for a two-year trade school by the time she turns eighty-five," he laments. (By the way, John inquired why that move had been made, but he never did get a straight answer.)

## UGMAs and UTMAs

Other common college savings methods include the Uniform Gifts to Minors Act (UGMA) and the Uniform Transfers to Minors Act (UTMA). Here's how these work:

Most states let you contribute to an account in a minor's name without setting up a formal trust. You can buy and sell securities in the child's name and, under the annual federal gift-tax exclusion, each donor may generally make gifts of $13,000 per year per child, without paying any federal gift taxes.

But here's the rub: You, as the custodian, only control the account until the child reaches the legal age of adulthood, which is as early as age eighteen in some states. After that, you have absolutely no legal control over how the money is used.

Let's assume, however, that your child *does* use the money for college. All withdrawals from the account are taxed at the student's rate. So far so good. But once again, there's a looming downside: Money in an UGMA or UTMA can decrease the student's chances for financial aid because colleges weigh children's assets much more heavily than parents' assets. If a college financial aid officer sees that an incoming student has a stash of cash, he'll assume the student doesn't need the money as much as other students. Not so good.

### Celebrity Financial Guru Plans

Coverdell Accounts, a type of government-blessed educational savings account, are another college funding option, particularly favored by financial gurus like Dave Ramsey. Ramsey says funding a college education is as simple as 1-2-3:

1. When your child is born, start putting $2,000 per year (the maximum allowed) into the plan.
2. Invest the money in a mutual fund that earns 12 percent per year.
3. Presto! You'll have $126,000 when your kid starts college.[46]

   Note to self: Find a mutual fund that *guarantees* to pay me at least 12 percent per year. There *must* be one *somewhere!*

## Student Loans

Here's where financing college really gets scary. Almost everyone knows a student who graduated from college with *ginormous* student loans. Since 1991, the number of American households owing student loan debt has doubled. According to FICO, two-thirds of college seniors in the class of 2012 graduated with loans averaging over $27,000. And *15 percent* of student loans made in the last two years are *delinquent.*

The Consumer Financial Protection Bureau reports that college student loans have ballooned into a *$1 trillion debt crisis.* That's more than our nation's total credit card debt or auto loan debt! [47]

And it's putting unimaginable pressure on graduates. As the cost of a college education spirals upward, students are being left with more and more debt. Meanwhile, the Bureau of Labor Statistics says the average pay for college grads has fallen 5 percent since 2007–2008.

- **Parent PLUS Loans**, the most popular federal aid student loan program, are currently charging 7.9 percent. Add the *4 percent loan origination fee*, and you can see these loans aren't cheap. Of course, like other government-approved programs, they come with plenty of strings attached.

- **Federal Stafford Loans** are charging a variable interest rate around 3.86 percent right now. The rate is based on the Federal ten-year Treasury rate, plus a margin, and can be adjusted annually. You also pay a 1 percent loan origination fee.

### Parent Loan Payments as Big as Mortgage Payments

An all-too-common scenario is the one faced by Diana Jackson, a parent I read about in a newspaper article. She had no student debt when she got her bachelor's degree in 1982. But when her daughter graduated in 2011, she was stuck with $33,000 in parent loans. As a fifty-one-year-old, Diana now faces a monthly payment of nearly $800 for those loans.

"I'll be in my mid-seventies before I get that paid off," says Ms. Jackson, a part-time college professor. "I am at the point in my life where I would like to be doing some of the things I really want to do. When you've got what is essentially another house payment, you can't do that."

Too bad Diana didn't know there's a better way to pay for college!

So what's the answer? With all the drawbacks to traditional college-funding strategies, how can *anyone* afford the college education they need, want, and deserve?

In my mind, the *best* option would be one that:

- Assures you guaranteed growth
- Allows flexibility in payments
- Can double as your retirement fund
- Has tax advantages
- Puts *you* in control

Does such a plan even exist? Yes! It's Bank On Yourself, of course. Just as you can borrow against your Bank On Yourself policy for other reasons, you can borrow against your policy to cover tuition costs. Bank On Yourself is the perfect vehicle to solve the college financing issues—*supporting your children's future while securing your own future.*

## A Smarter Way to Finance College

Using Bank On Yourself to finance a college education gives you flexibility and many advantages you won't find in traditional methods of saving for college. You don't have the risk of loss due to market fluctuations, and you can make your cash value do double duty. Take a policy loan to pay each year's tuition, and your policy continues to grow just as if you never touched a dime of it, if it's from the right company. As you pay back your loan, you're recapturing the money to set yourself up for a comfortable retirement—or anything else you want! And the interest you pay on your loans benefits *you*, as explained in Chapter 7.

In contrast with market-based 529 and other plans, your Bank On Yourself plan lets you know the *minimum guaranteed value* of your plan on the day your child starts *and* graduates from college. You'll never lose sleep wondering what the stock market will do next and whether you'll have enough when the big day comes.

## Seven Critical Questions Parents Should Ask

Let's compare the three most widely used methods—529 Plans, UGMAs/ UTMAs, and student/parent loans against Bank On Yourself by asking seven critical questions:

**1. Do you have full control over how and when the money is used?**

Only Bank On Yourself plans can answer "yes" to this one. With these plans, you *do* control how the money is used.

With limited exceptions, you can only withdraw money that you invest in a 529 Plan for eligible college expenses without incurring taxes and penalties. With UGMAs and UTMAs you lose all control the day your child legally becomes an adult—as young as eighteen in many states. Student loan proceeds are paid directly to the college, so you *never* have control.

**2. Can you avoid having the funds count against your kids when they apply for federal student aid?**

In most cases, the more resources a family has, the less aid the student will be offered. Student loans and the cash value in a Bank On Yourself plan are *not* considered as assets.

But the money in your 529 Plan is counted as *your* asset, and UGMAs and UTMAs will be treated as your *child's* assets. Either way, having these assets will likely penalize your child when they apply for need-based financial aid.

With a Bank On Yourself policy, your funds sit in the cash value account of a whole life insurance policy, and a life insurance policy's cash value does not count against you in the Department of Education's financial aid formula used to calculate a family's Expected Family Contribution for federal student aid. So your Bank On Yourself plan will *not* sabotage your chances for grants, scholarships, and interest-free loans from the federal and state governments.

**3. What if your child earns a full scholarship or decides to be an entrepreneur instead of going to college? Can you use the money for non-educational purposes?**

With 529 Plans, you definitely lose out in this case. 529 money must be used for qualified post-secondary education expenses. If you can't use it for your child, you'll have to use it for yourself or your spouse or someone else. And if you can't use the money for qualified educational expenses, you'll pay income tax on your gains (if you even have any gains!) plus a 10 percent penalty on those gains if you take money out before you turn 59½.

As for UGMAs and UTMAs, they can be used for whatever the *student* wants once they reach the legal age of adulthood—and you have no control. To some kids, this is like free money. We've all heard stories about students who use their UGMA or UTMA "windfalls" to buy everything from entertainment systems to snazzy cars. They have that right, but *you* cannot use the money for non-educational purposes without your child's permission.

Student and parent loans are only for college. Period.

Bank On Yourself plans are clearly superior here: Want to use the money for a purpose other than college? As the owner of the policy, that's entirely up to you.

### 4. Can you use the plan *beyond* college?

With 529 Plans, you face the taxes and penalties if you don't use it up for college expenses, and the funds typically have to be used within a four- to five-year window.

With UGMAs and UTMAs the money is not yours to use at all. As soon as your child is of legal age, they are in complete control of the money and can use it for whatever they want.

Student and parent loans definitely extend beyond college but only as a heavy burden of debt. These loans can haunt you or your child for decades.

Contrast those vehicles to Bank On Yourself plans where you—or your student, if you choose—can continue to use the policy for the lifetime of the person you've named as the insured. And, of course, Bank On Yourself has its death benefit, which none of the other vehicles can claim.

### 5. Are there tax benefits?

With 529 Plans the answer is "maybe." You *may* get a state income-tax deduction for your contribution, depending on where you live and the plan you have chosen. And if the money is used exclusively for college, any gains in your plan can be tax-free money.

Gains in UGMAs and UTMAs can be taxed at the minor's tax rate instead of yours, which may save you some money.

Student loans *may* give you a state income-tax interest deduction, depending on your income.

With Bank On Yourself, the answer is a definite "yes!" You can take money from the plan at any time, for any reason, with no taxes due under current tax law. (Learn more about the tax advantages of Bank On Yourself in Chapter 5.)

### 6. Can your plan be carried out if you die prematurely?

Can your plan finish funding itself if you pass away? That's a critical question that most families fail to ask. Only a Bank On Yourself plan comes with a death benefit that can make the plan self-completing. In all the other plans, your child will only have the value of the plan prior to death—which may not cover college expenses when the time comes.

### 7. Is growth of your money guaranteed?

In a 529 Plan, unless you have the money sitting in a money market account, absolutely not.

With UGMAs and UTMAs, probably not, since most families put the money in the stock or bonds markets. Bob Chambers, the retired Navy commander we met in Chapter 6, had this to say: "We started UGMA accounts for our sons as soon as they were born, but after several years of diligent saving and investing in those accounts, we lost fifty percent of their value when the market crashed in 2000. After a few more years of saving and investing, we still had very little to show for our efforts. So we took the money out, and we've used it for our boys in other ways."

With student loans, the only thing guaranteed to grow is the debt, especially if interest payments are deferred. But with Bank On Yourself, growth of your principal is both predictable and guaranteed.

Let's sum it all up with another picture worth a thousand words— and *thousands of dollars* to you and your college-bound child:

| Seven Questions Parents Should Ask When Choosing the Best Way to Pay for College | 529 Plans | UGMAS & UTMAS | Student & Parent Loans | Bank On Yourself |
|---|---|---|---|---|
| 1. Do you control how the money is used? | X | X | X | ✓ |
| 2. Can you avoid having the funds count against you when applying for federal student aid? | X | X | ✓ | ✓ |
| 3. Can you use the money for non-education purposes? | X | X | X | ✓ |
| 4. Can you use the plan beyond college – without owing taxes? | X | X | X | ✓ |
| 5. Are there tax benefits involved? | ? | ? | ? | ✓ |
| 6. Can your plan finish funding itself if you pass away? | X | X | X | ✓ |
| 7. Is growth of your money guaranteed? | X | X | X | ✓ |

## Show Me the Numbers

Let's see how Bank On Yourself could play out for a family and how it could double as a safe college savings plan *and* a way to provide you a passive retirement income stream you can count on.

Our hypothetical couple, Michael and Jennifer Johnson, are both thirty-five years old. Their ten-year-old daughter, Madison, plans to go to college and live in the dorm when she's eighteen.

They estimate that tuition and other expenses will be about $22,000 per year. The Johnsons are a two-income family bringing in $75,000 per year, and they've been socking away 5 percent of their income into savings for ten years. They are willing to use $40,000 of that money for Madison's Bank On Yourself college savings plan.

Their Bank On Yourself Authorized Advisor shows them a Bank On Yourself specially designed dividend-paying whole life insurance policy on Jennifer that will let them provide $20,000 each year toward their daughter's college education expenses. This will require only slight changes in their monthly spending habits, and if Madison takes a part-time college job, the end result should cover her expenses.

Michael and Jennifer will fund the policy with the $40,000 they've saved. In addition, they'll contribute the $312 per month they've been putting into savings, plus $108 per month they'll save by eating out twice a month instead of once a week.

When Madison starts college eight years after the policy has been put in place, the Johnsons will take out a $20,000 loan against their policy each year to cover most of Madison's expenses. Then Michael and Jennifer plan to pay the policy loans back—which is like paying *themselves* back—at $875 a month, an amount they feel they can comfortably handle at that time.

As we've discussed, Bank On Yourself policy loans have two great advantages you can't get anywhere else.

- You can pay back your loans on *your* schedule, not some bank's schedule
- You continue earning the same interest and dividends, even on the amount you borrowed (if your policy is from one of the handful of companies that offer this feature)

## The College Funding Plan That Doubles as a Retirement Plan

If Jennifer continues to make the same monthly contributions to her plan after Madison graduates, when she retires at age sixty-nine, her plan could give her $25,000 (with no taxes due on it) *each year* in additional retirement income until she's ninety-five years old. Plus, she could leave an income tax-free lump sum of more than $115,000 for her family when she passes away.

That's a perfect plan for the Johnsons. Would your plan look exactly like that? Probably not, because just as no two families are alike, no two plans are alike, either. Yours would be custom-tailored to *your* unique situation. For a free, no-obligation Bank On Yourself for College Savings Plan Analysis, go to **www.BankOnYourselfFreeAnalysis.com** or complete and submit the form on page 265. You'll also get a referral to a Bank On Yourself Authorized Advisor who can help you determine the best way to set up your plan and answer questions such as:

- Who should be the owner of the plan, and who should be the beneficiary?
- Who should be the insured?
- Where will you find the money to fund the policy?
- Is there lump-sum funding available to supercharge the policy?
- What other strategies should be considered to increase your child's likelihood of qualifying for financial aid and scholarships?
- At what point might you consider turning the policy over to your child, and what conditions should be met before doing that?

**Just-in-Time College Funding**

Tom Snyder didn't start a college fund until his daughter Kelsie was fourteen. Still, he discovered Bank On Yourself just in time.

"Kelsie is sixteen now," he explains. "Two years from now, when she's entering college, there's going to be about $35,000 in our Bank On Yourself policy. Basically, I'll be paying myself back instead of financing her college through a conventional bank.

"Where we live, colleges are funded heavily by the state. So if she goes to a state college, it's a good bargain. Even if she goes to our *best* state school, the tuition is only around $5,000 a year. And during the four years that she's on campus, my policy's cash value will continue to grow."

Even though Tom started late, his Bank On Yourself policy will still make college possible for his daughter.

## Grandparents Helping Fund Their Grandkids' College Education

Of course, college funding doesn't have to be a project just for parents and their college-bound children. Grandparents often want to help out, too. For the education of our two grandchildren, Larry and I started policies designed to maximize the power of the Bank On Yourself concept when they were six and four. The plan we set up for our grandson is projected to provide about $90,000 for his college education expenses by the time he graduates, based on the current dividends. Our granddaughter's plan is projected to have a value of about $125,000.

And if either of them decides to become an Internet entrepreneur, rather than go to college, the money could be used to help fund their dream.

Last year, when our grandkids were eleven and nine and they made their annual summer visit to our home, we started showing them the annual policy statements from the college funding policies we set up for them. It's been a lot of fun discussing the principles of money and finance with them (the principles that actually *work*, not the conventional wisdom).

We talk about the value of money, why it's important to pay policy loans back, even though no one's going to make you do it, opportunity cost, loan amortization tables, and more. Our grandkids are smart as whips, and that's not just Grandma braggin'. (Okay, maybe it is. But when you write a book, you can brag about your grandkids, too!)

 You'll find great ideas for teaching kids and teenagers about financial responsibility and money management at **www.BankOnYourselfNation.com**

We plan to turn the policies over to them once they've demonstrated financial responsibility, which includes taking a policy loan to make a purchase, and setting—and *meeting*—a repayment schedule of their choosing. (Turning ownership of these policies over to our grandkids is a simple process of filling out and sending in a change of policy ownership form.)

Our dream for our grandchildren is that they will *never* need to use the services of a bank, finance company, or credit card company, other than to have the convenience of a checking account and debit card, and a credit card they pay in full each month! They'll be using banks only for *their* convenience, and *not* to line the pockets of the banks!

## KEY TAKE-AWAYS

**1. The average college graduate earns almost twice as much as the average kid with just a high school diploma.** But the spiraling cost of higher education is putting college beyond the reach of many middle-class families.

**2. Far too many parents put their own financial futures at risk by raiding their retirement savings to pay for their kids' college.** Too often, this leads to Mom and Pop relying on Junior for financial assistance, just when Junior is trying to save for his *own* children's needs.

**3. Student and parent loans create a vicious circle.** Young people are collapsing under the burden of heavy student loan debt. And it's not uncommon for debt collectors to harass borrowers in their eighties over delinquent student loans that are decades old.

**4. Traditional college savings plans have their own "gotchas":**

- **529 Plans** *must* be used for qualified higher education expenses, even if your kid drops out or gets a full scholarship. Using the money for any other purpose results in tax consequences. The money in these plans is typically invested in mutual funds. Even the funds that are *supposed* to invest more conservatively as your child nears college age did not live up to their hype when the market crashed in 2008. Many parents would have been better off stuffing the money in the mattress! Have you considered what would happen to your plan if the market crashes *again*, right before your kid planned to go to college?

- Money in funds set up under the **Uniform Gifts to Minors Act** and **Uniform Transfers to Minors Act** belongs to the student, who, once they reach the legal age of adulthood (as early as age eighteen in some states), can use it for whatever they—not you—want. Legally, you can't touch the money. These funds are also typically invested in the volatile stock market.

5. **Using Bank On Yourself to finance a college education gives you flexibility and many benefits** you won't find in traditional methods of saving for college. Only a Bank On Yourself plan gives you *all* these advantages:

- Assures you guaranteed, predictable growth
- Puts you in control of your money
- Lets the money you pay for college expenses keep growing as though you hadn't spent it
- The cash value doesn't count against you when you apply for federal student aid
- Lets you use the money for non-educational purposes and beyond college—without tax consequences
- When you pay your Bank On Yourself policy loans back (on your schedule, not someone else's), you're recapturing the money back into your policy, so you can use it to fund a comfortable retirement

6. **Only a Bank On Yourself plan comes with a death benefit that can let your plan finish funding itself.** That gives you *real* financial peace of mind.

# CHAPTER 9

# Bank On Yourself for Business Owners and Professionals

*It's what you learn after you know it all that really matters.*

—JOHN WOODEN, LEGENDARY BASKETBALL COACH

I HAVE A SPECIAL affinity for professionals who run their own businesses, and all business owners in general, because I've been one myself for twenty-three years. I'll tell you more about my story at the end of this chapter. But because I've run my own businesses, I know that successful business owners have several things in common:

- **We're passionate.** Successful business owners are typically passionate about their product or service. Most are passionate about being excellent at whatever they do, and I suppose a few are passionate about just making money. But whatever the source, it's our passion that has us working those impossible hours, going above and beyond for our clients, customers, or patients.

> **INSIDE THIS CHAPTER...**
> - How to Be Prepared *Before* the Next Crisis Hits
> - How *You* Can Be the Lender Your Business Will Love
> - How to Attract and Retain Great Employees
> - Find the Funding for Your Start-Up
> - A No-Hassle $500,000 Loan

- **We're determined.** Successful business owners don't give up. We're told it will never work? We do it anyway. We hit an obstacle? We go over, under, or around it—or blast through it!

- **We're intelligent risk takers.** We've given up the security of a paycheck to run a business we believe in. We don't go jumping off cliffs but we know when to pull the trigger. We know that standing still is really moving backward.

- **We've got a lot on our shoulders.** We know that the success—or failure—of our business affects not only our own family but the families of our employees, vendors, and suppliers, as well.

- **We have to know about *everything*.** We may hire people to handle certain aspects of our business, but as responsible owners, we have to understand enough to determine if those people are doing a good job. That means a working knowledge of inventory control, accounts receivable and payable, HR, IT, customer service, marketing, tax laws, legal issues, industry trends, economic conditions, leasing facilities—are your eyes crossed yet?

- **We know the buck stops here.** If a poor decision is made or a plan fails, no matter who in our organization caused it, we are ultimately responsible.

- **We are self-reliant.** We may work with partners and vendors. We may have a bunch of employees and contractors working for us. But in the end, we've made the leap of faith to become business owners because we believe in ourselves and our abilities. We know that we are our own best resource. We bank on *ourselves*, not an employer.

- **We need capital to operate.** All businesses are different, but we all need capital to keep our businesses going, whether it's for payroll, expansion, facilities maintenance, new equipment, inventory, taxes, marketing, materials, or a myriad of other things. The need is constant, and when we need that money, we need it *now*.

If you write weekly payroll checks, you can't be at the mercy of customers or clients who pay you only when *they* have money. When orders pick up, you need cash to expand your business to handle the demand. And when the need arises, you need money to finance the big-ticket items that make your business more productive and competitive.

But that capital is no longer (if it ever really was) easy to come by, is it? Even five years after the credit bubble burst, banks are still very cautious about lending, especially to businesses.

In 2009, 55 percent of small employers attempted to obtain credit and *at least half of them failed* to obtain it, according to the National Federation of Independent Business (NFIB). One-third of business owners seeking to *renew their existing* lines of credit were rejected. Among the 61,148 businesses filing for bankruptcy that year, many failed because they simply ran out of fiscal fuel.

But you can have the capital you need whenever you need it. This chapter will show you how to:

- Become your *own* financing source for business vehicles, equipment, office buildings, and more
- Recapture interest you'd otherwise pay to financial institutions
- Fund a new business
- Afford the equipment or technology that puts you ahead of your competition
- Pay for the employees you need to take your business to the next level so you have more time to enjoy your family and your life
- Grow your retirement savings safely and predictably—with *no* government restrictions or penalties on when or how much income you can take from the plan
- Take a passive income stream in retirement, with no taxes due on it
- Take advantage of investment opportunities
- Attract and retain key employees, and be able to offer different employees different benefit amounts (from zero to whatever you choose), without running afoul of government regulations

## Home Equity Is No Longer an Option to Borrow Against

Many of us got comfortable using the equity in our homes as an ATM to cover cash needs. In a report titled *Small Business Credit in a Deep Recession*, the NFIB reported, "The net worth of residences was gold for securitizing purchases of business assets or pumping cash into a business's operation." And 93 percent of small business owners own their own residences.

But the one-two punch of the recession and the housing market collapse meant that this source of capital was no longer viable. Small business owners who have braved recessions dating back to the 1970s can't recall a time—*until now*—when they couldn't borrow against their homes to provide cash to keep their businesses afloat.

Real estate values took such a dive during the crash that the homes of many small business owners were worth less than they owed on them—and many still are. "The immediate business implication of the phenomenon for those affected was that their combined personal and business balance sheets contained a liability that formerly was an asset," says the NFIB.

## Are You Prepared for the *Next* Rainy Day?

One of the most important lessons business owners can learn from the recent turmoil is that the best time to begin preparation for the *next* recession is *right now*.

Small business owners who came through the crash solidly prepared for a downturn *ahead of time*. Many of those who merely tried to respond once the financial crisis hit didn't make it. The scary thing as I write this is that many people, fueled by the media and the false bravado and optimism of Wall Street, seem to have already forgotten that we even had a crisis a few years ago! They're taking up where they left off in 2006, when we were all fat and happy.

But do you really believe that was the *last* major downturn you'll ever see in your lifetime? Me neither. Grandma's old adage to prepare for a rainy day still holds true. And since ready cash is the oxygen every small business owner and self-employed professional requires to survive, we need to be prepared to have that oxygen available—no matter what the economy is doing.

---

### The best time to prepare for the *next* recession is *right now.*

---

I know of a business owner who got caught short in the recession who owns a company that builds modular office furniture. He had a $1 million line of credit from one of the major banks. He and his sales staff who had cards to access that credit were using it to the max. He was making interest-only payments of around $5,000 per month to the bank.

The first call he got from the bank informed him his credit line was being slashed in half to $500,000. Barely two weeks later, he got even worse news: The bank was calling in the loan *altogether*, and they gave him five years to pay back the $1 million of principal he was using to keep his business going, *plus* the interest he owed! His $5,000 monthly payment jumped to $19,247, and he no longer had the line of credit that had been the lifeblood of his business. It's as if the bank was doing all it could to deliberately drive him out of business!

Of course he's now become a Bank On Yourself revolutionary. He's building up his *own* Bank On Yourself "line of credit" so he and his business are never again at the mercy of a bank who puts their own profits before their customers' well-being.

## A Recession-Proof Source of Financing

As I finish writing this in the spring of 2013, many banks still have their money in indefinite lockdown. Capital is hard to get, and only those with impeccable track records need apply. Even business owners with A+ credit ratings are being told, "We'll loan you as much as you can put up in collateral." (Gee, thanks a lot!)

But members of the Bank On Yourself Revolution know that one of the best alternative financing options for small businesses is a loan taken against the owners' Bank On Yourself–type insurance policies. You can use the Bank On Yourself method to start or grow your business, even when no banker will loan you a dime. Business owners like Walt Disney and J. C. Penney successfully used this method decades ago. Policies designed the Bank On Yourself way are tax-advantaged, and they're no-hassle sources of the ready cash every small business owner needs.

## Gaining a Competitive Advantage *Plus* Retirement Security

Here's an illustration of how a medical professional could use Bank On Yourself to keep his practice on the cutting edge while growing a predictable retirement income. Say, for example:

- Dr. Jones starts his policy at age forty
- He pays an annual premium of $36,000 until age sixty-seven
- He uses his policy to finance a total of four $50,000 state-of-the-art equipment purchases, one every five years starting in his third year
- He pays each policy loan back
- When he's sixty-seven, Dr. Jones may start taking $100,000 a year from the plan until he's ninety—tax-free (based on the current dividend scale)
- That's a total retirement income of $2,300,000 ($100,000 x 23 years)
- If Dr. Jones saved $2.3 million in a traditional tax-deferred plan and retired in a 39.6 percent tax bracket, that plan would have to throw off $165,563 per year to net (after taxes) the $100,000 per year he could take from his Bank On Yourself policy. *And* he would never have had the benefit of using that plan to purchase the equipment he needs to keep up with advancing technologies.
- With Bank On Yourself, Dr. Jones could not only purchase the equipment he needs, but he could also retire comfortably and still have a death benefit of $329,000 remaining at age 100 to leave a legacy for his family and/or his favorite charity.

| | |
|---|---|
| **Total premium:** | **$972,000** |
| **Total benefit to Dr. Jones and his family:** | **$2,629,000** |

This is just an example. Regardless of your profession, age, income, or other circumstances, you can find out how Bank On Yourself can help you reach both your business *and* personal goals, and what *your* bottom line numbers and results would be, when you request a free Analysis at **www.BankOnYourselfFreeAnalysis.com** or by completing and submitting the form on page 265.

## Bridging Receivables

Ah, receivables! Unlike an employee whose paycheck shows up like clockwork every two weeks, small business owners often sweat bullets waiting for the mailman to come! Why is it that clients and customers tend to be *particularly slow* in paying right at those times when *you* need that cash the most? And there's only so much nagging and cajoling you can do before you lose their business. So how do you handle those short-term shortfalls?

Small business owner Jerry Thiebold ran into this issue.[48] Major clients of his ten-year-old medical equipment–repair business were late in paying him. "Great receivables, no cash," Thiebold lamented. He needed $15,000 to make his September fifteenth estimated tax payment—and, as we all know, the IRS does *not* take kindly to payments that are late. So the fifty-five-year-old proprietor considered asking his commercial bank to help tide him over—but only for a heartbeat. "You know what that would have been like," he said, noting the iffy and laborious process of winning a loan approval, even for those borrowers with good credit.

But Thiebold had shown foresight. A few years earlier, looking to diversify his 401(k) portfolio, he had taken out a dividend-paying whole life insurance policy designed to maximize the Bank On Yourself concept. At the time, the move was prompted by his desire for retirement savings, not alternative business funding.

But when his tax bill came due, Thiebold realized that he could lend his business $15,000 from his personal Bank On Yourself policy. Now his medical equipment–repair business is repaying the loan, paying interest that is tax-deductible just like business interest in general. Thiebold set his own repayment schedule on a timeline that makes sense for his business—not at the whims of the bank. And if he has to skip a payment, he won't be getting any collection calls during dinner.

---

While the money in Thiebold's policy is on loan to his business, his policy continues to grow as if he never touched a penny.

---

While Thiebold's $15,000 is on loan to his business, his policy continues to earn the exact same guaranteed annual cash value increase, plus any dividends the company declares, just as if he never touched a penny, thanks to a feature offered by the insurance company his Bank On Yourself Authorized Advisor recommended. So while his business's needs are being met, the policy keeps working for his personal retirement needs as well. (For more details about this, see Chapter 7.)

Thiebold got the money he needed, on time, and without a credit check, without having to submit financial statements, without needing the approval of a loan committee, and without any bureaucratic hassles. (Personally, I prefer this method to groveling on my hands and knees to beg for a loan from my friendly banker!)

## Avoid Crushing Interest Payments

Many small businesses have *constant* needs for cash infusions for all kinds of reasons. A loan for this and a loan for that ends up in creating some pretty hefty interest payments—which only increase whatever shortfall or capital need your business is experiencing. Adding insult to injury, depending on your amortization schedule, your initial payments to repay those loans are usually primarily interest, with little of your payment actually paying down your debt. Rather than digging you out of a hole, it's almost making that hole deeper!

Veterinarian Guy Ellis is a case in point. Ellis received his veterinary degree in 1996, and when the opportunity to buy a retiring vet's practice opened up, he seized it. He started with an animal clinic and gradually expanded to include a supply store and kennel. The veterinary hospital now has one part-time and five full-time employees, not counting his wife, Robin, who handles the bookkeeping.

The lively Ellis household includes a stable of three dogs, six horses, one cat, one mule, and four kids. Ellis and Robin perpetually require cash for supplies for the clinic as they juggle payables and receivables. As importantly, the Ellises have a strong commitment to doing good work in the community. For example, they recently used their policies to purchase and remodel a nearby home they plan to donate to a non-profit pregnancy crisis center.

A few years back, Ellis says his balance sheet was a financial mess. He and Robin were very concerned about saving for their children's college as well as for their own retirement. So they got a referral to a Bank On Yourself Authorized Advisor for financial advice and planning assistance.

As Ellis came to understand more about how the Bank On Yourself strategy works to build guaranteed and predictable growth *and* to act as a self-financing vehicle, he began relying on it more and more. He gradually pulled his funds out of the stock market and even decided to redirect his IRA money to his Bank On Yourself policies. Despite the 10 percent early withdrawal penalties on his IRA and the loss he incurred on liquidating his stocks, Ellis simply says, "I'm better off now." Ellis and his family currently use business profits to fund four personal Bank On Yourself policies, and they're getting ready to purchase a fifth. (Refer back to Chapter 7 for reasons some Bank On Yourself revolutionaries have more than one policy.)

Through his policies, Ellis has self-financed purchases of animal pharmaceuticals, x-ray and other diagnostic equipment, barn doors, and personal and business vehicles, and has set aside money for his children's college educations.

> The Ellis family has used their Bank On Yourself plans
> to finance everything from diagnostic veterinary
> equipment to personal and business vehicles, to
> supporting a pregnancy crisis center, to paying
> for their children's college educations.

He pays these loans back on a schedule he created. The interest he pays is not only at a better rate than he could get through a financial institution, it ultimately benefits *him* when dividends are paid to policy owners. (We covered how that works in Chapter 7.) By financing these expenses through his Bank On Yourself plan, Ellis saved a good portion of the $36,000 in annual interest he was paying to banks and finance companies.

The policies, whether targeted to fund the kids' college or his and Robin's retirement, continue to grow as if these loans had not been taken. And as Ellis points out, "I can look years ahead and know *exactly* where I'll be."

So what do you think? Would you rather pay thousands—or even tens of thousands—of dollars in interest to fatten the coffers of banks or other commercial lenders, or use that money in a way that benefits you, your family, and your business? Just sayin'.

### TIP  BUSINESS BONUS: ATTRACT AND RETAIN KEY EMPLOYEES

Attracting and *keeping* great employees is an ongoing challenge for most small and medium-size business owners. Bank On Yourself–type policies make an excellent—and meaningful—way to attract key employees with a **"Section 162" Executive Bonus Plan**.

For example, a software firm in Southern California was hiring MBAs out of college and training them—at an average cost of $150,000. These young key employees were making about $150,000 a year. But it's a very competitive industry, and, once these employees got up to speed, the company was losing them to competitors willing to offer them $10 an hour more.

By setting up Bank On Yourself plans for these employees and putting in an amount equal to 10–20 percent of their salary per year that vested over ten years, the company ensured these key people weren't going to leave big bucks on the table a couple years down the road to get more per hour.

*You* choose which employees receive the benefit, the amount to put in their plans, and the vesting period. You have total flexibility. And you don't have the administrative nightmares and expenses of 401(k)s, profit-sharing plans, and other government-sponsored plans.

Your key people will have an advantage that your competition probably doesn't even know about: a plan that gives them the ability to finance their lifestyle, while growing a retirement fund they can predict and count on.

**But what about your rank-and-file employees?**

According to a 2012 Towers Watson survey, 55 percent of employees would pay a higher amount out of their paychecks each month if they could have a guaranteed retirement benefit that doesn't rise and fall with the stock market.

Today, savvy business owners are offering their employees the guaranteed growth of a Bank On Yourself plan as a supplement—or even as an alternative—to a company-sponsored 401(k) plan.

If you'd like to have a Bank On Yourself Authorized Advisor do a free educational Lunch-and-Learn Workshop on Bank On Yourself for your employees, contact us at info@BankOnYourself.com.

## Where to Find Money for Those Wise Investments

We entrepreneurs are intelligent risk takers. And sometimes the opportunities we see are not *specifically* connected to our business. You are usually the best judge of when to step on the gas and when to hit the brakes. But just try approaching your friendly banker with "Hey, I know this idea is a little outside the box, but I want some cash to invest in XYZ." Did you hear that door slam in your face? But the Calendos found another way to take advantage of a good opportunity.[49]

Like many Bank On Yourself revolutionary business owners, Barb Calendo, a partner in a jobs shop that her father founded in 1967, first diversified into a Bank On Yourself policy to augment her family's retirement savings, *not* to invest in business opportunities. Yet when opportunity knocked, Calendo and her husband, Richard, both fifty-four, were able to access cash via a loan against their Bank On Yourself policies.

Barb Calendo's business makes custom parts for high-tech and other large corporate users. Richard works alongside her and runs his own small machine company as well. "The machine shop works for us now," Barb says, but she doesn't think it has the potential to yield the $5,000 to $10,000 a month they'd like to have available when they walk away from the lathes and mills.

The couple tried the stock market to build more retirement funds. But in 2007, their stock portfolio tanked. Because Richard previously worked with oil companies, he felt comfortable with the industry and the potential for strategic investments to produce big returns. So they funneled some of their machine shop profits into oil and gas well partnerships in Texas.

But Barb wanted something that was safer and more predictable. So she responded to a radio advertisement highlighting the guaranteed growth of Bank On Yourself–type life insurance policies. Originally, the Calendos intended to use their Bank On Yourself policies strictly to grow their retirement fund safely and predictably. But when Richard wanted some cash to acquire an interest in a Texas oil well, they realized that their policies gave them another advantage.

Though their local bank *might* have been willing to loan them the money they needed for the investment, after weighing the pros and cons, they decided to borrow against the cash value in their Bank On Yourself policies to make it happen. They are now repaying the loans at their own pace, while at the same time growing their cash value safely and predictably, to help provide a comfortable retirement.

## What's the Worst-Case Scenario?

When policy owners want to borrow against their policies to make an investment, I always recommend they play the "worst-case scenario" game. What if the investment doesn't pay off? What if you are unable to keep up with payments on the loan, or at the least make the interest payments—and you also find yourself unable to pay the premium? Do you have enough confidence in the investment you are considering that you are willing to risk lapsing the policy and losing some of the money you paid into it, as well as the death benefit if you have to default?

The risk of a policy lapsing for these reasons is greater in the early years of the policy, but asking yourself these questions first is a good litmus test of how comfortable you *really* are in taking a gamble with your safe money.

---

Before using your Bank On Yourself plan for a potentially risky investment, ask yourself what's the worst-case scenario if the investment doesn't pay off. It's a good litmus test of how comfortable you really are taking a gamble with your safe money.

---

The Calendo family chose to use some of their cash value to invest in the oil wells because they believed it could be very profitable and because Richard has intimate knowledge of the industry.

Another example of a Bank On Yourself policy owner who did his homework before deciding to use a policy loan to make an investment is surgeon Dr. Jerry West.[50] Dr. West decided to use his policy equity to buy shares in the surgical center—a medical building with four operating rooms and all the related equipment and facilities—where he performed much of his surgery.

Obviously, Dr. West knew the ins and outs of the facility well, and he felt confident his investment would return 20 percent or more each year. And since his Bank On Yourself Authorized Advisor put his plan with a company that pays the same dividends regardless of any policy loans, Dr. West's funds are working for him in two different ways simultaneously.

When I asked Dr. West to describe how it feels to take advantage of this remarkable feature of Bank On Yourself, he said, "You feel like you've been getting ripped off, and now you're not getting ripped off anymore. Knowing that your money is truly doing double duty for you, it's just the best of both worlds."

When asked what advice he would give people considering Bank On Yourself, he replied, "Don't discount this idea. It's a long-term solution to take control of all your finances. You need to be patient with it in the beginning, but it's a terrific long-term strategy."

## Starting a New Business

You've carefully researched your potential new business and built a conservative business plan. You've talked to other business owners, experts in your industry, and you've conducted market studies. Of course, nothing is a sure thing, but you're fully convinced that your new venture will be profitable and sustainable. You're excited to get started!

Then you go visit your friendly banker. Who is *not* excited. Who *might* be willing to lend you some money—not as much as you need, of course—but at an *exorbitant* rate. With a repayment plan—that will put you six feet under within twelve months—using your home, your car, and your pet iguana as collateral.

How about another option?

John Phillips (the Bank On Yourself revolutionary in Chapter 8 who got an unpleasant surprise funding his newborn daughter's 529 college fund) lives on the West Coast with his wife and two young children. He retired from law enforcement and started a security company providing protection to prominent individuals. Some of his high-profile clients encouraged him to start a gun shop and shooting range that they could use without attracting media attention.

Because John worked closely with some *very* affluent, successful people, he observed firsthand what *really* works when it comes to money and finances. The wealthy, he discovered, do *not* do what everyone else is doing. That's what made him receptive to Bank On Yourself.

---

John used his Bank On Yourself plans to start a successful business from scratch, in an industry where bank financing is almost impossible to obtain.

---

John started his gun shop and range with a $35,000 loan he took against two of his Bank On Yourself policies, one and a half years after starting them. He's since paid back those loans and used the money four or five times more to continue building his business. Not only has the business taken off, it may ultimately become one of the largest gun ranges in the country—open for law enforcement training and to the general public.

John told me that obtaining bank financing in his industry is next to *impossible*. But by becoming his own financing source, he created a major enterprise seemingly out of nothing, while maintaining control of his business.

 **BUSINESS BONUS: BUY-SELL SOLUTION**

---

One of the concerns of a new business or any small business is the issue of partners. You may have entered your business with the business partner of your dreams. He or she complements your skills, thinks like you do, and has the same work ethic, passion for the business, and dedication to quality. Yay!

But one thing many business partners *neglect* to consider is: "What if my perfect business partner dies? Is the spouse or child who will inherit their share the same dream partner I had?" Probably not.

Many business owners think about this. But even partners who realize they need to have a buy-sell agreement in place don't think about how they're going to *fund* the agreement. The partners may agree on a purchase price of $500,000 to buy out the other partner's interest, but if one of them passes away, now what?

The partner who is left will be saying, "Yikes! Where do I get my hands on half a million dollars to buy out the deceased partner's interest?"

And that's why so many businesses fail when something happens to one of the partners—no money to buy out the heirs who are probably not all that interested in the business (or maybe aren't the people you'd *want* to be in business with).

One of the most effective ways to cover everyone's interest is for the partners to take out Bank On Yourself policies on each other, to be used to fund the buy-sell agreement. If one partner dies prematurely, the remaining partner can have confidence that their business will continue because the funds will be available to compensate the heirs of the deceased partner and buy out their interest. The remaining partner can carry on.

## Cutting Out the Middleman and Pocketing More Profits

Entrepreneurs in certain industries are typically stuck with an intermediary who ends up with a lot of control and a big chunk of the profit of the business in exchange for producing the product. For example, movie producers end up with the lion's share of profits for most movies, and book publishers typically make more off a best-selling book than the author. And maybe most extreme of all is the music industry, where a gold record can make a lot of money for the producer, who then turns around and pays a pittance to the artist who laid that golden egg!

But is there a viable way to cut out that middle man? Yep. Ask Karyn White.

When she was in her early twenties, Karyn was the first female artist to have her first three solo releases hit #1 on the R&B charts. She has collaborated with industry legends, including Kenneth Brian "Babyface" Edmonds and L.A. Reid. But after a successful run of songs and a Grammy nomination, Karyn decided to devote herself to raising her family.

During her eighteen-year hiatus from recording, her fan base never forgot her. So with the family grown, Karyn decided to record again. Only this time she decided to produce her new CD, *Carpe Diem*, herself and pocket the profits the record companies previously made off her. Here's how she did it:

During her full-time mom years, Karyn heard about Bank On Yourself and got a referral to a Bank On Yourself Authorized Advisor. Although Karyn had been extremely successful in her career and also in her investments, the recession of 2008 hit her hard, and she lost a ton of money. That wake-up call scared her.

Her Authorized Advisor looked at her overall financial situation, reviewed what investments and assets she had, and discussed with her how much she would be comfortable putting into her new Bank On Yourself policy each year. Karyn had an old life insurance policy that she'd owned for years. It wasn't structured to optimize the growth of the cash value, but it was old enough that it had built up a fairly significant amount. Since her old policy was underperforming, her Advisor suggested doing a rollover of the cash value, called a 1035 Exchange, and replacing the old policy with a Bank On Yourself policy. (See "Business Bonus Tip: 1035 Exchange" later in this chapter.)

So on the day her new Bank On Yourself policy was issued, not only did Karyn have the initial premium amount that she had just paid, but she also had all the cash value that had built up in the old policy as well. That way Karyn started off with a much higher cash value.

"At that time I was wanting to sing again, and I was looking for a way that made sense." Karyn didn't want to give away all her profits to a producer, but credit was tight. "I don't know if I could have even gotten a loan. I have a lot of real estate debt, a lot of holdings, and with the industry the way it is, that probably would have affected me."

Karyn's Bank On Yourself Advisor had a better idea. He showed her how she could get the money she needed without dealing with a producer *or* begging for it from the bank. "I thought, 'This is awesome. I'm able to finance my album with my Bank On Yourself policy.'"

---

**Karyn White financed her new album through her Bank On Yourself policy and pocketed the profits record producers used to make off her.**

---

She took out a policy loan for $60,000. She didn't have to fill out a credit application to get it. She simply picked up the phone and signed a paper. It all happened quickly—in about a week.

"We planned a minimal repayment schedule," she recalled, "because I knew that I was getting back into the industry after eighteen years, and I wasn't quite sure what was going to happen. I knew I had to reconnect both with my fans and with promoters, and I didn't want to lock myself in. That's a great part of Bank On Yourself. There was no one saying you have to pay back a certain amount every month. There's just so much flexibility."

She began by paying back $100 per month. Then, as she started getting singing engagements and money from licensing deals, she periodically called her Authorized Advisor to say, "Okay, I want to pay more money back." This arrangement worked perfectly for Karyn. "Everything was simple, and it's a great liberating feeling to be able to be in control and not feel the pressure, because there's already enough pressure just getting back into the industry." Being out of the music business for eighteen years, she knew her comeback was kind of a crapshoot. Maybe she would be very successful, maybe a little bit successful, or she could flop altogether.

Karyn notes that this is a situation that *many* entrepreneurs face. You don't want to lock yourself into a bank loan or credit card or finance company loan. Lenders will dictate the repayment terms to you, and if you have to skip some payments or reduce payments, you can count on getting collection calls. And you'd for sure get a black mark on your credit report.

But thanks to Bank On Yourself and her 1035 Exchange, Karyn had $60,000 she could borrow against in her policy a mere two years after starting it.

## Estate Planning Made Easy

Karyn couldn't be happier. On top of everything else, her policy provides a substantial death benefit that will go to her daughter to help pay inheritance taxes that will be assessed when she passes away. Karyn's Authorized Advisor explained it to her this way:

"The estate you plan to leave for your daughter is significant—particularly when you include your real estate holdings and the residuals from your albums. And that estate is going to be taxed. However, the income tax-free death benefit of your Bank On Yourself policy may be enough to pay the taxes on your estate if something happens to you."

Karyn's thirst for knowledge about growing and protecting her money taught her a lot. "Unfortunately," she notes, "most people aren't taught about money while they are growing up, at least not the principles that really, really work. There's no school for learning what really works."

If you've been thinking about adding Bank On Yourself to your financial plan, you might benefit from what Karyn has learned since she has joined the Bank On Yourself Revolution. "My advice would be to start now," she says. "To me, Bank On Yourself is like a dream come true. I tell all my friends, 'Do your due diligence, and you'll find that Bank On Yourself is a great tool, and it resolves so many challenges. People can achieve their goals, but in order for you to have options, you have to take control of your destiny and not leave it in the hands of someone else.'"

 To listen to or read the interview I did with Karyn White, go to **www.BankOnYourself.com/karyn**

---

**TIP** **BUSINESS BONUS: 1035 EXCHANGE**

---

When you exchange the cash value of one life insurance policy for cash value in another policy, following the guidelines spelled out in Section 1035 of the tax code, the IRS says you don't owe any taxes on the transaction.

Another bonus, as we saw in Karyn's case, is that the entire cash value of the old policy can be used as a one-time drop-in into a Paid-Up Additions Rider. And that can be in *addition to* your annual PUAR. Recall that the PUAR is the most efficient way to grow cash value, so this option can give you even more cash value that you can access in the early years of your policy.

But don't transfer out values of any older policy that you have without having an Authorized Advisor run the numbers on it. It may or may not make sense to cash in that old policy.

---

## Taking Your Business to the Next Level

As business owners, we know when it's time to pull the trigger and take a giant leap. I'd like to share my own experience with taking my business to that next level.

Right before my first book came out in early 2009, I made the big, bold decision to make a giant splash with it. Our country was in the depths of the financial crisis. People all across the nation were suffering while the financial gurus and talking heads on Wall Street wailed, "There's no place to hide from this crash."

But I, along with hundreds of thousands of other Bank On Yourself revolutionaries, knew otherwise. *Not one of us lost a penny in our Bank*

*On Yourself plans when the stock and real estate markets crashed.* Our plans *continued growing* each year, just as promised. *And* we even had easy access to money to help get us through the crisis.

So I was committed to educating as many people as possible about this little-known and much-misunderstood wealth building method. I knew if my book got some major publicity and hit the bestseller lists, millions of people would know how to avoid another such financial devastation.

I sat down with my team and we listed everything we thought we'd need to make this happen and to be fully prepared for the interest and inquiries that would follow. Our list included everything from hiring a top PR firm, to having a generous advertising budget, to buying new computers and software and pulling together a team to design a new, more comprehensive website—the list seemed endless. Estimated price tag? *$500,000!*

Half a million bucks? I'm a big thinker, but that number made my eyes pop out like one of those cartoon characters. Where on earth were we gonna come up with that much money? I knew that banks had their money on total lockdown at the time, and getting credit was even *more* impossible for business owners!

But I had an ace in the hole: our Bank On Yourself plans, our specially designed dividend-paying whole life policies. My husband and I had been living well below our means and pouring every dollar we could find into these policies from the moment we discovered their potency. I checked our annual policy statements and saw I could easily get $500,000 by borrowing on the cash value of three of our policies.

We didn't sit down with a banker, trying to convince him that our expansion idea was valid and the time was right. We didn't fill out extensive credit applications and spend hours justifying our ability to repay the loan. We didn't pledge our firstborn. We didn't spend days haggling over exorbitant interest rates or shopping around. We simply made a quick phone call, then filled out a short little form to tell the insurance company how much to send us.

Bingo! One week later, we had all $500,000 in our checking account, and we were ready to rock and roll!

---

During the darkest days of the credit crisis, I was able to get $500,000 within one week, to take our business to the next level—no questions asked other than "How much do you want, and where do you want it sent?"

---

Yes, my first book *did* hit all the bestseller lists, including the *New York Times* list. And interest and inquiries *flooded* in, exceeding even my own enthusiastic expectations. The return on my investment was phenomenal. Had we not taken the steps to upgrade all of our company systems, we would not have been able to leverage the book's success and respond to the thousands of people who wanted our help.

It was so easy and simple to get the money. I have to pinch myself every once in a while when I realize how great it is to be out from under the thumb of some faceless, heartless (brainless?) banking institution.

During that same time, I was curious how the most successful business owners and entrepreneurs were handling the crisis. Did they have better connections? Better relationships with their bankers? Strings they could pull that the rest of us can't?

I decided to survey my Mastermind group, made up of some very successful, forward-thinking entrepreneurs (a group that often hosts guest speakers like Sir Richard Branson and Steve Forbes). My main question was: "How were you able to get access to capital to expand your businesses during the credit crisis?"

Guess what? I couldn't find a *single* business owner in that elite group who had been successful in getting the capital they needed.

It didn't matter that they had a perfect record of making their payments on time for twenty years. It didn't matter that they and their banker had a regular tee time at the club every Thursday morning. It didn't matter that their expansion plans were brilliant. They were told that there was simply *no money to lend.*

In fact, some told me their lines of credit had been shut off with no warning. Some even had loans suddenly called due by their banker buddies.

> Bank On Yourself policy owners were able to get access
> to the capital they needed for their businesses during
> the credit crisis—while other business owners were told
> there was simply no money to lend.

When I told my Mastermind colleagues how easily I had gotten access to the capital I needed, their jaws dropped. But when I told them that my policies continued growing as if *all* $500,000 were still in them and *kept growing* even while the markets were crashing, they nearly wept. Their own retirement accounts had been slashed by an average of 50 percent. (By the way, many of them asked for a referral to an Authorized Advisor, so they could join me and do this, too. Turns out nobody enjoys being held hostage by bankers and financial institutions!)

Like me, many business owners believe that investing in their businesses gives them the best possible return on their investment of time and money. Time is the easy part. We can usually find time to do things we really want to do. But money to grow your business? It can be impossible—*unless* you become your own source of financing!

### BUSINESS BONUS: HOW TO FINANCE BUSINESS CARS AND EQUIPMENT

For the past ten years, my husband and I have used the Bank On Yourself method to finance cars we use primarily for our business. I am *not* a CPA—nor have I ever played one on TV!—but here's the simple process our CPA recommended:

1. Start one or more individual policies.
2. When you have sufficient cash value built up to cover the cost of a big-ticket item, negotiate your best deal for paying cash for it. Remember: Cash is king, and when *you're* the one who has it, you call the shots!
3. Lease the equipment to your corporation or partnership at a market value rate.

4. The corporation rent or lease payments are paid to *you*.
5. You pay it back.
6. When the loan is paid back, you can repeat the process with another piece of business equipment.
7. Repeat as many times as desired!

The usual tax deductions for interest and depreciation can be taken. Structured properly, this can be a net zero tax transaction. Plus, you get the capital you need without filling out any lengthy applications. And you can't be turned down!

Of course, this process can be used for leasing any business equipment, not just cars. It's a far better method than traditional leasing, which is actually the *least* efficient way to finance big-ticket items. At the end of a lease, you typically have nothing to show for all the money you spent. And the Bank On Yourself strategy beats directly paying cash for business purchases. Refer back to Chapter 7 (How to Fire Your Banker) for more details.

Again, this is not intended to be tax advice, and you should do this with the guidance of a Bank On Yourself Authorized Advisor and a tax professional who understands the concept.

---

## A Sad Story

I recently received this letter from a business owner, begging for a solution to an all-too-common problem:

I've owned a successful wholesale business for eleven years. I supply 3,000 customers in seven states. Now my bank has shut down all commercial lending. They called my loans, and they've shut down my line of credit. My inventory is almost gone, and I'm barely hanging on. I have plenty of orders from my customers, but I don't have the cash flow to replenish inventory to supply my customers. My vendors require up-front payment on my purchases. Is there any solution to my problem, or do I have to shut down my business? I laid off seven employees, including my own daughter, which has crushed my spirit. It's now only my son and me running routes, making deliveries, and rationing what inventory we have left. I need funding, and I need it now. Today! We are dying here. Can the Bank On Yourself method help me?

How sad! Of course, this gentleman did not own a Bank On Yourself policy. I'm not sure what happened to him, but I'm guessing he had to close his business's doors. If he had just found out about the Bank On Yourself Revolution sooner...

It's another reminder that the *best* time to prepare for the next recession or downturn in your industry is now—*today*.

## KEY TAKE-AWAYS

1. **A business needs access to cash to keep going.** Whether for the next opportunity or lagging receivables, businesses need a source of ready capital at hand.

2. **Your Bank On Yourself plan also doubles as a safe, predictable way to grow your nest egg**, providing you with an income stream that can last as long as you do (with no taxes due on it).

3. **Even when available, a loan from your friendly banker ain't a great option.** With banks reeling from their self-inflicted losses, they've become incredibly tight-fisted when it comes to small business loans. Even when you can get a loan, the amount you get, the repayment schedule, and the interest rate are all *under the bank's control*—and not necessarily beneficial to the health of your business.

4. **Using your Bank On Yourself policy for financing, you're in control.** You can arrange to pay yourself back on a schedule that works for your business. And the interest you pay (often lower than the bank's rate) can ultimately benefit you through policy dividends. Even better, if your policy is from a company

offering this feature, it can continue growing, even on the money you're using elsewhere!

**5. With a Bank On Yourself loan, you gain a competitive advantage and can seize opportunities that come up.** You can finance new business equipment that gives you an advantage over your competition, purchase new properties that can expand the business, cut out the middleman and pocket more profits, and hire new personnel.

**6. With a Bank On Yourself plan, you can pull the trigger when you know it's time.** You can expand your business to the next level or branch out into totally new fields. You don't need to justify your decisions to your friendly banker, the guy who knows a whole lot less about your business than you do. Your success is limited only by your own good sense in business.

# CHAPTER 10

# Bank On Yourself for Seniors

*The best time to plant a tree is twenty years ago.*
*The second best time is today.*

—ANONYMOUS

I'M FREQUENTLY ASKED, "Does the Bank On Yourself method work well for people in their sixties, seventies, and eighties, and for people who've already retired?" After all, the concept relies on a life insurance product and ongoing premiums. Does it still make sense to start a life insurance policy when you're older?

My answer is a resounding "Yes!" And this chapter explains the details of a unique variation of a dividend-paying whole life policy that addresses the specific concerns of seniors and retirees.

In general, we seniors have different concerns than when we were younger. (Yes, I turned sixty this year, so I qualify as "we"!) We're not planning for retirement; we're often already retired or about to retire. We're not thinking about paying for college for our kids, we're thinking about long-term care for ourselves. Though we'd like to maximize the growth of our money, we sure as heck want

> **INSIDE THIS CHAPTER . . .**
> - The Perfect Plan If You're Between Sixty and Eighty-Five
> - Get a Better Yield Without Increasing Your Risk
> - Will You Live Longer Than Your Money?
> - How to Avoid Required Minimum Distributions
> - The Real Skinny in a Senior's Own Words

to avoid taking risks with it. Our biggest worry is: Will our money last as long as we do?

That said, we're each aging uniquely. Some of us are running marathons and still active in our careers at eighty-six. Others are winding down and retiring in Puerto Vallarta at sixty-two. Still others are now raising their grandchildren because their children are unwilling or unable to do so. In fact, the U.S. Census of 2010 reports that about 5.8 million children (almost 8 percent of all children) are living with a grandparent as the head of the household.

## Where Traditional Planning Has Left Us

Even if you've done all the right things to plan for retirement, now that you're there, in the words of Dr. Phil, "How's that working for ya?" Unfortunately, if it wasn't obvious before, many of us now realize that the traditional retirement planning we relied on isn't panning out as we thought it would. Is it too late to change direction? Nope. But before we get into what really *could* work for you, let's take a look at the results of traditional retirement and investment planning for seniors overall:

- Seniors are carrying far more debt than ever before—the median amount of debt held by households headed by someone sixty-five or older rose almost 120 percent between 2000 and 2011. A significant portion of this increase is from rising mortgage debt.[51]

- According to the Center for Responsible Lending, more than 25 percent of bank "payday loans"—short-term loans with interest rates as high as 300 percent!—are now taken out by *Social Security recipients.*

- The Federal Reserve has kept interest rates at rock-bottom lows for so long, many seniors have seen their income from CDs, savings, etc. reduced significantly.

- The nonprofit group Wider Opportunities for Women reports that many seniors are now forced to choose between putting food on the table and paying the gas bill or getting needed medical care.

- Studies show a sixty-five-year-old couple retiring now will need $220,000 to cover out-of-pocket health care costs during retirement[52]—but many don't have that much in *total* savings. In case you think that staggering number must include possible nursing home and long-term care costs, it doesn't. *And* it assumes you have Medicare insurance.

Many of us who are retiring (or hoping to retire) today do not have a company pension plan guaranteeing a lifetime income. We relied on 401(k)s and IRAs and the Wall Street Casino for retirement security. But the financial debacle beginning in 2008 gutted those vehicles. And that was the *second* time in a decade that the market plunged by 49 percent or more.

While seniors are often told they can plan on needing *less money* to live on in retirement, our surveys of seniors haven't unearthed many who've found that to be true. Most laugh when it's mentioned. Their utility bills aren't lower. Their grocery bills haven't gone down. They still need haircuts, visits to the dentist, and oil changes, and all of it seems to cost more every year. They don't have fewer children or grandchildren. Was that big reduction supposed to come from the afternoon matinee Super Senior Discount?

Traditional financial advice has failed us. And though this advice was *supposed* to answer the specific concerns of seniors, it really hasn't. The good news? You still have another option.

## Bank On Yourself for Seniors Options

Recognizing where conventional financial vehicles have gotten them, it's not uncommon for people in their sixties to start regular Bank On Yourself–type policies (the policies where you pay monthly, quarterly, or annual premiums). For example, this year, at age sixty, I started another Bank On Yourself policy. It's my biggest policy yet, and it was designed so that I could be done paying premiums out of my cash flow in about five years (the premiums could be paid from the policy's values), and so that I could stop paying them *altogether* in approximately seven years, if I choose.

But there is *another* type of dividend-paying whole life insurance policy designed for people between age sixty and eighty-five that may be more appropriate for some, especially for people in their seventies and eighties. It's still a dividend-paying whole life policy, but you only pay a single one-time premium for it. I call it a **Bank On Yourself for Seniors Plan**, and I'll show you how it works in this chapter.

A Bank On Yourself for Seniors Plan is based on a unique kind of dividend-paying whole life insurance: **single-premium** whole life insurance. You pay a one-time lump-sum premium, and no additional premiums are due. Because you're putting in a lump sum rather than making periodic premium payments, that money goes to work for you *immediately*.

How do you know which type of policy makes the most sense for you? It's best to get a referral to one of the Bank On Yourself Authorized Advisors by going to **www.BankOnYourselfFreeAnalysis. com** or completing and submitting the form on page 265. They'll take a look at your unique situation and goals and make an appropriate recommendation.

## Does Low Risk Always Equal Slow Growth?

We're taught we must become more conservative with our investments as we grow older, to avoid taking a big loss right before or during retirement. That makes sense, doesn't it? Many of us won't be working any longer to create income, so we don't want to risk the income streams we have.

But on the flip side, the problem with this strategy is that it pretty much ensures your returns will be the *lowest* during what are supposed to be your golden years. In these years, many of us could use as much extra income as possible, especially if like many folks, your 401(k) or IRA took a huge hit in the recent stock market crash. Your money in very conservative vehicles is pretty safe—but it's not maximizing your income stream!

Case in point: If you're retired and you have $250,000 in a CD or money market fund that today is giving you only a 1 percent return, that's all of $2,500 a year. Or about $6.84 per day—which will buy you a Senior Grilled Cheese at Denny's (though your spouse will have to go hungry). Not exactly what you had in mind after forty-plus years of working hard and trying to build a nest egg?

But wait! We've still got Social Security!

As of the beginning of 2012, the average monthly Social Security benefit for a retired worker was about $1,230, according to the Social Security Administration website. That *might* work out—if you don't have medical expenses or mortgage payments or utilities or auto repairs or... okay, so it's gonna be tough.

Of course, the government has plans in the works to raise the age at which you can start taking Social Security. And to make matters worse, now they're trying to tie your paltry Social Security cost-of-living increases to a different measure, which *assumes* you'll just switch to buying cheap brands when your favorites become more expensive due to inflation. Really? They *assume* we want to spend our golden years using scratchy toilet paper and brushing our teeth with baking soda?

So you're forced to eat into some of your principal to make ends meet. What if you have to supplement your post-retirement income with $25,000 of your savings each year? That's $25,000 you'll never earn interest or growth on again! So each year, your interest income drops, and within a decade you've run through your entire savings!

## Enhanced Growth Without Added Risk

But a Bank On Yourself for Seniors Plan works just the opposite. The growth curve gets *steeper every year* you have it—that's the way these policies are *designed*. With a Bank On Yourself plan, both your principal and growth are locked in. Your policy doesn't go backward when the stock or real estate markets crash. A Bank On Yourself plan increases by a contractually guaranteed amount each year, with additional growth potential from dividends. The companies recommended by Bank On Yourself Authorized Advisors are among the strongest financial services companies in the country. Although dividends aren't guaranteed, these companies have paid dividends *every single year* for more than one hundred years.

## Bank On Yourself vs. CDs or Money Market Accounts

Let's revisit the situation we discussed earlier in this chapter: the retiree who has $250,000 in a CD or money market account, giving them a 1 percent return. This return is pretty common today, and it's been that way for longer than most seniors care to remember.

At 1 percent interest, that's $2,500 per year in income. But if you were to put that same $250,000 into a Bank On Yourself for Seniors Plan, you'll typically be able to withdraw 5–6 percent of that amount every year *for the rest of your life*. If we use the 5 percent withdrawal figure, that's $12,500 per year—*five times* as much as the CD was paying. And you'd *still* have some death benefit left, to leave a financial legacy to your loved ones or favorite charity.

---

A Bank On Yourself for Seniors Plan can enable you to withdraw five times as much money than you could from today's CD or money market accounts—and *still* be able to leave a legacy to your loved ones.

---

If you'd *planned* on earning 4 percent on your $250,000 CD, which is $10,000 per year, what happens if the interest rate drops to 1 percent? You end up with only $2,500 per year—and *now* you've got to make some hard choices. Should you skip doctors' visits or turn the thermostat down to fifty degrees in the winter…or start eating into your principal? If you take the latter option, it will lower your future income potential even more. Do you really want to be forced to make choices like these in your golden years?

If you're between the ages of sixty and eighty-five, a Bank On Yourself for Seniors Plan may be the answer. It gives you *safety* for your money. It gives you *guaranteed* growth—but more than what you're getting with today's CDs and savings or money market accounts, which have been losing value every year to inflation.

Your Bank On Yourself policy gives you some built-in protection from inflation so you can continue using squeezable Charmin rather than that industrial-grade TP. And if you want to go to Denny's, you and your spouse can *both* eat—or you can go to a place with no pictures on the menu instead!

In addition, gains on Bank On Yourself for Seniors Plans are *tax-deferred* until you withdraw them. That's different from a CD or savings account, where you're barely earning anything, yet you have to pay taxes on that gain each year—whether you use the money or not!

You don't have to be an investing genius for a Bank On Yourself plan to work as it's designed to work. You don't have to spend hours and hours worrying about your investments. You can spend more time enjoying your life.

## How to Avoid Burdening Your Kids

Let's see how a Bank On Yourself for Seniors Plan could look in action. For the first example, we'll suppose that Jane Smith wants to receive a lifetime income that will ensure she'll never have to be a burden to her loved ones—or a bag lady. When she's sixty-two, she starts a Bank On Yourself for Seniors single-premium dividend-paying whole life plan with $100,000, and she never puts in another dime. She has an initial death benefit higher than the premium she paid in. In this particular example, her death benefit is more than $207,000.

Five years later, when she's sixty-seven, Jane starts taking 5¼ percent of her original $100,000 annually to supplement her living expenses. That's $5,250 every single year for the rest of her life. If Jane passes away at age ninety, she could have received $126,000 of income—all without the risk or volatility of stocks, real estate, and other investments.

And even after Jane took all that income, her loved ones could *still* receive an income tax-free death benefit of more than $84,000.

---

You can typically take 5–6 percent of the amount you funded your plan with every year for life (based on the current dividend scale), and still leave an income tax-free financial legacy to your loved ones.

---

So Jane's purchase of a Bank On Yourself for Seniors policy gives her *living benefits* of more than $126,000, and gives her loved ones and favorite charities more than $84,000, for a total of more than $210,000—all based on that one-time payment of $100,000 into her policy.

Jane also has peace of mind, knowing she has a **long-term** or **home health-care benefit** of $2,000 per month for thirty-six months, if she needs it. In most states, it's included in her Bank On Yourself for Seniors Plan *at no extra cost*! She won't have to worry about her daughter having to quit her job to take care of her (or find herself a shopping cart).

### How Safe Is Your Retirement Money?

"I would recommend Bank On Yourself to everyone," wrote Jake Hightower, a telephone engineer in Colorado. "The conservative life insurance companies used by Bank On Yourself Advisors are the closest possible guarantees in today's financial market. I'm almost sixty-five, and my term insurance policies are about to expire. I will cancel them and buy a Bank On Yourself policy."

## Will You Live Longer Than Your Money?

Many financial planners will base their projections on your living to age eighty-five or so. After all, they figure, a man reaching age sixty-five today can expect to live, *on average*, until age eighty-three, and a sixty-five-year-old woman will live *on average* until age eighty-five. But those averages are just that—averages of the total population. It doesn't tell you how long *you* will live.

According to the Social Security Administration, the reality is that 25 percent of people turning sixty-five today will live past ninety, and one out of ten will live past ninety-five.

What if you're the lucky one who hangs on until 100 or longer? You don't know for sure, do you? But just how lucky will you feel if you can't provide for yourself in those final years? Doesn't it make sense to plan for your money to last as long as you might? How confident are you that, if you continue to save and invest the way you've been doing it, your money will last until you're 90, 100, or even 110 years young?

## Cash That Outlasts You

A Bank On Yourself for Seniors policy lets you know the guaranteed minimum value of your plan at any given point in time. You can take predictable withdrawals and even use the money in the plan to finance whatever you need while your plan continues to grow just the same.

## Control, Timing, and Taxes

One of the biggest complaints we hear from seniors who've been able to sock money away in retirement accounts is this: "The government is forcing me to take income I don't need! Then they're telling me I have to pay taxes on it!" 401(k)s, 403(b)s, IRAs, and other government-controlled retirement plans all have restrictions and penalties regarding distribution of the funds you've accumulated. With the exception of Roth plans, they all have the dreaded Required Minimum Distribution (RMD), which means that no matter what your financial situation at the time or your intentions for the money you've put aside in these plans, you *have* to take a specific percentage out starting at a specific age.

For example, if your retirement funds are in a 401(k), you must begin taking money out—and paying taxes on it!—every year once you turn 70½. And even if you're healthy as a horse with genes that indicate you'll make it to ninety-nine, the amount you *must* take out is calculated based on how long some government actuarial assumes you'll live (balance in your plan divided by assumed number of years left equals annual minimum required distribution).

The following example shows how this might play out, and another option to consider.

## How to Avoid the Dreaded RMDs and Leave a Legacy

Let's say that Juan Garcia is seventy years old. He has $200,000 in his IRA, earning 2 percent interest each year, and the IRS says he's going to have to start taking Required Minimum Distributions (RMD) next year and *pay taxes* on each withdrawal.

Juan's not happy about that because *he doesn't need the money* and doesn't want to be forced to pay taxes on money he doesn't even need! He'd rather leave that money as a legacy for his children and his grandchildren. But if he leaves his money in his IRA, next year his required minimum distribution will be $7,300, on which he'll have to pay income tax. The year he turns eighty-five, the IRS says he'll *have* to withdraw $8,600—*and* pay taxes on that.

If Juan passes away *this* year, his family will have to pay taxes on the *entire* $200,000. So his family might net just $144,000—or less, if they're in a high tax bracket. If, instead, Juan passes away ten years from now, his $200,000 IRA will have dwindled to $156,000. After paying tax on that amount, his family would receive only $112,000. And if he lives to age ninety, his loved ones will receive *less than $70,000* of Juan's original $200,000 legacy.

But what if Juan chose instead to go the Bank On Yourself for Seniors route? Juan could pay the income tax on his $200,000 IRA now and put his after-tax balance of $144,000 into a Bank On Yourself for Seniors Plan. That would create an *immediate* legacy of $210,000 for his children and grandkids, because the moment his policy is issued, Juan has a death benefit that's larger than the lump sum he put in—*and* larger than the original $200,000 he had in his IRA. Plus, this money will go to his family with no income taxes due on it.

In addition, Juan will have $4,000 per month, available for long-term care or home health care, for up to thirty-six months if he needs it.

If Juan leaves his money in his IRA, the balance available to his beneficiaries goes *down* every year, and it's *taxable*. But in a Bank On Yourself for Seniors Plan, his legacy actually goes *up* every year, and it's *income tax-free* to his beneficiaries. For example, in ten years, based on the current dividend scale, his policy would have a cash value of about $190,000, with a projected death benefit of about $250,000, based on the current dividend scale. If Juan were to pass away then, that death benefit of nearly $250,000 would go to his family. If he continues living, his cash value continues to grow.

## You Have Flexibility if Your Situation Changes

Juan never thought he'd need the money in his IRA. He planned to leave it as a legacy for his family. But what if Juan's situation changes when he's eighty, and he actually *does* need income? He could then begin withdrawing 5 percent of his cash value—about $6,650—every year *for the rest of his life.*

In twenty years, if he takes no income, Juan's policy's projected cash value is almost $273,000, and should he pass away, the income tax-free legacy for his family could be nearly $314,000. But if he lives, and if he finds he needs income, he can start withdrawing 5–6 percent of his cash value every year, knowing he'll never run out of money.

Which legacy would you prefer to leave for your family if you pass away at age ninety: $70,000 from your IRA, or nearly $314,000 from your Bank On Yourself plan?

## Other Bank On Yourself Strategies for Seniors

The two examples we just went through show how two individuals with different goals and unique situations could use a Bank On Yourself for Seniors Plan. There are other strategies you could use to begin a Bank On Yourself policy. For example, if you don't want to pay taxes all at once by taking a lump sum from your current plan, you could take your RMDs each year, pay the taxes on them, then put the balance into a traditional Bank On Yourself plan for your spouse, your children or grandchildren, or some other beneficiary—even a favorite church or charity.

Bank On Yourself for Seniors Plans have none of the restrictions and none of the penalties that come with 401(k)s, 403(b)s, IRAs, and other government-sponsored retirement plans. You can take retirement income when you choose, with no penalties for waiting too long and no Required Minimum Distributions.

Finally, the built-in death benefit can potentially give your family and favorite charity as much money as you started with or even more, income tax-free. And it bypasses the expense, publicity, and delays of probate.

---

A Bank On Yourself for Seniors Plan can enable you to leave more money than you started with to your loved ones or favorite charity.

---

## Covering Major Expenses

It just doesn't stop, does it? We're no longer in our biggest income-producing years, but the roof starts leaking and the car decides to die anyway. We still have relatives we want to help out and, often even more than before, unexpected medical expenses. And we still have items on our bucket list that we'd like to cross off before we kick that bucket!

### Sixty-Seven-Year-Old Minister Gains Financial Flexibility

"I recommend Bank On Yourself to anyone," commented Dr. Harry Peatt, a Connecticut minister. "The first thing I did is use my Bank On Yourself plan to pay off my debt, to be able to retain the interest I was paying to banks. I started this when I turned sixty-seven. I'm using it to finance home improvements and to provide a legacy for my children."

We've talked about being your own source of financing through Bank On Yourself throughout this book, and a Bank On Yourself for Seniors Plan can be used in the same way. You can borrow your equity in a Bank On Yourself plan and use it for anything you want, while your money in the plan continues to grow as though you never touched a dime of it.

# Assistance with Skyrocketing Long-Term Care Costs

Long-term care costs can be devastating for seniors. At least 70 percent of people over age sixty-five will require long-term care services at some point, and more than 40 percent will need nursing home care, according to the U.S. Department of Health and Human Services. Based on the average cost of a private nursing home and the average length of stay, you would need more than $225,000 to cover a stay.[53] And many people don't realize that Medicare does *not* pay your long-term care expenses.

One great benefit of a Bank On Yourself for Seniors policy is that, in most states, a long-term care benefit is included at no additional cost. And it's not just for stays in a long-term care facility. You can also use it for home health care, which many seniors prefer. This coverage can last up to thirty-six months, which is longer than the average stay in a nursing home of 2.8 years.

---

A Bank On Yourself for Seniors Plan has a long-term care benefit included at no extra cost, in most states.

---

Are you concerned that you might not qualify for life insurance because of health reasons? Relax. Underwriting requirements are easier to meet for single-premium policies like Bank On Yourself for Seniors Plans than for traditional whole life policies, where you pay premiums over time. And besides, you don't even have to be the insured person. Your spouse, child, or grandchild may meet the requirements. As long as you're the *owner* of the policy, you are in control of the policy and get to call all the shots about the policy and what happens with the money in the policy. (Any long-term care benefits, however, are paid only if the *insured person* needs care.)

# What About Annuities?

With a Bank On Yourself policy, your money is available when you need it, without all the restrictions of an annuity.

Compared to annuities, you'll typically get a higher return with Bank On Yourself policies, and you'll have much more flexibility and liquidity. With a Bank On Yourself for Seniors Plan, you can be confident that the income will last as long as you do. And Bank On Yourself plans provide a death benefit to leave your family or favorite charity as a financial legacy when you pass on, which an annuity does not provide.

There may be situations where an annuity is a good solution for a specific situation. A Bank On Yourself Authorized Advisor can help you determine if buying an annuity makes sense for you.

## A Senior Sums It Up

Bill Williams discovered Bank On Yourself as a senior. He described his experience this way in a letter he wrote to me:

> Thanks for all the good things you are doing, Pamela. I am working with my Bank On Yourself Advisor to set up my third policy, and I am so appreciative of her guidance and expertise. She has been tremendously supportive.
>
> The real "snake oil" is all of the purported advice about savings and investing we have been fed by the "experts" in the past. I get so upset by the advice to invest with before-tax dollars into 401(k)s or 403(b)s. I'm over sixty years old and know when I turn 70½, I'm going to have to take required withdrawals from my plans and have the added burden of paying taxes on them. After all, the IRS wants to get its hands on the taxes they let me avoid paying all those years. I wish that not only I had learned about Bank On Yourself earlier, but that the concept could be taught to the masses when they are young enough to get the maximum benefit from it.
>
> Here's why I say that. I think of all of the purchases I've made through the years where Bank On Yourself would have been a much better means to fund them. As an example, my sons' college expenses, which I paid every cent by selling stock and mutual funds and taking a loan from a 401(k). Needless to say, my son received a great education (to his credit), but dear old dad has nothing to show for it. I had to put money into the stocks, 401(k), and mutual fund, so I had the resources at the time which could have been so much more powerful in a Bank On Yourself policy!

It's as simple as that. And now I would still have the policies, which would have even more value.

I am depleting an IRA to fund my third policy and to help fund policies one and two. I just hope I live long enough to enjoy all the benefits.

Couldn't have said it better myself! Maybe I'll get Mr. Williams to write my next book.

## KEY TAKE-AWAYS

With a Bank On Yourself for Seniors lump-sum plan, we seniors have several great reasons for becoming Bank On Yourself revolutionaries:

**1. To grow wealth safely and predictably** *every* **year**—even when the markets are tanking.

**2. To get a better return than savings and money market accounts, CDs, annuities, and other conservative investments** *without* **increasing our risk.**

**3. To be able to get our hands on our money whenever we need it**—without government restrictions or penalties. A Bank On Yourself plan lets us avoid the annual Required Minimum Distributions (RMDs) that the IRS forces us to take from 401(k)s, IRAs, etc., once we turn age 70½.

**4. To ensure our money will last as long as we do.**

**5. To provide an income tax-free financial legacy** to our family and/or favorite charity (even after receiving a lifetime income from the plan).

**6. To become our own source of financing for major purchases**—remember that financing things through a Bank On Yourself plan beats financing or leasing them, and even beats directly paying cash for them, as we discussed in Chapter 7.

**7. To provide a long-term care benefit at no extra cost,** for stays in a long-term care facility or for home health care (in states where it's available).

## CHAPTER 11

# The Path to a Lifetime of Financial Freedom

*We can't solve problems by using the same kind of thinking*
*we used when we created them.*

—ALBERT EINSTEIN

WE'VE SHOWN YOU how Bank On Yourself–type policies work in different stages of your life and for various situations. Now I'll give you an example of what happens when you put it all together and use Bank On Yourself as a system for managing your money and reaching your goals, from cradle to grave. I'll be sharing the story of Tim Austin who—though he's definitely not at the *grave* stage of life yet!—began successfully using this method for himself and his clients when he was still in his twenties.

As you'll see, Tim built that pyramid we talked about in Chapter 6 the *right* way, creating a solid foundation from the get-go, so that he and his family could live a life that is financially stress-free.

> **INSIDE THIS CHAPTER . . .**
> - Financial Advisor Learns the Hard Way
> - What Our Grandparents Knew That We've Forgotten
> - How Young Couples End Up in Debt
> - Reaching Your Financial Milestones Without Taking Unnecessary Risks
> - How to Prepare for the Unexpected

# How Tim Began His Journey

Even as a young boy, Tim wanted to make his mark in the world, and from the time he was twelve years old, he showed his very strong work ethic. "I did everything from delivering two paper routes to cutting lawns to shoveling snow in the winter. The good news is that, growing up in Michigan, I never ran out of snow to shovel!"

By the age of fourteen, Tim started working in restaurants and even worked his way up to night manager by the age of sixteen. At the same time, Tim was trying to earn good grades in high school so he could get into college, as well as playing sports, especially tennis. "I became pretty proficient in tennis and even reached #2 in the region."

But when Tim headed to college, he gave the sport up. "My father was a pipefitter and my mom raised foster children, so we really didn't have a lot of money. From my dad, I had learned, 'If you need to get something or buy something, well, you've got to go out and work for it.'"

When Tim figured out that he wasn't going to get a whole bunch of grants and scholarships to pay for college and that he'd be paying his own way, he realized he needed something with better pay than his current jobs. "I also was looking at a way to start building a career. I needed to make some money while I was in college, but at the same time, I wanted to get into something other than working in a restaurant."

# A Lesson Learned the Hard Way

Tim answered an ad for a job in financial services that was extremely attractive, where he could work his own hours and get licensed to sell securities. He studied hard and got all the licenses he needed pretty quickly. He became a financial securities specialist in early 1989.

"Basically, I was a stock jockey. They sat me down at a table with ten other investment specialists. Then they would hand you a phonebook and a script. That script told you what mutual fund you were supposed to sell to prospects that day. You'd make 200 phone calls to perfect strangers, until you met your sales quota.

"The script might go something like, 'This particular fund is on the move! This is going to be a great mutual fund! This is what you're going to want to get involved in. Have you ever invested in mutual funds before? What if you had an opportunity to make $5,000 by next month? If this thing comes through, it could be $20,000.' Blah, blah, blah."

If you've ever seen the movie *Boiler Room*, that's what Tim was describing. That's what some securities companies still do today. Tim lasted about eight months there, then thought, "This is crazy. This is *not* for me. This isn't where I want my career going."

But before he came to that realization, as a brand-new financial securities specialist, Tim's bosses encouraged him to start with the people he knew and give his sales pitch to family and friends.

"I have a family that loved me, especially my grandma. My grandma had lived through the Depression and shared her story with me many times. In 1933, they lived above a grocery store, and they had to work and basically fend for whatever they could. Once she found a dime on the sidewalk and told me that was the happiest day of her life because she was able to buy tomato soup to feed the whole family for two days.

"Grandma never put money anywhere except in cash hidden in the home and CDs and savings accounts in the bank. But my sales manager, who went with me to make a presentation to my grandmother, convinced her to pull $10,000 out of her CD and put that money into a bond fund. He told her, 'Bonds are very safe, and this bond fund is going to earn an 11 percent rate of return. It's done very well over the years, and you're going to really love this.' My grandma looked at me, not the manager, and the only thing she said was, 'I am not concerned about a big return on my money. Just make sure I don't *lose* any money.'

"Well, in October of 1989, just six months later, I had to tell Grandma that her $10,000 was now only worth $6,000. I felt sick to my stomach—and I'll never forget that feeling.

---

Grandma told me to make sure I didn't lose any of her money, but just six months later, I had to tell her that her $10,000 was now worth only $6,000. I felt sick to my stomach—and I'll never forget that feeling.

---

"And it was really from that point forward that I started on my mission of figuring out really appropriate types of solutions for my clients of all ages. Solutions that made sense and reflected their true comfort levels. At the same time, I wanted to figure out how the heck you can help somebody to reach their financial goals without taking all that unnecessary risk."

Tim moved to one of the largest financial services companies in the country and got licensed to sell virtually every financial services product there is, from property and casualty insurance to health insurance, to annuities, to life insurance, to securities. Though this position was better, Tim realized that the entire industry was all about sales and more sales.

"Literally we were taught that, if a person can fog a mirror, you can sell them something. The idea was to get in front of as many people as you can and figure out *what* you can sell them. We were taught that you can sell them just about anything because what you're really selling is the sizzle. That just didn't feel right to me either."

## The Wisdom of Our Grandparents

It took Tim about two years, but he finally came across someone who showed him what permanent whole life insurance could do within an overall financial plan, how clients could use their policies (based on the same structure Bank On Yourself uses) to accomplish their financial goals without taking on a lot of risk. That was in 1991, and Tim was just twenty-seven years old.

During that time, Tim found another excellent source of education. He was pretty successful with the company, so he earned the right to work with their "orphan accounts"—accounts whose original salesperson was no longer with the company. These accounts were small whole life policies people had kept for twenty, thirty, forty, or even fifty years. Tim's job was to go out and meet these people and see if they needed anything else.

"Most of these people were in their seventies, eighties, and even nineties. I got to meet all of them and listen to their stories. I was young, and I was a pretty good listener, so I heard all about how they purchased these policies, and why they purchased them, and what they did with them. They loved to share their financial successes and failures with me.

"I would hear about when their daughter got married and they borrowed the $3,000 they needed to pay for the wedding from the policy. Then they'd pay it back in. I'd hear about how they paid cash for their first car by saving the cash for it in their life insurance policy. And I'd hear about how they used their policy when some emergency medical expenses came up.

---

These families knocked the wind out of the claim that you need to be wealthy to use the Bank On Yourself method. They were ordinary blue-collar and middle-class families building their financial foundation on whole life insurance.

---

"Their stories really helped me understand and solidify the value of Bank On Yourself–type whole life contracts. I began to understand why these people became successful and how they used their policies to respond to life's roadblocks and challenges. These families, with policies costing a relatively few dollars each month, knocked the wind out of the argument that you need to be wealthy to use the Bank On Yourself method. These were ordinary folks—blue-collar and middle-class families—building their financial foundation on whole life insurance."

Tim recognized that what was common to people who were raised in the 1920s through the 1950s became more rare when the era of speculation started in the 1960s. It became more common to invest in the stock market because you thought you could earn more than the interest you'd get from a savings account.

People became comfortable taking risks. But Tim had seen the downside, and he didn't want his future family or his clients to end up there. "Their parents or grandparents would *never* have put their money into the market in risky or long-term investments *before* they built up a substantial emergency fund that they could get their hands on when they needed it."

## Today's Typical Young Couple

In 1994, Tim started specializing in the type of whole life policies that the Bank On Yourself method uses today, within the specific market-place of young families: parents in their mid-forties who were concerned about how they would get all their kids through college yet still be able to retire comfortably someday.

As he started working extensively in his marketplace (people in their mid-forties), he realized that their stories were drastically different than those he'd heard from older folks.

"For example, when I was visiting with people who were already in their seventies, eighties, and nineties back in 1991, they still lived in the same house that they got married in. But if you talk to anybody today who's between forty and sixty years old, you'll find they're on their fourth home. They buy nicer cars than their parents and grand-parents ever did. They go out to eat a heck of a lot more, yet they say that they're not any better off, and that 'times are tough.' They say they can't save any money. Yet their grandparents were able to save a lot of money."

Unfortunately, as Tim sees every day, the typical young couple start-ing out today does it differently. "They don't save up to create an emer-gency fund. They might put a couple thousand dollars in the bank, but then they're told to put as much as they can into their 401(k) plans. This not only puts their money at risk, but it also ties their money up so they can't use it without penalties.

"At the same time, they're trying to purchase a home to get out of the apartment or maybe even move out of their parents' home. They need to save up for the down payment on a home, and they do that. They save just enough to be able to buy that home, and—*boom!*—they have no money left. Then suddenly they realize they need to put furniture in that new home. They save up for furniture, and—*boom!*—they have no money again.

"They need to paint the walls. They need to do this and do that. Almost without realizing it, they've sunk a whole bunch of money into their house. Then, oops! Here comes the firstborn. And they need money for their child. 'Whoa! A kid costs more than we thought!'

---

Many of us will have to reduce our lifestyle in retirement
because things just keep "coming up," and we simply
didn't save enough.

---

"Uh-oh! Another financial emergency: The roof leaks or the car breaks down. Or maybe they think the house isn't big enough anymore so they purchase another home, using the equity (if they have any) they built up in their first one. Then not only do they sink more money into the second home, but now they also have bigger utility bills, house payments, insurance payments, and property taxes. And the story goes on and on.

"This is why too many of us are moving into retirement having to reduce our lifestyle. We simply did not save enough. Too many things 'came up.'"

## How to Map the Milestones

Tim saw that pattern over and over again, and he figured there had to be a better way. So for his clients and for himself, he developed a way to map out *primary financial milestones*—creating a plan for how to prepare for those milestones while still building wealth and avoiding debt.

"When I do this with clients, my goal is to come up with a plan you can follow so you never have to borrow from a bank for your cars again, a plan that provides an adequate emergency fund, that puts the kids through college, and that gives you plenty of retirement income, income tax-free. And, after the human game is over, a plan that lets you leave an estate that bypasses probate and is income tax-free. *And the plan must accomplish all this without your taking unnecessary risk.*

"We know that certain things are probably going to happen, right? You'll get married. You'll probably have kids. And when you have kids, you may need a larger home. Or a minivan rather than a sports car. And what about childcare?

"With a new home, you'll have additional expenses. Maybe remodeling or replacing major appliances. When your kids grow up, they may need cars themselves, and odds are they'll want to go to college. Oh, and they'll probably get married.

"None of these expenses should come as a surprise."

Even before Tim and his wife Chris got married, he drafted a primary financial milestones breakdown for his future family that incorporated the purchase of a total of five Bank On Yourself policies over the years. The "Life Milestones for the Austin Family" chart that follows shows the plan Tim envisioned.

The first dividend-paying whole life policy Tim bought had a premium of $25 per month. "Twenty-five dollars doesn't get you much today. But, as I always tell my clients, you start wherever you are." When he and Chris became engaged in 1994, he started an action plan that included several policies, and when the two tied the knot in 1995, he was putting a whopping (for him) $1,000 into his policies every month. As the couple could afford more, they started putting more money into their policies each month.

"We needed an emergency fund, so I made sure that was taken care of. I knew we'd need new cars at some point. So I thought, 'Let's eliminate the need for banks to finance those cars.'

"How about college? Our intent at the time was to have two kids. Okay, so what rule says you have to wait to start saving for their college education until *after* they're born? These policies allow you to use the money whether you end up having kids who go to college or not." (Learn more about the advantages of using Bank On Yourself for college funding in Chapter 8.)

---

### What rule says you have to wait to start saving for your children's college education until *after* they're born?

---

Tim's objective was to use Bank On Yourself–type policies so the family could *self-finance* virtually every major purchase they would encounter through the years—just as he had seen his elderly clients from previous generations do.

| Life Milestones for the Austin Family | Cash Value at end of Period [1,2] | Death Benefit at end of Period [1,2] |
|---|---|---|
| **1st Five Year Period: 1993-1997** | | |
| • In 1993, at age 30, Tim starts his first policy. Total premium: $12,000 per year<br>• Finance a car for Tim at $25,000 | $48,515 | $689,187 |
| **2nd Five Year Period: 1998-2002** | | |
| • In 1998, Tim starts his second policy. Total premium for two policies: $18,000 per year<br>• Finance a car for Tim and a car for Chris at $25,000 each | $157,716 | $1,330,265 |
| **3rd Five Year Period: 2003-2007** | | |
| • In 2003, Tim starts his third policy. Total premium for three policies: $24,000 per year<br>• Finance a car for Tim and a car for Chris at $25,000 each | $335,289 | $1,926,434 |
| **4th Five Year Period: 2008-2012** | | |
| • In 2008, Tim starts his fourth policy. Total premium for four policies: $30,000 per year<br>• Finance a car for Tim and a car for Chris at $25,000 each<br>Finance Bradley's first year in college at $30,000 | $599,352 | $2,537,174 |
| **5th Five Year Period: 2013-2017** | | |
| • In 2013, Tim starts his fifth policy. Total premium for five policies: $36,000 per year<br>• Finance a car for Tim and a car for Chris at $25,000 each<br>Finance Bradley's last three years in college at $30,000 each<br>• Finance Sarah's four years in college at $30,000 each<br>• Finance Bradley's wedding at $30,000 | $876,253 | $2,721,824 |
| **6th Five Year Period: 2018-2022** | | |
| • Finance a car for Tim and a car for Chris at $25,000 each<br>• Finance Sarah's wedding at $30,000 | $1,200,394 | $3,062,543 |
| **7th Five Year Period: 2023-2027** | | |
| • Finance a car for Tim and a car for Chris at $25,000 each<br>• Pay off the mortgage at $210,500 | $1,604,263 | $3,419,969 |
| **8th Five Year Period: 2028-2032** | | |
| All loans fully repaid by 2030 | $2,165,656 | $4,075,785 |
| **9th Five Year Period: 2033-2037** | | |
| • In 2034, at age 72, Tim starts drawing passive income of $182,350 per year[2] | $2,101,229 | $3,484,936 |

[1] Cash Value and Death Benefit values are *after* loan balances have been deducted.
[2] Projected values reflect the 2011 dividend scale. Dividends are not guaranteed and may change.

"Our grandparents and great-grandparents instinctively followed a 10/10/10 style of saving: 10 percent of their gross income was saved for short-term expenses such as a vacation or gift-giving; 10 percent was put aside for mid-term needs and potential emergencies, such as a new car, a new roof, or college tuition; and 10 percent was socked away for long-term retirement planning. They lived on the remaining 70 percent." (See Chapter 6 for more on the 10/10/10 Savings Formula.)

"But today, it's typical for families to spend 30 percent or more of their gross income on mortgage interest, credit card debt, car payments, and other installment loans. They're now putting 30 percent or more of their income toward debt payments, rather than into savings as their great-grandparents did. No wonder they're in trouble!"

## Increasing Lifetime Wealth Without Increasing Risk

By anticipating primary financial milestones and self-financing and avoiding debt, Tim knew that he and his clients could build a strong financial future for their families. In fact, after working with thousands of clients over more than twenty years, Tim estimates that the average family could increase their lifetime wealth by *$500,000 or more* simply by financing their major purchases and expenses through their Bank On Yourself–type dividend-paying whole life insurance policies. No gambling in the Wall Street Casino is required.

---

The average family could increase their lifetime wealth by $500,000 *or more,* simply by financing their major purchases through their Bank On Yourself–type dividend-paying whole life insurance policies.

---

Through his experience, Tim has seen that a typical family can get their needs met by having five policies (though he and many others in the Bank On Yourself Revolution have chosen to purchase more).

"I have policies that are set up for the kids' weddings. I have two policies that are earmarked for car purchases. I have four policies that we plan to use for college education and retirement income, and then I have other policies that can provide near-instant cash for emergencies. I have separate policies because the IRS limits the amount of premium you can deposit into each policy without the policy becoming a modified endowment contract (MEC)." (We covered the modified endowment contract issue in Chapter 4.) "So, when I want to add additional money, sometimes the best way is simply to start a new policy."

"For example, on one of my policies, my current monthly premium is $1,000. If I were to put in any more, the policy becomes a MEC. If that were to happen, all my gains in the policy would become taxable upon withdrawal. If it becomes a MEC and I borrow or withdraw from the policy before age 59½, the IRS would charge a penalty equal to 10 percent of the gain. So, when I was ready to contribute more, I avoided the MEC issue by simply starting another policy."

Over the years, of course, Tim and Chris have revised their projection of primary financial milestones. They ended up with three children, not two, and Chris sold her travel agency business to run their busy household. "We moved into a bigger home and bought more property. I hadn't planned on that, and I hadn't anticipated the cost of building our dream home," Tim recalls. But with each big decision, Tim figured out a way to handle the changes financially so they could remain stress-free and wouldn't have any debt to banks and credit card companies. "It was the cushion of our policies that made me comfortable with things. I am very blessed that things have really gone pretty much as planned."

## The $1,000 Wager

Tim Austin has been a believer in dividend-paying whole life insurance policies as ideal savings vehicles ever since he bought his first policy in 1993. He teaches others to use whole life polices to avoid the volatility and uncertainty inherent in universal life and variable life policies. And he has practiced what he preaches.

In 2009, Tim found himself at a life insurance convention in Bermuda, playing golf with the president of a large, prestigious life insurance company. As they played, Tim offered the man a wager—not about golf, but about life insurance.

*continued*

*continued from previous page*

"I bought my first whole life insurance policy sixteen years ago," Tim said to the man. "You've sold tens of thousands of variable life insurance policies. If you can show me just *one* of your company's policies that's at least fifteen years old and has a long-term performance record equal to my whole life policy, *I'll pay you $1,000.*"

The prestigious company president looked sheepish. "Keep your checkbook in your pocket," he said. "I can tell you right now that *none* of our variable life insurance policies can match the performance record of your simple dividend-paying whole life policy. Not one."

## Being Ready for the Unanticipated

By following his plan and consistently putting money into his Bank On Yourself–type policies, Tim and Chris have also been able to comfortably handle even those situations that they *couldn't* have anticipated. For example, the sudden illness of their son, Bradley:

"I had set up a policy for Bradley while he was still in the cradle. My main focus was that by the time he was sixteen, he would have enough cash value in his policy to borrow against it to buy his first car and then pay back the loan. Then, by the time he was eighteen, he'd be in a position to borrow seed money from his policy for college."

Bradley grew up as a bright, athletic, active boy. And Tim looked forward to the talk he knew he'd have with his son when he reached sixteen and Bradley was thinking about how to pay for his first car.

"What I couldn't have known was that, right after he turned fifteen, Bradley would be diagnosed with Stage III Hodgkin's lymphoma—cancer."

Bradley has since fully recovered. But a diagnosis like that means that he probably will not be insurable in the future.

"Well, Bradley has had a life insurance policy since he was a one-year-old. That policy currently has $29,000 of cash value in it. Today Bradley is uninsurable. If I hadn't started that policy for him then, he might not ever be able to qualify for one.

"Did I plan for Bradley to get cancer? Did I plan for him to become uninsurable? Absolutely not. But I *did* plan that I was going to sit down with Bradley when he turned sixteen and educate him on his policy. And I did that just a few months ago.

"I explained that he has the ability to borrow a certain amount of money to go out and get his first car, and that he can pay that money back to his own policy. I showed him how he's going to have the ability to help pay for college expenses with some of those funds.

"But what was the most rewarding was that I was also able to show him that, even though he's now uninsurable, he's going to be able to get married some day with no worries that he doesn't have any protection for his family. The death benefit on that policy now is almost $700,000."

Tim doesn't know if Bradley will grow up to be on the PGA Tour or in the NBA, or whether he'll be a politician or a chef. "I see Bradley being extremely successful, whatever route he takes. It's really up to him. I just know that, because of what I came to believe in twenty years ago, Bradley's got a good start."

## When Opportunity Knocks, Are You Able to Take Advantage of It?

Sometimes it's not just roadblocks and potholes that we don't anticipate. Sometimes we run into unexpected but *terrific* opportunities. If we don't have the wherewithal to take advantage of them, these opportunities disappear and we're out of luck. As the ancient Roman philosopher Lucius Annaeus Seneca said, *"Luck is a matter of preparation meeting opportunity."*

Tim was fully prepared to get lucky in 2008.

The real estate market had tanked. The burst of the bubble left millions of homeowners and real estate investors underwater. Banks foreclosed, and people walked away from properties that were no longer affordable. Houses were available at exceptionally discounted rates in Tim's area. But at the same time, credit was so tight that even buyers with impeccable credit histories couldn't get loans.

To cash in, you needed cash.

"My brother is in real estate. He hunted for really solid opportunities and found one—but the seller wanted cash and wanted it quickly. Within a few days, I was able to borrow the $40,000 we needed from one of my policies. So we paid him in cash, and we got the property.

"I set it up so that the rental money would pay back the policy loan. Over time, my brother was able to flip that property, and it snowballed so that we now have nineteen rental properties. The best part is that the income from the rental property paid back all of that loan to my policy—and it took just five years."

Tim was able to take advantage of a great opportunity for two reasons: First, he realized that, even though the purchase price was highly discounted, there's a risk with any investment. And he knew that he could afford to risk that money because he had built a very solid financial foundation. He had plenty socked away to cover his family's financial milestones and plenty in his emergency funds to cover whatever challenges life might throw at him and his family.

Second, he had fast access to cash that other potential real estate investors simply didn't have because he had been building up funds in his Bank On Yourself–type policies.

---

**When the opportunity arose, Tim had fast access to cash that other potential real estate investors simply didn't have because he had been building up funds in his Bank On Yourself–type policies.**

---

"It's funny, but I keep building my policies and I've become very comfortable with saving more and more money over the years. I know it's because I have confidence that I can still use that money at any point in time, whether it's for some unexpected crisis or some great opportunity. I don't have to worry about the risk of the market or that I've locked up my savings in a government-controlled retirement plan and can't get to it. I don't have any of those worries.

"And most importantly, if I don't make it home one day, my family will have the dollars they need to move on."

# Helping Others Get an Early Start

In addition to working with parents of college-age students, Tim now spends a good amount of his time educating young people who are in high school and even elementary school.

"If I can teach them how to build a solid financial foundation early on, they can avoid the stresses and problems too many baby boomers face today." Rather than building their futures on an upside down pyramid or a house of cards, Tim teaches them the solid fundamentals from generations past that will set these kids up for a lifetime of fiscal stability and growth. (Learn more about these fundamental financial principles in Chapter 6.)

"It's really not rocket science. But it does go against the grain of what everybody's touting today, and it runs counter to that 'buy more to be happy, and buy it now' mentality that recent generations have adopted. I've seen from my own experience and the experience of thousands of my clients that building a strong financial foundation is one of the best gifts you can give yourself and your family."

By the way, that very first policy that Tim bought for $25 per month? Tim increased his premium as his income grew, and today it has a cash value of about $170,000. Contrast that with the investment Tim's uncle made back in 1987 when Tim was a brand-new financial securities specialist.

"My uncle put $1,000 in the same fund my grandmother did, and six months later, I had to tell him that his $1,000 was down to $600. Just to see what would happen, my uncle has kept his account open for all these years. In 2006—two decades later—his account *finally* got back up to $1,000."

## KEY TAKE-AWAYS

1. **Your grandparents got it right.** Save before you *ever* invest, using the 10/10/10 Savings Formula:

- Save 10 percent of your gross income for short-term expenses

- Save 10 percent for mid-term needs and potential emergencies

- Save 10 percent for long-term retirement planning

- Live on what's left

**2. Take stock of the rest of your life.** Think realistically of potential emergencies you might face and about the milestones you can expect to face, including buying automobiles, having children, purchasing a home, paying for college tuition, weddings, retirement, etc.

**3. Begin *now* to plan for those milestones.** Ignoring them now will almost always cost you more later.

**4. Plan not only for unexpected expenses but also for unanticipated opportunities.** Remember the wisdom of the ages: "Luck is a matter of preparation meeting opportunity."

**5. If you have children or grandchildren, remember it's never too soon to begin helping them understand how to use Bank On Yourself as a money management system.** Begin with simple concepts, such as saving for a rainy day. Continue sharing your wisdom as the children grow older. Leave a legacy of knowledge as well as a legacy of financial security.

# CHAPTER 12

# How to Get Started

*Even if you're on the right track, you'll get run over*
*if you just sit there.*
—WILL ROGERS

YOU NOW KNOW ABOUT a powerful and proven way to bypass Wall Street, build wealth safely, and beat the banks at their own game. Are you ready to join the Bank On Yourself Revolution so you can:

- Put your hard-earned money into a vehicle that guarantees it will grow every year by a larger dollar amount than it did the previous year, no matter what kind of shenanigans Wall Street is up to?

- Know your principal and growth are locked in, and you won't go backward when the markets crash?

- Keep your money safe while earning more than savings and money market accounts and CDs that can't even keep up with inflation?

- Fire your banker and self-finance *all* your major purchases and expenses, from cars to college tuition to roof replacements?

- Build a secure retirement fund where *you* call the shots about when and how you use your money?

> **INSIDE THIS CHAPTER...**
> - Who's Qualified to Design and Implement Your Bank On Yourself Plan?
> - The Pitfalls of Using Advisors Without Specialized Training
> - Best Companies for Your Bank On Yourself Plan
> - Getting Started Step by Step

- Sleep at night knowing your loved ones will be taken care of if something happens to you?

Did I hear "Yes!" to that? Good. Then let's get started!

## Find a *Qualified* Advisor

Bank On Yourself is not an off-the-shelf type of product. There are no cookie-cutter plans (and why would you want one like that anyway?). Yours *must* be custom-tailored if you want it to help you reach as many of your short-term and long-term goals and dreams as possible—in the shortest time possible. Sure, it would be spiffy if you could buy one of these plans from a vending machine, but that's not gonna happen. And it's critical that your plan be structured properly to give you all the benefits, growth, and protections.

You need a *qualified* advisor.

---

### Dentist Learns a Lesson

"I learned the hard way that most agents don't know which companies to use or how to set up a Bank On Yourself plan properly. So I would caution you to be sure to work with a Bank On Yourself Authorized Advisor."
—Tom Hesch, DDS

---

The financial advisor you need *must* have specialized training in properly structuring a policy designed to maximize the power of the Bank On Yourself concept. If the wrong company or product is used, your plan could grow much more slowly, or you could lose some of the tax advantages, or *both*. I found this out the hard way myself, and I want to make sure you don't run into the same problems.

The advisor who set up Larry's and my first two policies swore up and down that he knew *everything* there is to know about how to structure them properly. Turns out, he didn't. Unfortunately, about a year later, we got a notice that the policies had turned into modified endowment contracts, which means they lost a key tax advantage.

I spent more than *forty hours* on the phone with the insurance company, trying to figure out how to fix it. When I spoke with one of the company's top executives, she told me she wished their advisors had never heard of this concept because they had no clue how to structure them properly—even though these advisors were convinced they did— and it was causing the bulk of the complaints they were getting.

Although I was ultimately able to get our policies fixed, I wouldn't wish the hassle I went through on anyone.

During those early years of learning about and implementing this concept, I referred my sister to a different advisor who also said he knew how to set up the policies properly. We found out several years later that he *didn't* know what he was doing, and her policy has grown more slowly than it could have, forcing her to postpone her planned retirement for several years. My frustration led me to realize the need for a program to identify and train advisors *properly*, so no one would ever again have to go through what my sister and I did.

---

My frustration led me to realize the need for a program to identify and *properly* train advisors on the Bank On Yourself concept, so no one would ever again have to go through what my sister and I did.

---

The kind of policies, and the details of how they're structured to maximize the power of the Bank On Yourself concept, are *not* covered in the standard industry training programs taken by agents seeking licenses. Only a handful of companies offer policies that meet all the requirements. We've also found that even most experienced advisors require *at least one year* of additional specialized training in this concept to become truly proficient at it.

And these days, with the growing public awareness and popularity of Bank On Yourself, a lot of advisors and big-money marketing groups seem to be jumping on the bandwagon. That does *not*, however, ensure they have sufficient understanding of the concept or know the best companies and policies to use so that you get the maximum benefit possible from your plan.

Unfortunately, most financial advisors and insurance agents don't know what they don't know about Bank On Yourself. A little knowledge really *can* be a dangerous thing—and we've seen it happen more than it should. If you don't have a trained specialist helping you, it's more than likely that you *won't* reap all of the potential benefits. And don't you and your hard-earned money deserve those benefits? Yes, you do!

So how do you find someone with this expertise?

## The Authorized Advisor Training Program

Finding an advisor who could design and implement a Bank On Yourself–type plan properly was *so* frustrating. But I was still inspired to tell people about this concept because I knew from personal experience that it worked. As I did, people from all over the U.S. and Canada started asking me if I could refer them to an advisor who truly understands the ins and outs of the Bank On Yourself method. That led to the creation of the Bank On Yourself Authorized Advisor Program.

Today, there are approximately 200 highly qualified professionals across the U.S. and Canada who form the core of Bank On Yourself Authorized Advisors. Each is a licensed financial advisor or life insurance agent who has undergone many hours of additional training on the technical aspects that make these policies such a powerful financial tool. As part of this training, advisors learn how to coach their clients to become their own source of financing for all their needs in every stage of life while maximizing their retirement income and minimizing their taxes in the process.

Each of these 200 Authorized Advisors:

- Has passed a certification test and demonstrated his/her competency with the concept
- Takes continuing education classes
- Works under the guidance of a Bank On Yourself technical and policy-design specialist team that has collectively designed tens of thousands of policies
- Works with some of the financially strongest life insurance groups

in the country, and knows which companies have policies that meet all the requirements needed to maximize the power of the concept

The Bank On Yourself Authorized Advisor training program is sponsored by a separate company (in which I have *no* ownership) that was chosen for its outstanding history and success in training advisors to help their clients reach their financial and personal goals through the use of guaranteed, permanent life insurance products. Admission standards to be accepted into the program are high, and only about one out of every twenty applicants is accepted.

To be referred to one of these Advisors, request your free Analysis at **www.BankOnYourselfFreeAnalysis.com** or complete and submit the Analysis Request Form on page 265. You'll then be referred to a Bank On Yourself Authorized Advisor we've hand-picked for you because of their experience in working with people in situations similar to yours. Although these advisors have already been through a thorough screening process, we encourage you to speak with the advisor selected for you and to review their background so you feel confident and comfortable moving forward with them.

## The Money Was Only a Phone Call Away

Here is what Paul Hester, an environmental engineer in Alaska, had to say about signing up with Bank On Yourself:

"It took almost a year of research into the system before I took the plunge to give it a try. Now I recommend and discuss it with people all the time. The best part is that no matter how good anyone says they can do in any other investment strategy, you can come out ahead by using the Bank On Yourself system to fund that same investment strategy.

"Initially, I considered it a low-risk investment, as we needed life insurance for my wife, and this was a way to have both a method of savings and a death benefit. We started small, with only $200 a month, as it was all we could afford at the time. Initially, it was slow and worrisome, as there was very little cash value buildup, but there was still the death benefit, and I had faith in the projections.

*continued*

*continued from previous page*

"It was only about two years into the program when we needed a financial assist. It was only $2,500, but we really needed it, as my work was relocating me and we needed to self-finance part of the relocation expenses. A phone call was all it took, and we had the money we needed. And my Authorized Advisor showed me a way to repay that loan that supercharges the growth of our cash value."

## Beware of Untrained Advisors

You may be tempted to ask a financial advisor you already know if they can help you implement Bank On Yourself. However, if you talk to a financial advisor or insurance person who doesn't *thoroughly* understand this concept, or who is not familiar with the *proper* way to structure the policy, here's what you're likely to hear:

- "You should *never* buy that kind of life insurance."

Many advisors have received little or no training on dividend-paying whole life policies, and they have no clue about the riders used to turbocharge the growth of the policy. Adding these riders can give a policy owner up to forty times more cash value in the early years than the policies most financial experts and writers talk about.

Most advisors got their training at the same place Suze Orman, Dave Ramsey, and other gurus got it. They don't know how the policies used for the Bank On Yourself concept are different, as I proved in Chapter 3. Most industry training programs don't even cover this type of policy at all, partly because so few companies offer it.

In addition, an advisor who helps a client implement this policy receives 50–70 percent less commission—something not many advisors are willing to accept. Why the cut? It's because 50–70 percent of your premium will typically be directed into that *Paid-Up Additions Rider* that supercharges the growth of your cash value, but pays the agent virtually no commission. (See Chapter 4 for a refresher on how this works.)

Why would these advisors deliver *more* and get paid *way less*? Because by providing such a high level of advice, well-structured personalized plans, and long-term follow-up, their clients do more business with them, as well as happily and voluntarily refer family, friends, neighbors, and colleagues.

- **"It's a good idea, but you should use a different type of policy, like an equity indexed universal life or a variable life policy."**

*No* other life insurance product comes with as many guarantees as dividend-paying whole life insurance, and this is the *only* policy type recommended for Bank On Yourself! Period! See Chapter 3 for more on this.

(Also, some advisors will try to steer you toward a different product because their contracts restrict them to only use the products of specific companies.)

- **"It sounds too good to be true."**

The Bank On Yourself method is based on an asset class (whole life insurance) that has increased in value every single year for more than 160 years—even when stocks, real estate, and other investments tumble. Great entrepreneurs people like Walt Disney and J. C. Penney have used this time-tested method as a ready source of capital when no bank would lend them a dime, as we saw in Chapter 3. And whole life insurance was the bedrock of our grandparents' financial plan.

Bank On Yourself is *not* a magic pill, and you won't get all of its benefits and results overnight. However, if you have a little patience and discipline, it can soon turn your financial life around and give you peace of mind for a lifetime.

- **"Sure, I can help you do that."**

Uh-oh. If they haven't been specifically trained, you don't want their help with this! If your advisor tells you he already understands all the important details necessary to help you implement and benefit from Bank On Yourself, you may want to ask him, "If you *could* have done this for me before, *why didn't you?*"

As I've warned, if a financial advisor doesn't structure your policy properly or uses the wrong company or product, your plan could grow *much* more slowly, and you could lose the tax advantages. Is it worth the risk?

This book was never intended to be a training manual for advisors on how to implement this concept. *That* manual is equivalent to about 1,000 pages. (I don't have the time to write such a book, and, trust me, you wouldn't really enjoy reading it!)

And if you wish to verify that a financial advisor you already work with or who has told you about this concept or book is an Authorized Advisor, e-mail info@bankonyourself.com and provide their full name and state. We'll tell you within one business day if they're trained and authorized or not.

## Is There a Directory of Bank On Yourself Advisors?

Nope. That's a question we get from time to time. We have asked the Authorized Advisors if they would be willing to be listed in a public directory so that people could contact them, interview them, and so on.

But they've declined. Rather than fielding phone calls from people who may not be a match for their specific focus, these Authorized Advisors prefer to focus their time and efforts on designing the most effective plans for their clients, working with them on a continuing basis to ensure they reach their financial goals and objectives. This also leaves them time to take the continuing education classes that keep them on the leading edge of this very specialized field.

So by using us to sort through requests, they end up with referrals to new clients whose situations and goals really match their expertise. For example, some of the Authorized Advisors specialize in clients with young families planning for college educations. Others work mainly with seniors or business owners. We take the time to make sure referrals are going to the right Authorized Advisor so you get the expertise you need.

So how do I benefit from this? The advisors pay a fee for each referral they receive. I get the word out, let people know the benefits of Bank On Yourself, then refer them to an Authorized Advisor to answer their questions, design their plans, and handle their day-to-day needs. (Remember, I'm an educator, not a licensed financial advisor.) This process frees me up and allows me to pursue my mission of helping the greatest number of people find the peace of mind and financial security they deserve. *And* I can be confident that I've put you in good hands.

---

## Ⓜ Ⓨ Ⓣ Ⓗ Ⓑ Ⓤ Ⓢ Ⓣ Ⓔ Ⓡ

### Couldn't a Fee-Only Advisor Do This?

I get that question from time to time from people who wonder why a non-commissioned, fee-only advisor can't set up a Bank On Yourself plan.

One problem with this is that the payment of a fee has *never* been a guarantee of the best service or product. And a commission is still typically built into any policy you buy, which means if you use a non-commissioned advisor, you'll end up paying the commission *and* the advisor's fee.

Bank On Yourself Authorized Advisors don't charge a fee to design and implement your plan. They receive a commission from the insurance company (a commission that is typically 50–70 percent lower than with a traditionally designed policy), and that commission and *all* other costs have *already* been deducted from the bottom-line numbers you'll see when you request a free Analysis. There is *no* surprise or added-on fees.

---

## Which Are the Right Companies?

Out of approximately 1,000 major life insurance companies, we've found only a handful that offer policies that meet all four requirements needed to maximize the power of the Bank On Yourself concept. When your plan is designed by one of the 200 Bank On Yourself Authorized Advisors, they recommend companies that have the following features and advantages:

1. **Dividend-paying:** These companies offer dividend-paying whole life policies and have paid dividends every single year for at least the last 100 years. They are participating companies, which means the policy owners (you!), rather than stockholders, share in the profits.

**2. Non-Direct Recognition:** They offer *non-direct recognition* policies, which means they credit you *the exact same dividend* even when you've taken a loan on your policy. That lets you *use* your money and *still* have it growing for you as though you never touched it.

Some companies (which Bank On Yourself Advisors would *not* recommend) discourage policy owners from taking policy loans. Discouraging people from taking loans doesn't make much sense to me. A company must either lend or invest the premiums in order to deliver on their promises to policy owners. And policy loans are perhaps the most reliable place the company can put money to work, because either policy owners are going to pay their loans back with interest while they're alive, or the company will get the money back when the insured dies. Since the death benefit is used as collateral for policy loans, the company deducts any outstanding loans and any interest due before paying out the death benefit.

One well-known company, which you'll sometimes hear suggested by some people and advisors (but *not* by Authorized Advisors) for the Bank On Yourself concept because of its dividend-paying track record, pays policy owners a different dividend on the money they have borrowed. The company is quick to warn you how much your dividend will be lowered if you don't pay the loan back immediately. And to make matters worse, this company reduces their agents' compensation if their clients have what the company deems too many policy loans, so their advisors may discourage you from taking policy loans.

Using your cash value to become your own source of financing is one of the most popular benefits of the Bank On Yourself concept. So you want to work with a company that understands and supports that aspect of the plan.

**3. Flexible PUAR:** Recommended companies offer a flexible Paid-Up Additions Rider (PUAR). At least 50 percent of your premium will typically be directed into this rider, which makes your cash value grow much faster than a policy that doesn't include it, especially in the early years of the policy. See Chapter 3 for a side-by-side comparison of how much more growth you'll have in a properly structured plan.

Some companies that offer this rider don't give you much flexibility in paying for it. Bank On Yourself Advisors prefer companies that allow you to pay a portion of your PUAR premium when and how you want, and that allow you to make partial payments or skip payments and make up for them later. In addition, some companies allow you to withdraw some or all of your paid-up additions and put them back in later.

**4. Financial Strength:** The insurance companies recommended by the Bank On Yourself Authorized Advisors are among the financially strongest in the country, as determined by several independent rating agencies.

## Is There a List of Recommended Companies?

Because I am an educator and not a licensed financial advisor, I'm prohibited from recommending or naming any specific companies. *And just having a list and knowing that the company is sound isn't enough.* It's equally important to have your policy *designed* properly. If it isn't, your plan could grow much more slowly, lose the tax advantages, or both. So, no, we don't just hand you a list and wish you luck!

It's the job of the Bank On Yourself Authorized Advisors to look at your overall financial picture in order to design a customized plan that will help you reach as many of your long-term and short-term goals as possible. Only then can they recommend the company that's most suitable for *your* situation. And you can then do your own research and make sure you're comfortable with the recommendation.

**Guaranteed Growth and Less Government Interference**

"Tax advantages, guaranteed growth, less government interference." That was the snap reply of Jody Cooper, a real estate agent in Florida, when she was asked what she liked best about her policy. "It sounded too good to be true, but I read everything I could find, and even the bashings couldn't

*continued*

*continued from previous page*

turn away my interest. Just a few months after starting, I feel great, having dual results—a process to prepare for my retirement years, and knowing I'll leave a legacy for my family."

## Getting Started: Step by Step

You may be wondering about the actual process you'll follow to implement a Bank On Yourself plan. As soon as you request your free Analysis at **www.BankOnYourselfFreeAnalysis.com** or by completing and submitting the form on page 265, you'll be connected with a Bank On Yourself Authorized Advisor who will arrange a time to speak with you to discuss the details of the concept and your specific situation. Here are the typical steps in the process:

**Step 1.** Your advisor will answer all your questions and help you identify your key short-term and long-term personal and financial goals.

**Step 2.** Your advisor will create a Personalized Solution and Recommendations report that will show you how the Bank On Yourself program can help you reach your primary goals. Each policy is custom-designed. There is no one-size-fits-all policy. Your Personalized Solution report will reveal:

- The guaranteed minimum value of your plan on the day you plan to tap into it—and at *every* point along the way
- How much income you can *count* on having during your retirement years
- How much you could increase your lifetime wealth simply by using a Bank On Yourself plan to pay for major purchases, rather than by financing, leasing, or directly paying cash for them
- Answers to any other questions you may have

**Step 3.** Your Advisor will then help you determine how much you need to fund your policy and where you'll find the funds to do it. As a general guideline, plans funded with a minimum of

$250 a month grow more efficiently. But don't rule yourself out if you're not sure you can set aside at least $250 a month to grow your wealth safely and predictably. Bank On Yourself Advisors are skilled at helping you restructure your finances to free up additional seed money to fund your plan.

---

## MYTHBUSTER

### Only Wealthy People Can Benefit from Bank On Yourself

This is an urban legend that *desperately* needs to be put to rest. We explained in Chapter 3 that whole life insurance was part of the financial foundation of half the population around 1900, and one-third of the population in 1950. And as Tim Austin mentioned in Chapter 11, it was common for blue-collar and middle-class families to own these policies. There are Bank On Yourself revolutionaries who make $20,000 or $30,000 a year, as well as those who make $300,000 to $3,000,000 per year.

If you're determined to build a solid financial foundation and take control of your own financial future, *you can do this*. (For some helpful money management strategies, check out Chapter 6.)

---

**Step 4.** Your Advisor will help identify who should be the **owner** of the policy, who should be the **beneficiary**, and who should be the **insured**. As long as you are the owner of the policy, you control the policy *and* the money in the policy. (Because you can have all the benefits of ownership without necessarily being the insured person, neither your health nor your age is necessarily a barrier.) Many couples start two policies at the same time, one for each of them, and may also start policies for each of their children.

If you own a business, you may also want to start one or more policies for the purpose of financing major business purchases.

**Step 5.** Your Advisor will recommend the best company for your situation and will help you complete the insurance company's application. The first premium is typically submitted with your application.

**Step 6.** Your application goes to the insurance company's underwriting department, which, in most cases, will require that the proposed insured take a medical exam. The insurance company pays all costs for the exam, which is conducted by a licensed medical professional, typically in the privacy of the insured's home or office. Policy approval usually takes about thirty days, although in some cases it can take up to sixty days.

**Step 7.** If the insurance company has additional questions about your health or driving record, they may request information from your physician or from your state department of motor vehicles.

**Step 8.** When the policy is issued, your Authorized Advisor will review it with you, and you'll have a free look period (typically thirty days, although it varies by state) during which you may reject the policy. If you decide you don't want the policy, the insurance company will promptly refund any premium you have paid.

**Step 9.** Premium payments begin on the schedule you've chosen (monthly, quarterly, semi-annually, or annually). An exception is a Bank On Yourself for Seniors Policy, which involves a one-time premium. (See Chapter 10 for more details.)

**Step 10.** Next, you'll meet semi-annually with your Bank On Yourself Advisor to review your policy, track your progress, and make any adjustments dictated by changes in your situation.

**Step 11.** Based on initial and ongoing planning with your Bank On Yourself Advisor, you can start using your policy to become your own source of financing (typically one to three years after starting the policy, although you always have access to the equity in your plan). Make sure you pay your loans back just as you would be required to do by a traditional financial institution. Your advisor will assist you in strategically planning the best way to pay back your policy loans.

Step 12. Based on your needs and cash flow, you may want to start new policies periodically to assist you in achieving new or bigger goals.

Step 13. Once you're ready to enjoy your golden years, you can start taking a passive retirement income stream. Your Advisor will assist you in structuring a schedule so that you receive this income with little or no income tax liability according to the then-current tax laws.

Step 14. Though nothing is certain except death and taxes, you can at least *minimize* your taxes. Under current tax law, your death benefit (less any outstanding loans) passes income tax-free to your loved ones, favorite charities, or other beneficiaries. It's the final grand gesture following years of great benefits that will have improved and enhanced your lifestyle.

---

### Only One Regret

*"I'm using Bank On Yourself as a source of financing, savings and financial security. And anyone who wants some **economic sanity** in their life ought to think about doing the same. My only regret is that I wish I learned about this sooner."*
—D.J. Simon, IT Consultant

---

## Ready, Set, Go!

If you're ready to take the next step, you can request a free Analysis at **www.BankOnYourselfFreeAnalysis.com** or by completing and submitting the form on page 265. You'll receive a referral to an Authorized Advisor who will contact you by phone or e-mail within two business days to review your unique situation and goals, in order to prepare your custom-tailored Analysis and Personalized Solution report.

So within the next forty-five to sixty days, you could be on your way to a level of financial security and flexibility that most people desire, but few know how to actually achieve. It doesn't matter what your age or life circumstances are. It doesn't matter what your financial past has been. It doesn't matter if you don't yet know where you'll find the money to fund the plan. The Bank On Yourself method is a strategy that has been proven to be viable, valuable, and powerful for more than 160 years.

---

### A Different Way of Looking at Money

*"Thanks for planting the seed about Bank On Yourself. There's a huge need for a different way to look at money. I've shared this with a number of family members, and we all agree our only regret is that we didn't start our plans sooner."*

—Janel Baca

---

It won't happen overnight. It will take some patience and some discipline. But if you don't begin today, *will you be any further ahead a year from now?* Two or three or thirty years from now? Will banks still have control over your ability to finance what is important to you? Will Wall Street still play poker with your retirement funds? Will the security and well-being of your family still be *out* of your control and in the hands of too-big-to-fail institutions that don't know or care about what happens to you?

Or, now that you know what you know, will you take the first step and join the Bank On Yourself Revolution?

I've laid it all out. Now it's up to you.

## KEY TAKE-AWAYS

1. Bank On Yourself Authorized Advisors know how to properly structure a policy designed to maximize the power of the

**Bank On Yourself concept.** A little knowledge is a dangerous thing. You want the advisor who has scads of knowledge about and experience with this concept. If your plan isn't structured correctly, it could grow much more slowly, lose the tax advantages, or both. You should definitely *avoid* using a financial advisor who is unfamiliar with the concept or who thinks reading a book about it is all that's needed to be an expert at it.

**2. Bank On Yourself Authorized Advisors have specialized training and extensive resources.** Each Authorized Advisor has passed a series of examinations to demonstrate his or her professional knowledge and skills, takes continuing education classes, and works under the guidance of a Bank On Yourself technical and policy-design specialist team that has collectively designed tens of thousands of policies.

**3. Insurance companies recommended by Bank On Yourself Authorized Advisors are among the financially strongest in the country.** They provide dividend-paying whole life policies and have paid dividends every single year for at least 100 years. They offer *non-direct recognition* policies, which means they credit you the exact same dividend even when you've taken a loan against your policy. These companies also offer flexible Paid-Up Additions Riders in order to supercharge the values of your policy.

**4. Your Advisor can answer all your questions and help you identify your key short-term and long-term personal and financial goals.** They will create a Personalized Solution and Recommendations report that will show you how the Bank On Yourself program will help you reach these goals. Your policy is custom-designed to fit *your* individual needs. Your Authorized Advisor will also look at ways to help you find the dollars to fund your plan.

**5. The most common regret people express about Bank On Yourself is that they wish they'd started sooner.** I want to make *sure* that's one regret *you* never have. The *best* time to take the steps needed to take control of your financial future and enjoy financial security for the rest of your life is *today*. The first step is to request your free, no-obligation Analysis and get a referral to an Authorized Advisor by going to **www. BankOnYourselfFreeAnalysis.com**, or by completing and submitting the form on the next page.

# Free No-Obligation Analysis Request Form

☐ Yes! I want to find out how to grow wealth I can predict and count on and become my own source of financing. Please have a Bank On Yourself Authorized Advisor contact me, so I can receive my free, no-obligation Bank On Yourself Analysis. I understand there will be *no* high pressure and I will *not* be asked to buy anything during this meeting. (Note: Please **use black ink** for readability.)

Name: _____

Address: _____

City: _____ State _____ Zip _____

Day phone: _____ Eve. Phone: _____

Primary Email Address: _____

Best time to speak briefly during business hours: _____

NOTE: We *never* trade, rent, sell or abuse your contact or other personal information. We ask for email and phone to make it easy to put you in contact with the Bank On Yourself Authorized Advisor we refer you to, who will prepare your Analysis. By giving us this information, you authorize Bank On Yourself and the Advisor we select for you to contact you regarding your Analysis.

Please tell us about you – this information will be held in <u>strict confidence</u>:

|  | *You* | *Spouse or Significant Other* |
|---|---|---|
| Age: | _____ | _____ |
| Occupation: | _____ | _____ |
| Annual Income: | _____ | _____ |

Your biggest financial concern: _____

Do you own your home? _____ Approx. mortgage balance: _____

Approx. total credit card debt: _____ Interest rates: _____

Do you own a business? _____ If yes, type: _____

How did you hear about Bank On Yourself? _____

If you learned about it from someone, please list their name and state: _____

_____

**How to arrange for your free Bank On Yourself Analysis:**

1. **Fax** this form to **505-466-2167** (no cover sheet necessary)
2. *Or* **mail** the form to: Bank On Yourself, 903 W. Alameda St. #526, Santa Fe, NM 87501
3. *Or* **request it online at: BankOnYourselfFreeAnalysis.com**

# Bank On Yourself Is Looking for a Few Good Men and Women

BEING A BANK ON YOURSELF Authorized Advisor is a challenging but very rewarding career. It's challenging because Bank On Yourself goes against the grain of what we've been taught about money and finances, and because of the investment of time needed to master the ins and outs of the concept, technical information, and plan design.

For those who stick with it, however, the benefits are many. Perhaps the greatest satisfaction comes from knowing you are changing your clients' lives by helping them achieve the financial peace of mind they seek and deserve.

Though there is a need for additional Bank On Yourself Authorized Advisors throughout the U.S. and Canada, not everyone has what it takes to be successful with this concept, and not everyone is accepted into the training program.

If you have a life insurance license and at least one year of experience in financial services, you may qualify to be accepted into the Bank On Yourself training program. Please understand that it's not just past success that is considered. Attitude and a willingness to be mentored are key factors. To learn more, and to see if you qualify for the Program, go to **www.BankOnYourself.com/authorized-advisors**.

# Acknowledgments

I AM GRATEFUL FOR so many people who helped me get this massive project done! And specifically, I'd like to acknowledge:

Lee McIntyre, for his heroic dedication to detail and accuracy, burning the midnight oil, and skipping vacations to make sure we got it *right*. ("Really, Lee? Are you *sure* they charged me an amount that equals an annual interest rate of 1,600 percent for paying my credit card off *one* day late?") I knew you had my back at every turn.

To Heather Estay, for her wit, indestructible optimism, and dogged persistence to make sure concepts were clear. ("Pamela, if *I* don't get it, they won't either.") My book therapist, you talked me down from more than a couple of ledges.

To Glenn Yeffeth, my publisher at BenBella Books, for his enthusiasm, his ability to see beyond the same-old, same-old, and his constant support. ("Glenn, about that deadline...") I felt totally confident putting my baby into your hands.

To my literary agent Bill Gladstone, who tenaciously encouraged (pushed? goaded?) me to write this second book. And who had the wisdom to introduce me to the perfect publisher, BenBella. ("Thanks, Bill. And don't even *think* about book number three!") Thank you for your persistence—now lose my phone number.

To two of my favorite Bank On Yourself revolutionaries, Navy Commander Bob Chambers and Dan Proskauer, who generously shared their personal stories, painstakingly reviewed drafts, and gave sincere, detailed feedback. ("Okay, team, on page forty-seven, Dan and Bob are questioning our use of the word *equity*. And Dan says, "The *London Whale* debacle has now caused over $6 billion in losses.") I am inspired by your heartfelt dedication to all that Bank On Yourself stands for!

To all of the Bank On Yourself Authorized Advisors who generously shared their insights, stories, and technical expertise for this project. ("Wait! One of the Advisors just sent me this awesome story! We've *got* to fit it in somewhere...") You are the troops on the ground, and I so appreciate your commitment to making sure that families all across the nation achieve the financial peace of mind they deserve.

To Tim Austin, who was so open about his personal philosophies, triumphs, and disappointments in Chapter 11, giving others a peek into how Bank On Yourself can contribute to all stages of life. ("Tim, I'm pretty sure your grandmother has forgiven you.") I value your sincerity and dedication to the families you serve and the Advisors you support and train.

To Nelson Nash, my first mentor on this concept, who never tires of pushing back the frontiers of ignorance.

And most importantly, to my husband Larry. He has been my rock. Reminding me of what is really important when the going got tough and when I couldn't see any light at the end of the tunnel. Believing in me more than I could believe in myself at times. Reading every draft, listening to my every rant and rave, contributing to every meeting, keeping me within the generally sane zone. I love you.

# References

1. "2010 Survey of Consumer Finances." Federal Reserve. <http://www.federalreserve.gov/econresdata/scf/scf_2010.htm>

2. Patterson, Scott, Jenny Strasburg, and Liam Plevin. "Speedy Traders Exploit Loophole." *Wall Street Journal*, May 1, 2013, sec. A1.

3. Ahrens, Robert W., Denny Gainer, and Jerry Mosemak. "Why Does This Bull Market Get No Respect?" *USA Today*, Jan. 17, 2013. <http://www.usatoday.com/story/money/markets/2013/01/17/raging-stock-bull-market-gets-no-respect/1839971/>

4. Scaggs, Alexandra and Steven Russolillo. "Investors Rediscovering Margin Debt." *Wall Street Journal*, May 18, 2013, sec. C1.

5. Summers, Nick. "Behold the Ghosts of Bubbles Past." *Bloomberg Businessweek*, Apr. 1, 2013. Cited at <http://magsreview.com/bloomberg-businessweek/bloomberg-businessweek-april-1-2013/3974-behold-the-ghosts-of-bubbles-past.html>

6. Weiss, Martin D., Ph.D. "How Long Can This Rally Last?" *Money and Markets*, May 18, 2013. <http://www.moneyandmarkets.com/how-long-can-this-rally-last-51887>

7. Lanman, Scott. "Fed Raises Target Rate to 4.5 percent to Cap Greenspan Era." *Bloomberg*, Jan. 31, 2006. <http://www.bloomberg.com/apps/news?pid=newsarchive&sid=aPmQp.NDe7Sw&refer=news_index>

8. Laise, Eleanor. "Best Stock Fund of the Decade: CGM Focus." *Wall Street Journal*, Dec. 31, 2009. <http://online.wsj.com/article/SB10001424052748704876804574628561609012716.html>

9. "2013 Retirement Confidence Survey: Perceived Savings Needs Outpace Reality for Many." Mar. 2013, Employee Benefit Research Institute (EBRI). <http://www.ebri.org/surveys/rcs/2013/>

10. Bogle, John C. *Common Sense on Mutual Funds*. Hoboken, NJ: Wiley, 2009, p. 436.

11. de Soto, Jesús Huerta. *Money, Bank Credit and Economic Cycles*. Auburn, AL: Ludwig von Mises Institute, 2009, p. 590.

12. *The Facts of Life and Annuities,* 2009, LIMRA, Windsor, CT.

13. Dyke, Barry James. *The Pirates of Manhattan II: Highway to Serfdom.* 2012. <http://thepiratesofmanhattan.com/the-book/>

14. *Life Insurers Fact Book 2012.* American Council of Life Insurers. Dec. 5, 2012. <http://www.acli.com/Tools/Industry%20Facts/Life%20Insurers%20Fact%20Book/Documents/factbook2012_entirety.pdf>

15. Beard, Patricia. *After the Ball.* Bloomington, IN: Xlibris, 2009, p. 10.

16. American Council of Life Insurers. *Life Insurers Fact Book 1950,* as reported by ACLI researcher Jiangmei Wang to the author, Jun. 5, 2013.

17. Munnell, Alicia H., Anthony Webb, and Francesca Golub-Sass. "The National Retirement Risk Index: An Update." Center for Retirement Research at Boston College, Oct. 2012. <http://crr.bc.edu/wp-content/uploads/2012/11/IB_12-20-508.pdf>

18. "The Retirement Crisis and a Plan to Solve It." U.S. Senate Committee on Health, Education, Labor, and Pensions, Jul. 2012. <http://www.harkin.senate.gov/documents/pdf/5011b69191eb4.pdf?>

19. Olshan, Jeremy. "Father of the 401(k)'s Tough Love." *MarketWatch,* Nov. 22, 2011. <http://blogs.marketwatch.com/encore/2011/11/22/father-of-the-401ks-tough-love/>

20. "2011 Survey of Income and Program Participation." U.S. Census Bureau. 2011.

21. Dyke, Barry James. "The 401(k) Mutual Fund Retirement Plan: A Failed Experiment, a Recipe for Disaster and a Greater Fool Pump and Dump Ground for Wall Street." *The Economic Warrior.* May 10, 2012. <http://economicwarrior.org/2012/05/10/the-401k-mutual-fund-retirement-plan-a-failed-experiment-a-recipe-for-disaster-and-a-greater-fool-pump-and-dump-ground-for-wall-street/>

22. "Defined Contribution Plans: Key Information on Target Date Funds as Default Investments Should Be Provided to Plan Sponsors and Participants." U.S. Government Accountability Office. Jan. 2011. <http://www.gao.gov/new.items/d11118.pdf>

23. "The Accidental 401(k) Planner." *SmartMoney,* Nov. 2009.

24. Olen, Helaine. "IBM Makes Changes to Its 401(k) Plan." *Forbes,* Dec. 10, 2012. <http://www.forbes.com/sites/helaineolen/2012/12/10/ibm-makes-changes-to-its-401k-plan/>

25. Rubin, Richard and Margaret Collins. "Obama's Budget Would Cap Romney-Sized Retirement Accounts." *Bloomberg*, Apr. 5, 2013. <http://www.bloomberg.com/news/2013-04-05/obama-budget-calls-for-cap-on-romney-sized-iras.html>

26. "Self-Directed IRAs and the Risk of Fraud." North American Securities Administrators Association (NASAA). <http://www.nasaa.org/5866/self-directed-iras-and-the-risk-of-fraud/>

27. Lieber, Ron. "When Credit Gets Tight, a 401(k) Loan Becomes Tempting." *New York Times*, Jul. 5, 2008. <http://www.nytimes.com/2008/07/05/business/yourmoney/05money.html>

28. Greene, Kelly. "Congress Eyes 401(k)s Again." *Wall Street Journal*, Apr. 20, 2012. <http://online.wsj.com/article/SB1000142405270230433120457735402420725532.html>

29. "The 401(k) Fallout." *60 Minutes*. CBS, Apr. 19, 2009.

30. Lambert, Emily. "Find the Fees." *Forbes*, May 19, 2011. <http://www.forbes.com/forbes/2011/0606/investing-401k-retirement-savings-aarp-brightscope-find-fees.html>

31. Choi-Allum, Lona. "401(k) Participants' Awareness and Understanding of Fees." *AARP Research*. Mar. 2011. <http://www.aarp.org/work/retirement-planning/info-02-2011/401k-fees-awareness-11.html>

32. "401(k) Plans: Labor and IRS Could Improve the Rollover Process for Participants." Government Accounting Office, Mar. 7, 2013. <http://www.gao.gov/products/GAO-13-30>

33. Coombes, Andrea. "With 401(k) Disclosure, Some Fees Still Hidden." *Wall Street Journal's Market Watch*, Jun. 25, 2012.

34. "2013 Retirement Confidence Survey – 2013 Results." Employee Benefit Research Institute (EBRI). <http://www.ebri.org/surveys/rcs/2013/>

35. "2012 'Getting Paid in America' Survey Results." National Payroll Week, American Payroll Association. <http://www.nationalpayrollweek.com/documents/2012SurveyResults_nodemo.pdf>

36. Leamy, Elisabeth. "When to Pay a Higher Health Insurance Deductible." *ABC News*. Jun. 19, 2012. <http://abcnews.go.com/Business/pay-higher-health-insurance-deductible/story?id=16597067#.UZea0spqM70>

37. Mirhaydari, Anthony. "Beware: Market insiders are selling." *MSN Money*, May 22, 2013. <http://money.msn.com/investing/beware-market-insiders-are-selling>

38. "The Big Payoff: Educational Attainment and Synthetic Estimates of Work-Life Earnings, July 2002." U.S. Census Bureau. <http://www.census.gov/prod/2002pubs/p23-210.pdf>

39. Prior, Anna and Matthew Heimer, "Which colleges help grads snare top salaries?" *MarketWatch*, Sep. 25, 2012. <http://www.marketwatch.com/story/which-colleges-help-grads-snare-top-salaries-2012-09-25-121034742>

40. "Fast Facts." *National Center for Education Statistics*. <http://nces.ed.gov/FastFacts/display.asp?id=76>

41. Bigelow, William. "Tuition Rising at Record Rate at Public Colleges, Universities." *Breitbart*, Mar. 8, 2013. <http://www.breitbart.com/Big-Government/2013/03/06/Tuition-Rising-At-Record-Rate-At-Public-Colleges-And-Universities>

42. Chilingerian, Natasha. "Student Loan Debt Piles Up." *Credit Union Times*, Jun. 4, 2012. <http://www.cutimes.com/2012/06/04/student-loan-debt-piles-up>

43. "For Unpaid College Loans, Feds Dock Social Security." *SmartMoney*, Aug. 7, 2012.

44. Mui, Ylan Q. "Senior Citizens Continue to Bear Burden of Student Loans." *Washington Post*. Apr. 1, 2012. <http://articles.washingtonpost.com/2012-04-01/business/35450643_1_student-loans-william-e-brewer-debt-collectors>

45. Zweig, Jason. "Did Your College Savings Plan Blow Up on You?" *Wall Street Journal*, Mar. 20, 2009. <http://online.wsj.com/article/SB123758112211598861.html>

46. Ramsey, Dave. "Saving for College Is Easier Than You Think." Daveramsey.com. Oct. 27, 2009. <http://www.daveramsey.com/article/saving-for-college-is-easier-than-you-think/lifeandmoney_college/>

47. Coy, Peter. "Student Loans: Debt for Life." *Bloomberg Businessweek*, Sep. 18, 2012. <http://www.businessweek.com/articles/2012-09-06/student-loans-debt-for-life>

48. This is a true story; however, some identifying details have been changed to protect the client's privacy.

49. This is a true story; however, some identifying details have been changed to protect the client's privacy.

50. This is a true story; however, some identifying details have been changed to protect the client's privacy.

51. "Fewer U.S. Households Have Debt, But Those Who Do Have More." U.S. Census Bureau. Mar. 21, 2013. <http://www.census.gov/news-room/releases/archives/income_wealth/cb13-51.html>

52. "Fidelity Estimates Couples Retiring in 2013 Will Need $220,000 to Pay Medical Expenses Throughout Retirement." May 16, 2013. <http://www.fidelity.com/inside-fidelity/individual-investing/fidel-ity-estimates-couples-retiring-in-2013-will-need-220000-to-pay-medical-expenses-throughout-retirement>

53. "Genworth's 2013 Cost of Care Survey." Conducted by CareScout, Genworth. Mar. 18, 2013. <https://www.genworth.com/corporate/about-genworth/industry-expertise/cost-of-care.html>

# General Disclaimer

WHILE A GREAT DEAL of care has been taken to provide accurate and current information regarding the subject matter covered, neither the author, Pamela Yellen, nor the publisher, BenBella Books, is responsible for any errors or omissions, or for the results obtained from the use of this information. The information contained in this book is intended to provide general information and does not constitute financial or legal advice.

All information in this book is provided "as is," with no guarantee of completeness, accuracy, or timeliness regarding the results obtained from the use of this information. And without warranty of any kind, express or implied, including, but not limited to warranties of performance, merchantability, and fitness for a particular purpose. Your use of this information is at your own risk. You assume full responsibility and risk of loss resulting from the use of this information. Pamela Yellen will not be liable for any direct, special, indirect, incidental, consequential, or punitive damages or any other damages whatsoever, whether in an action based upon a statute, contract, tort (including, but not limited to negligence), or otherwise, relating to the use of this information. In no event will Pamela Yellen, BenBella Books, their related partnerships or corporations, or the partners, agents, or employees thereof be liable to you or anyone else for any decision made or action taken in reliance on the information in this book or for any consequential, special, or similar damages, even if advised of the possibility of such damages.

Neither Pamela Yellen nor BenBella Books is engaged in rendering legal, accounting, or other professional services. If accounting, financial, legal, or tax advice is required, the services of a competent professional should be sought.

Information that was accurate as of the time of publication may become outdated by marketplace changes or conditions, new or revised laws, or other circumstances. Any slights against individuals, companies, or organizations are unintentional. All figures and examples in the book (except the Milestones Chart in Chapter 11) are based on rates and assumptions that were in effect in March 2013, thus, these rates and assumptions are not guaranteed and may be subject to change. As in all assumptions and examples, individual results may vary based on a wide range of factors unique to each person's situation.

# About the Author

Financial Security Expert Pamela Yellen investigated more than 450 savings and retirement planning strategies seeking an alternative to the risk and volatility of stocks and other investments. Her research led her to a time-tested, predictable method of growing and protecting wealth now used by more than half a million people. Pamela Yellen's first book, *Bank On Yourself: The Life-Changing Secret to Growing and Protecting Your Financial Future*, is a *New York Times* bestseller.

Pamela has appeared on every major TV and radio network and served as a source for organizations such as the Associated Press, Fox News, Bloomberg Businessweek, and AARP. Her articles have been featured in thousands of major publications and websites.

Pamela was born in Buffalo, New York, and has lived in Sarasota, Phoenix, and the San Francisco Bay area. She graduated from the University of San Francisco with a degree in psychology. Pamela and her husband Larry currently live outside of Santa Fe, New Mexico. They enjoy theatre and the arts, hiking, biking, bird watching, traveling, gourmet cooking, working out (Pamela can leg press 200 pounds!), reading, spoiling their two grandkids, and are involved in supporting numerous charitable causes.

Ten percent of all author royalties are donated to educational not-for-profits, such as The Smile Train, The Nature Conservancy, Susan G. Komen for the Cure, Heifer International, and Hawk Watch.

About the Author